Lecture Notes in Computer Science   9533

Commenced Publication in 1973
Founding and Former Series Editors:
Gerhard Goos, Juris Hartmanis, and Jan van Leeuwen

More information about this series at http://www.springer.com/series/7407

Pierre Ganty · Michele Loreti (Eds.)

Trustworthy Global Computing

10th International Symposium, TGC 2015
Madrid, Spain, August 31 – September 1, 2015
Revised Selected Papers

 Springer

Editors
Pierre Ganty
IMDEA Software Institute
Pozuelo de Alarcón, Madrid
Spain

Michele Loreti
Università degli Studi di Firenze
Florence
Italy

ISSN 0302-9743   ISSN 1611-3349   (electronic)
Lecture Notes in Computer Science
ISBN 978-3-319-28765-2   ISBN 978-3-319-28766-9   (eBook)
DOI 10.1007/978-3-319-28766-9

Library of Congress Control Number: 2015959594

LNCS Sublibrary: SL1 – Theoretical Computer Science and General Issues

Printed on acid-free paper

This Springer imprint is published by SpringerNature
The registered company is Springer International Publishing AG Switzerland

Preface

This volume contains the proceedings of TGC 2015, the 10th International Symposium on Trustworthy Global Computing. The symposium was held in Madrid, Spain, from August 31 to September 1. The TGC Symposium was co-located with CONCUR, QUEST, and FORMATS. Informal pre-symposium proceedings were made available in electronic form to the attendees of the symposium. The papers in this volume were further improved by the authors in response to helpful feedback received at the symposium.

The Symposium on Trustworthy Global Computing is an international annual venue dedicated to safe and reliable computation in the so-called global computers, i.e., those computational abstractions emerging in large-scale infrastructures such as service-oriented architectures, autonomic systems, and cloud computing. The TGC series focuses on providing frameworks, tools, algorithms, and protocols for designing open-ended, large-scaled applications and for reasoning about their behavior and properties in a rigorous way. The related models of computation incorporate code and data mobility over distributed networks that connect heterogeneous devices and have dynamically changing topologies.

The first TGC event took place in Edinburgh in 2005, with the co-sponsorship of IFIP TC-2, as part of ETAPS 2005. TGC 2005 was the evolution of the previous Global Computing I workshops held in Rovereto in 2003 and 2004 (see LNCS vol. 2874) as well as of the workshops on Foundation of Global Computing held as satellite events of ICALP and CONCUR (see ENTCS vol. 85). Four editions of TGC were co-located with the reviews of the EU-funded projects AEOLUS, MOBIUS, and SENSORIA within the FP6 initiative. They were held in Lucca, Italy (TGC 2006, LNCS vol. 4661); in Sophia Antipolis, France (TGC 2007, LNCS vol. 4912); in Barcelona, Spain (TGC 2008, LNCS vol. 5474); and in Munich, Germany (TGC 2010, LNCS vol. 6084). Further editions of TGC were held in Aachen, Germany (TGC 2011, LNCS vol. 7173), Newcastle upon Tyne, UK (TGC 2012, LNCS vol. 8191), Buenos Aires (TGC 2013, LNCS vol. 8358), and Rome (TGC 2014, LNCS vol. 8358). TGC 2015 solicited contributions in all areas of global computing, including (but not limited to) languages, semantic models, and abstractions; security, trust, and reliability; privacy and information flow policies; algorithms and protocols; resource management; model checking, theorem proving, and static analysis; and tool support.

The fruitful collaboration with CONCUR, initiated in 2013, was continued this year allowing for concurrent submissions to CONCUR and TGC, with the reviewing schedule of TGC slightly delayed with respect to that of CONCUR and submissions accepted by CONCUR were automatically withdrawn from TGC. This year there were seven papers concurrently submitted to TGC and CONCUR and 12 papers were submitted only to TGC. As with the last edition, the papers submitted at CONCUR and TGC were also reviewed by the Program Committee of TGC, which was provided with the CONCUR reviews.

The Program Committee selected ten papers to be included in this volume and to be presented at the symposium. The program was structured in four sessions chaired by Lenore Zuck, Giorgio Delzanno, Michele Loreti, and Pierre Ganty. Finally, the TGC program had invited talks by Andrey Rybalchenko (Microsoft Research Cambridge, UK) and, jointly with CONCUR, by Gianluigi Zavattaro (University of Bologna/INRIA, Italy).

We would like to thank the Steering Committee of TGC for inviting us to chair the conference; the members of the Program Committee and external referees for their detailed reports and the stimulating discussions during the review phase; the authors of submitted papers, the invited speakers, the session chairs, and the attendees for contributing to the success of the event. Finally, we thank the providers of the EasyChair system, which was used to manage the submissions.

November 2015   Pierre Ganty
                                                                Michele Loreti

Organization

Program Committee

Myrto Arapinis	University of Birmingham, UK
Alessandro Armando	DIBRIS, Università di Genova, Italy
Laura Bocchi	University of Kent, UK
Luis Caires	Universidade Nova de Lisboa, Portugal
Marco Carbone	IT University of Copenhagen, Denmark
Ilaria Castellani	Inria Sophia Antipolis, France
Pedro R. D'Argenio	Universidad Nacional de Córdoba - CONICET, Argentina
Giorgio Delzanno	DIBRIS, Università di Genova, Italy
Fabio Gadducci	Università di Pisa, Italy
Pierre Ganty	IMDEA Software Institute, Spain
Rolf Hennicker	Ludwig-Maximilians-Universität München, Germany
Christos Kaklamanis	University of Patras and CTI, Greece
Steve Kremer	Inria Nancy - Grand Est, France
Alberto Lluch Lafuente	Technical University of Denmark
Michele Loreti	Università degli Studi di Firenze, Italy
Parthasarathy Madhusudan	University of Illinois at Urbana-Champaign, USA
Matteo Maffei	CISPA, Saarland University, Germany
Gennaro Parlato	University of Southampton, UK
Michael Rusinowitch	LORIA - Inria Nancy, France
Davide Sangiorgi	Università di Bologna, Italy
Emilio Tuosto	University of Leicester, UK

Additional Reviewers

Accattoli, Beniamino
Bartoletti, Massimo
Calzavara, Stefano
Cirstea, Horatiu
Costa, Gabriele
Fabre, Eric
Jorge A., Pérez
Kissig, Christian
Klarl, Annabelle
Lee, Matias David
Peressotti, Marco

Petri, Gustavo
Prasad, K.V.S.
Radhakrishna, Arjun
Reniers, Michel
Ruffing, Tim
Schrammel, Peter
Turuani, Mathieu
Villard, Jules
Zhang, Lijun
Zucca, Elena

Contents

Secure Two-Party Computation in Applied Pi-Calculus: Models
and Verification 1
    Sergiu Bursuc

Multiparty Testing Preorders................................. 16
    Rocco De Nicola and Hernán Melgratti

Data Tracking in Parameterized Systems 32
    Giorgio Delzanno

Modular Monitor Extensions for Information Flow Security in JavaScript ... 47
    José Fragoso Santos, Tamara Rezk, and Ana Almeida Matos

Hybrid Typing of Secure Information Flow in a JavaScript-Like Language ... 63
    José Fragoso Santos, Thomas Jensen, Tamara Rezk, and Alan Schmitt

Fault Ascription in Concurrent Systems........................ 79
    Gregor Gössler and Jean-Bernard Stefani

Disjunctive Information Flow for Communicating Processes............. 95
    Ximeng Li, Flemming Nielson, Hanne Riis Nielson, and Xinyu Feng

Near-Optimal Scheduling for LTL with Future Discounting 112
    Shota Nakagawa and Ichiro Hasuo

A Switch, in Time.. 131
    Lenore D. Zuck and Sanjiva Prasad

Verification of Component-Based Systems via Predicate Abstraction
and Simultaneous Set Reduction 147
    Wang Qiang and Simon Bliudze

Author Index 163

Secure Two-Party Computation in Applied Pi-Calculus: Models and Verification

Sergiu Bursuc[(✉)]

School of Computer Science, University of Bristol, Bristol, UK
s.bursuc@bristol.ac.uk

Abstract. Secure two-party computation allows two distrusting parties to compute a function, without revealing their inputs to each other. Traditionally, the security properties desired in this context, and the corresponding security proofs, are based on a notion of simulation, which can be symbolic or computational. Either way, the proofs of security are intricate, requiring first to find a simulator, and then to prove a notion of indistinguishability. Furthermore, even for classic protocols such as Yao's (based on garbled circuits and oblivious transfer), we do not have adequate symbolic models for cryptographic primitives and protocol roles, that can form the basis for automated security proofs.

We propose new models in applied pi-calculus to address these gaps. Our contributions, formulated in the context of Yao's protocol, include: an equational theory for specifying the primitives of garbled computation and oblivious transfer; process specifications for the roles of the two parties in Yao's protocol; definitions of security that are more clear and direct: result integrity, input agreement (both based on correspondence assertions) and input privacy (based on observational equivalence). We put these models together and illustrate their use with ProVerif, providing a first automated verification of security for Yao's two-party computation protocol.

1 Introduction

In secure two-party computation, two parties with inputs a and b wish to compute a function $f(a, b)$ such that each party can both preserve the privacy of its inputs and be sure to receive the correct result of the computation [1]. Even more, each party would like assurance that the other party does not learn more from the protocol, like the evaluation of the function f on other inputs, e.g. $f(a', b')$, or the evaluation of another function on the same inputs, e.g. $g(a, b)$. A classic, and still most efficient, way of achieving secure two-party computation is Yao's protocol [2]. It allows two parties to exchange a garbled circuit and garbled inputs for a function, and compute the corresponding output, without leaking private inputs. In addition, zero-knowledge proofs can be incorporated into this protocol to ensure that any party cannot cheat [3,4].

This work has been supported in part by ERC Advanced Grant ERC-2010-AdG-267188-CRIPTO.

© Springer International Publishing Switzerland 2016
P. Ganty and M. Loreti (Eds.): TGC 2015, LNCS 9533, pp. 1–15, 2016.
DOI: 10.1007/978-3-319-28766-9_1

Security Proofs in Computational Models. The active security of Yao's protocol has been defined and proved in the simulation-based model [3,5,6], which states that, by executing a two-party computation protocol for a function f, an attacker can obtain essentially nothing more than the output of the function. First, this requires the definition of an ideal model where the desired functionality can be securely computed in a trivial manner, for instance relying on a trusted third party and private channels. Secondly, one has to show that the view of every attacker on the real protocol can be matched by a computationally indistinguishable view that comes from the ideal model. This requires a simulator, whose role is to decorate an ideal run with innocuous data that makes it look like a real run to any polynomially bounded adversary. This level of generality comes however at a cost, the security proofs being complex and challenging to automate.

Security Proofs in Symbolic Models. On the other hand, significant progress has been made in the field of automated verification of security protocols in formal (or symbolic) models [7,8]. However, even symbolic definitions of simulation-based security, e.g. [9,10] or [11,12] (in applied pi-calculus), are still a challenging task for such methods, which are tailored for basic properties like secrecy, authentication or privacy. Indeed, recent work aiming to automate verification for multi-party computation protocols is either relying on additional manual input [12,13], or only captures properties of correctness [14]. For Yao's protocol in particular, we also lack symbolic models for the required cryptographic primitives of garbled computation and oblivious transfer. Overall, we do not yet have the models that could be given directly to a verification tool and ask the basic question: is a particular two-party computation protocol secure or not? We propose such models for Yao's protocol.

Our Approach and Contributions. The main challenge in automating simulation-based security proofs comes from the fact that a simulator first needs to be found, and, for some methods (e.g. [12,13]), processes need to be rearranged to have the same structure in order to check indistinguishability - this requires some human input in order to be tractable by tools. In this paper, we propose an alternative approach, formulating two-party computation security for Yao's protocol as a conjunction of three basic properties: result integrity, input agreement and input privacy (Sect. 5). They are based on the standard symbolic notions of correspondence assertions and observational equivalence (of two processes with the same structure), do not require a simulator, and are directly amenable to automation. We also propose formal models in applied pi-calculus for the cryptographic primitives (Sect. 3) and the processes (Sect. 4) of Yao's two-party computation protocol. We show that our models can be combined and verified with ProVerif, deriving a first automated proof of security for Yao's protocol.

Relations Among Notions. Computational soundness results in [9,10,13,14] show that it is sufficient to prove security in the symbolic model, in order to derive security guarantees in the corresponding computational model. The models in [11,12] have not yet been shown to be computationally sound, to our knowledge. Our models are related to [11–14], being formulated in the same language of applied pi-calculus. In future work, we aim to show an even stronger relation, deriving conditions under which our properties imply, or not, simulation-based security in these formal models. We discuss this open problem and related work in more detail in Sect. 6.

2 Preliminaries

2.1 Secure Two-Party Computation with Garbled Circuits

Assume two parties $\mathcal{A}$ (with secret input x) and $\mathcal{B}$ (with secret input y) want to compute $f(x, y)$, for a function f. The basic tool in Yao's two-party computation protocol [2,6] is a garbling construction that can be applied to any circuit representing the function f. For a fresh key k, it generates a garbled circuit $GF(f, k)$ and garbled input wires $GW(x, k, a), GW(y, k, b)$, where a and b mark the circuit wires corresponding to the input of $\mathcal{A}$ or $\mathcal{B}$. Then: (i) the output of the circuit $GF(f, k)$ on inputs $GW(x, k, a), GW(x, k, b)$ is equal to $f(x, y)$, as depicted in the left part of Fig. 1; and (ii) without access to the key k, $f(x, y)$ is the only meaningful information that can be derived from $GF(f, k), GW(x, k, a), GW(y, k, b)$. In particular, the values x and y remain secret and, for any $\{x', y'\} \neq \{x, y\}$, these garbled values do not allow to compute $f(x', y')$. Relying on garbling, one of the two parties, say $\mathcal{A}$, can play the role of a sender and the other party, say $\mathcal{B}$, can play the role of a receiver. The role of the sender, as depicted in the right part of Fig. 1, is to garble the circuit and the inputs of the two parties. The role of the receiver is to execute the garbled computation and send the result back to $\mathcal{A}$. Note, however, that the party $\mathcal{A}$ does not have access to the private input of $\mathcal{B}$, so we need another tool to ensure that $\mathcal{A}$ and $\mathcal{B}$ can agree on a garbled input for $\mathcal{B}$.

Fig. 1. Garbled computation and Yao's protocol for two parties

This is where $\mathcal{A}$ and $\mathcal{B}$ rely on oblivious transfer [15,16]. An oblivious transfer protocol allows a receiver to obtain a message from a set computed by the sender such that: (i) only one message can be received and (ii) the sender does not know which message has been chosen by the receiver. In Yao's protocol, the receiver $\mathcal{B}$ can then get one message, which is the garbling of his desired input for the function, and nothing else, whereas the sender $\mathcal{A}$ does not learn what value $\mathcal{B}$ has chosen as input. Having obtained $GF(f, k), GW(x, k, a)$ and $GW(y, k, b)$, $\mathcal{B}$ can evaluate the garbled circuit and obtain $f(x, y)$, which can be sent back to $\mathcal{A}$ as the result of the computation.

Active Security. In the case when $\mathcal{B}$ might be malicious, we have to ensure that $\mathcal{A}$ can obtain from $\mathcal{B}$ the correct result. For this, the functionality of the garbled circuit is modified such that its output is a pair of values $f(x,y)$ and $enc(f(x,y),k)$, where k is a fresh secret key chosen by $\mathcal{A}$ for each protocol session. Then, instead of $f(x,y)$, $\mathcal{B}$ returns $enc(f(x,y),k)$ to $\mathcal{A}$: the result $f(x,y)$ is authenticated by the key k. To counter the case of a malicious $\mathcal{A}$, the sender $\mathcal{A}$ can prove that the garbling is correct, relying on cut-and-choose techniques [3,17] or zero-knowledge proofs [4,18].

2.2   Applied Pi-Calculus and ProVerif [19–23]

Term Algebra. We are given a set of *names*, a set of *variables* and a *signature* $\mathcal{F}$ formed of a set of *constants* and *function symbols*. Names, constants and variables are basic *terms* and new terms are built by applying function symbols to already defined terms. The signature $\mathcal{F}$ can be partitioned into *public* and *private* symbols. A *substitution* σ is a function from variables to terms, whose application to a term T is the term $T\sigma$, called an instance of T, obtained by replacing every variable x with the term $x\sigma$. A *term context* is a term $\mathcal{C}[\_1,\ldots,\_n]$ containing special constants $\_1,\ldots,\_n$ (also called holes). For a context $\mathcal{C}[\_1,\ldots,\_n]$ and a sequence of terms $T_1,\ldots,T_n$, we denote by $\mathcal{C}[T_1,\ldots,T_n]$ the term obtained by replacing each $\_i$ with the corresponding T_i in $\mathcal{C}$.

An *equational theory* is a pair $\mathcal{E} = (\mathcal{F},\mathcal{R})$, for a signature $\mathcal{F}$ and a set $\mathcal{R}$ of rewrite rules of the form $U \to V$, where U, V are terms. A term T_1 rewrites to T_2 in one step, denoted by $T_1 \to T_2$, if there is a context $\mathcal{C}[\_]$, a substitution σ and a rule $U \to V$ such that $T_1 = \mathcal{C}[U\sigma]$ and $T_2 = \mathcal{C}[V\sigma]$. More generally, $T_1 \to^* T_2$, if T_1 rewrites to T_2 in several steps [24]. We assume convergent theories: for any term T, there is a unique term $T\!\downarrow$ such that $T \to^* T\!\downarrow$. We write $U =_{\mathcal{E}} V$ if $U\!\downarrow = V\!\downarrow$. A term T can be deduced from a sequence of terms S, denoted by $S \vdash_{\mathcal{E}} T$ (or simply $S \vdash T$), if there is a context $\mathcal{C}[\_1,\ldots,\_n]$ and terms $T_1,\ldots,T_n$ in S such that $\mathcal{C}[T_1,\ldots,T_n]\!\downarrow = T$ and $\mathcal{C}$ does not contain function symbols in $\mathcal{F}^{priv}$. Such a context, together with the positions of terms $T_1,\ldots,T_n$ in S, is called a proof of $S \vdash_{\mathcal{E}} T$.

0	null process	$P \mid Q$	parallel composition
$!P$	replication	$new\ n; P$	name restriction
$in(c,x); P$	input x on c	$out(c,T); P$	output T on c
$if\ U = V\ then\ P\ else\ Q$	conditional	$let\ x = T\ in\ P$	term evaluation
$event\ T; P$	event occurence		

Fig. 2. Process algebra

Processes of the calculus, denoted by $P, Q, \ldots$, are built according to the grammar in Fig. 2, where c, n are names, x is a variable, T, U, V are terms. Replication allows the creation of any number of instances of a process. Names introduced by *new* are called *private*, or *fresh*, otherwise they are *public*, or *free*. The term

T in *event T* is usually of the form $\mathcal{A}(T_1,\ldots,T_n)$, where $\mathcal{A}$ is a special symbol representing the name of an occuring event (e.g. the start of a protocol session), while the terms $T_1,\ldots,T_n$ represent the parameters of the event (e.g. the names or inputs of parties). A variable x is *free* in a process P if P does not contain x in any of its input actions and any term evaluation of the form $x = T$. A process P with free variables $x_1,\ldots,x_n$ is denoted by $P(x_1,\ldots,x_n)$, i.e. $x_1,\ldots,x_n$ are parameters of P that will be instantiated in the context where P is used. We denote by $sig(P)$ the set of function symbols that appear in P. A *process context* $C[\_]$ is defined similarly as a term context.

Formally, the operational semantics of processes is defined as a relation on tuples of the form $(\mathcal{N},\mathcal{M},\mathcal{L},\mathcal{P})$, called configurations, whose elements represent the following information in the execution of a process: $\mathcal{N}$ is the set of freshly generated names; $\mathcal{M}$ is the sequence of terms output on public channels (i.e. to the attacker); $\mathcal{L}$ is the set of occured events; $\mathcal{P}$ is the multiset of processes being executed in parallel. The rules that define the operational semantics, presented in the associated research report [25] and adapted from [21,22], are quite standard and correspond to the informal meaning previously discussed. We denote by $P \to^* (\mathcal{N},\mathcal{M},\mathcal{L},\mathcal{P})$ if the configuration $(\mathcal{N},\mathcal{M},\mathcal{L},\mathcal{P})$ can be reached from the initial configuration of P, which is $(\emptyset,\emptyset,\emptyset,\{P\})$.

Security Properties. We rely on *correspondence assertions* [21] and *observational equivalence* [22]. Correspondence assertions allow to specify constraints for events occuring in the execution of the protocol. They are based on formulas Φ, Ψ whose syntax is defined as follows:

$$ev : T \qquad att : T \qquad U = V \qquad \Phi \wedge \Psi \qquad \Phi \vee \Psi \qquad \neg\Phi$$

Their semantics, for a configuration $\mathcal{C} = (\mathcal{N},\mathcal{M},\mathcal{L},\mathcal{P})$ and equational theory $\mathcal{E}$, is defined by $\mathcal{C} \models_\mathcal{E} ev : T \Leftrightarrow \exists T' \in \mathcal{L}.\ T' =_\mathcal{E} T$, and $\mathcal{C} \models_\mathcal{E} U = V \Leftrightarrow U =_\mathcal{E} V$ and $\mathcal{C} \models_\mathcal{E} att : T \Leftrightarrow \mathcal{M} \vdash_\mathcal{E} T$, plus the usual semantics of boolean operators. Note, a predicate $ev : T$ is true for a configuration if the event T occured in the execution trace leading to it, and $att : T$ is true if the attacker can deduce T from the public messages of the configuration. A *correspondence assertion* is a formula of the form $\Phi \rightsquigarrow \Psi$. Such a formula is satisfied for a process P if and only if, for every process Q, with $sig(Q) \cap \mathcal{F}^{priv} = \emptyset$, and every configuration $\mathcal{C}$ reachable from $P \mid Q$, i.e. $P \mid Q \to^* \mathcal{C}$, and any substition σ, we have that $\mathcal{C} \models \Phi\sigma$ implies $\mathcal{C} \models \Psi\sigma'$, for some substition σ' that extends σ, i.e. if $x\sigma$ is defined, then $x\sigma' = x\sigma$. Intuitively, a correspondence assertion requires that every time the formula Φ is true during the execution of a process, the constraints specified in Ψ must also be true for the same parameters. The process Q stands for any computation that may be performed by the attacker.

Observational equivalence, denoted by $P_1 \sim P_2$, specifies the inability of the attacker to distinguish between two processes P_1 and P_2. Formally, $P_1 \sim P_2$ is true if and only if, for every process Q, with $sig(Q) \cap \mathcal{F}^{priv} = \emptyset$, and every configuration $(\mathcal{N}_1,\mathcal{M}_1,\mathcal{L}_1,\mathcal{P}_1)$ reachable from $P_1 \mid Q$, there is a configuration $(\mathcal{N}_2,\mathcal{M}_2,\mathcal{L}_2,\mathcal{P}_2)$ reachable from $P_2 \mid Q$, such that for any term T_1 and any two different proofs π_1, π_2 of $\mathcal{M}_1 \vdash_\mathcal{E} T_1$, there is a term T_2 such that π_1, π_2 are also proofs of $\mathcal{M}_2 \vdash_\mathcal{E} T_2$ [19, 22, 23, 26].

3   Equational Theory for Garbled Computation

In this section we present an equational theory to model the cryptographic primitives used in garbled computation protocols like [2, 3, 6]. We will refer to a party $\mathcal{A}$ as *the sender* (who garbles and transmits data), and to a party $\mathcal{B}$ as *the receiver* (who receives and ungarbles data). The equational theory, presented in Fig. 3 and discussed below, allows $\mathcal{B}$ to evaluate a garbled circuit on garbled inputs; $\mathcal{A}$ to prove that the circuits and its inputs are correctly garbled; $\mathcal{B}$ to obtain by oblivious transfer $\mathcal{B}$'s garbled input.

Garbled Circuit Evaluation. The term $eval(T_\mathcal{F}, T_\mathcal{A}, T_\mathcal{B})$ represents the result of evaluating a circuit, represented by the term $T_\mathcal{F}$, on inputs of $\mathcal{A}$ and $\mathcal{B}$, represented by terms $T_\mathcal{A}$ and $T_\mathcal{B}$ respectively.

The term $gf(T_\mathcal{F}, T_\mathcal{K})$ represents the garbling of a circuit $T_\mathcal{F}$, given a garbling key $T_\mathcal{K}$. The term $gw(T, T_\mathcal{K}, i)$, with $i \in \{a, b\}$, represents a garbling of the input T with a key $T_\mathcal{K}$, where T corresponds to the input wires of party $\mathcal{A}$, when i is a, or of party $\mathcal{B}$, when i is b.

The term $geval(gf(T_\mathcal{F}, T_\mathcal{K}), gw(T_\mathcal{A}, T_\mathcal{K}, a), gw(T_\mathcal{B}, T_\mathcal{K}, b))$ represents the computation performed on the garbled function and garbled inputs given as arguments to $geval$, the result of which is $eval(T_\mathcal{F}, T_\mathcal{A}, T_\mathcal{B})$, as specified by the rewrite rule $\mathcal{R}_1$.

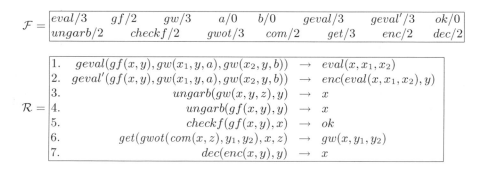

Fig. 3. Equational theory $\mathcal{E}_{GC}$ for garbled computation

In addition, the function $geval'$ specified by $\mathcal{R}_2$ provides an encryption of the function output. As explained in Sect. 2.1, this ciphertext can be sent as response to $\mathcal{A}$, providing confidence that the final result correctly reflects $\mathcal{A}$'s inputs in the protocol, even while interacting with a malicious $\mathcal{B}$. For brevity, the key in the encryption returned by $\mathcal{R}_2$ is the same as the one used for garbling, but the model can be easily adapted for more complex scenarios.

Overall, $\mathcal{R}_1$ and $\mathcal{R}_2$ are the only operations that can be performed on garbled values without the key, this way enforcing several security properties. First, the function and the inputs of the garbled circuit cannot be modified. Second, the computation in rules $\mathcal{R}_1, \mathcal{R}_2$ succeeds only for circuits and inputs that are garbled with the same key y (otherwise, a malicious party may combine garbled values from different sessions of the protocol in order to derive more information than it should). Third, the inputs must be used consistently, e.g. the garbled input of $\mathcal{A}$ cannot be substituted with a garbled input for $\mathcal{B}$ (ensured by the constants a and b). Garbled data can only be ungarbled by the key holder, as specified by the rule $\mathcal{R}_3$ for garbled functions and the rule $\mathcal{R}_4$ for garbled inputs.

These features ensure that a malicious receiver cannot cheat. In addition, we need to ensure that a malicious sender cannot cheat. This is the role of $\mathcal{R}_5$, which allows a party to check that a function is correctly garbled, without access to the garbling key. Cryptographically, there are various ways in which this abstraction can be instantiated, e.g. by zero-knowledge proofs [4] or cut-and-choose techniques [3,27]. The model of oblivious transfer that we explain next will also allow the receiver to be convinced that his input is correctly garbled.

Garbled oblivious transfer is modeled relying on functions $gwot, get, com$, and the rewrite rule $\mathcal{R}_6$, as follows: the term $com(T_\mathcal{B}, V)$ represents a commitment to a term $T_\mathcal{B}$, which cannot be modified, and is hidden by a nonce V; such a term will be used by $\mathcal{B}$ to request a garbled version of $T_\mathcal{B}$ without disclosing it.

The term $gwot(com(T_\mathcal{B}, V), T_\mathcal{K}, T)$ is an oblivious transfer term, obtained from a commited input $com(T_\mathcal{B}, V)$ and a garbling key $T_\mathcal{K}$; such a term will be constructed by $\mathcal{A}$ and sent in response to $\mathcal{B}$'s commitment.

The term $get(gwot(com(T_\mathcal{B}, V), T_\mathcal{K}, T), T_\mathcal{B}, V)$ allows to obtain $gw(T_\mathcal{B}, T_\mathcal{K}, T)$ from an oblivious transfer term, if a party has the secret input $T_\mathcal{B}$ and the nonce V that have been used to construct the corresponding commitment. The term T would be equal to the constant b in a normal execution of the protocol.

This way, we capture formally the security properties of oblivious transfer protocols like [15,16,27,28]: for a sender $\mathcal{A}$ and a receiver $\mathcal{B}$: $\mathcal{B}$ should only learn one garbled value among many possible ones; and $\mathcal{A}$ should not learn which value $\mathcal{B}$ has chosen. The first property is ensured in our model by the fact that a dishonest $\mathcal{B}$ cannot change the commitment $com(T_\mathcal{B}, V)$ in an oblivious transfer term $gwot(com(T_\mathcal{B}, V), T_\mathcal{K}, T)$. The only way to obtain a garbling of a second message would be to run a second instance of the protocol with $\mathcal{A}$, involving another commitment and corresponding oblivious transfer term - this is a legitimate behaviour that is also allowed by our model. The second property is ensured by the fact that a commitment $com(T_\mathcal{B}, V)$ does not reveal $T_\mathcal{B}$ or V. Furthermore, only the holder of $T_\mathcal{B}$ and V can extract the respective garbled value from an oblivious transfer term, ensuring that $\mathcal{B}$ is in fact the only party that can obtain $gw(T_\mathcal{B}, T_\mathcal{K}, T)$.

4   Formal Protocol Specification

In this section, we show how the equational theory from Sect. 3 is integrated into higher level protocols modeled by processes communicating over a public network. Figure 4 contains the process specifications of the two roles in Yao's protocol for secure two-party computation: the sender process $\mathcal{A}$ and the receiver process $\mathcal{B}$. Text within (* and *) represents comments. The public parameter of $\mathcal{A}$ and $\mathcal{B}$ is the function to be evaluated, represented by the free variable $x_{\mathcal{F}}$. The private parameters of $\mathcal{A}$ and $\mathcal{B}$ are their respective inputs, represented by the free variables $x_{\mathcal{A}}$ and respectively $x_{\mathcal{B}}$. The goal of $\mathcal{A}$ and $\mathcal{B}$ is therefore to obtain $eval(x_{\mathcal{F}}, x_{\mathcal{A}}, x_{\mathcal{B}})$, without disclosing $x_{\mathcal{A}}$ to $\mathcal{B}$ and $x_{\mathcal{B}}$ to $\mathcal{A}$. A public name c represents the communication channel between the two parties, possibly controlled by an attacker.

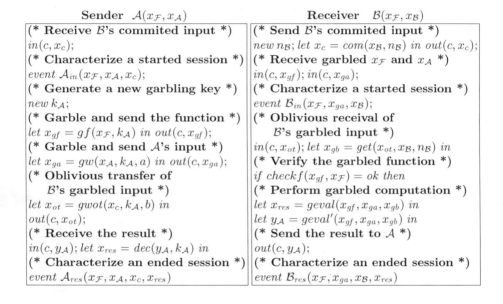

Sender $\mathcal{A}(x_{\mathcal{F}}, x_{\mathcal{A}})$	Receiver $\mathcal{B}(x_{\mathcal{F}}, x_{\mathcal{B}})$
(* **Receive** $\mathcal{B}$**'s commited input** *)	(* **Send** $\mathcal{B}$**'s commited input** *)
$in(c, x_c)$;	$new\ n_{\mathcal{B}};\ let\ x_c = com(x_{\mathcal{B}}, n_{\mathcal{B}})\ in\ out(c, x_c)$;
(* **Characterize a started session** *)	(* **Receive garbled** $x_{\mathcal{F}}$ **and** $x_{\mathcal{A}}$ *)
$event\ \mathcal{A}_{in}(x_{\mathcal{F}}, x_{\mathcal{A}}, x_c)$;	$in(c, x_{gf}); in(c, x_{ga})$;
(* **Generate a new garbling key** *)	(* **Characterize a started session** *)
$new\ k_{\mathcal{A}}$;	$event\ \mathcal{B}_{in}(x_{\mathcal{F}}, x_{ga}, x_{\mathcal{B}})$;
(* **Garble and send the function** *)	(* **Oblivious receival of**
$let\ x_{gf} = gf(x_{\mathcal{F}}, k_{\mathcal{A}})\ in\ out(c, x_{gf})$;	$\mathcal{B}$**'s garbled input** *)
(* **Garble and send** $\mathcal{A}$**'s input** *)	$in(c, x_{ot}); let\ x_{gb} = get(x_{ot}, x_{\mathcal{B}}, n_{\mathcal{B}})\ in$
$let\ x_{ga} = gw(x_{\mathcal{A}}, k_{\mathcal{A}}, a)\ in\ out(c, x_{ga})$;	(* **Verify the garbled function** *)
(* **Oblivious transfer of**	$if\ checkf(x_{gf}, x_{\mathcal{F}}) = ok\ then$
$\mathcal{B}$**'s garbled input** *)	(* **Perform garbled computation** *)
$let\ x_{ot} = gwot(x_c, k_{\mathcal{A}}, b)\ in$	$let\ x_{res} = geval(x_{gf}, x_{ga}, x_{gb})\ in$
$out(c, x_{ot})$;	$let\ y_{\mathcal{A}} = geval'(x_{gf}, x_{ga}, x_{gb})\ in$
(* **Receive the result** *)	(* **Send the result to** $\mathcal{A}$ *)
$in(c, y_{\mathcal{A}}); let\ x_{res} = dec(y_{\mathcal{A}}, k_{\mathcal{A}})\ in$	$out(c, y_{\mathcal{A}})$;
(* **Characterize an ended session** *)	(* **Characterize an ended session** *)
$event\ \mathcal{A}_{res}(x_{\mathcal{F}}, x_{\mathcal{A}}, x_c, x_{res})$	$event\ \mathcal{B}_{res}(x_{\mathcal{F}}, x_{ga}, x_{\mathcal{B}}, x_{res})$

Fig. 4. Processes for two-party computation

Sender. The sender $\mathcal{A}$ creates a new key $k_{\mathcal{A}}$, which it uses to garble the circuit $x_{\mathcal{F}}$, its input $x_{\mathcal{A}}$ and, obliviously, the input of $\mathcal{B}$. As part of the oblivious transfer, $\mathcal{A}$ first receives the commited input of $\mathcal{B}$. The garbled values, as well as the corresponding oblivious transfer term, are sent to $\mathcal{B}$ over the public channel c. As response from $\mathcal{B}$, $\mathcal{A}$ receives the result of the computation encrypted with $k_{\mathcal{A}}$.

Receiver. The receiver $\mathcal{B}$ obtains garbled data from $\mathcal{A}$ and, to get a garbled version x_{gb} of its own input $x_{\mathcal{B}}$, engages in the oblivious transfer protocol: it makes a commitment to $x_{\mathcal{B}}$, sends the commitment to $\mathcal{A}$ and receives in response the corresponding oblivious transfer term containing the garbled input. Next, $\mathcal{B}$ verifies that the function is correctly garbled and performs the garbled computation. The value x_{res} is the result obtained by $\mathcal{B}$, while $y_{\mathcal{A}}$ is the encrypted result that is sent back to $\mathcal{A}$.

Events. The events $\mathcal{A}_{in}$, $\mathcal{A}_{res}$, $\mathcal{B}_{in}$ and $\mathcal{B}_{res}$ are used as part of the formal specification of security properties that we present in Sect. 5. The event $\mathcal{A}_{in}(x_\mathcal{F}, x_\mathcal{A}, x_c)$
records that $\mathcal{A}$ has engaged in a protocol session for the computation of $x_\mathcal{F}$,
having $\mathcal{A}$'s input equal to $x_\mathcal{A}$, and $\mathcal{B}$'s input being committed to x_c. The event
$\mathcal{A}_{res}(x_\mathcal{F}, x_\mathcal{A}, x_c, x_{res})$ records in addition that $\mathcal{A}$ has obtained the result x_{res} as
outcome of the protocol session.

The event $\mathcal{B}_{in}(x_\mathcal{F}, x_{ga}, x_\mathcal{B})$ records that $\mathcal{B}$ has engaged in a protocol session
for the computation of $x_\mathcal{F}$, having $\mathcal{B}$'s input equal to $x_\mathcal{B}$, and $\mathcal{A}$'s input being
garbled as x_{ga}. The event $\mathcal{B}_{res}(x_\mathcal{F}, x_{ga}, x_\mathcal{B}, x_{res})$ records in addition that $\mathcal{B}$ has
obtained the result x_{res} as outcome of the protocol session.

Attacker. As usual, the attacker can execute any of the operations that we have
described, as well as any other operations allowed by the equational theory, and
(pretend to) play the role of any party, while interacting with an honest party $\mathcal{A}$
or $\mathcal{B}$ on the public channel c. This is captured formally by the semantics of the
applied pi-calculus and the definition of the security properties that we present
in the next section.

5   Formal Models of Security for Two-Party Computation

Informally, we require the following security properties for a two-party computation protocol:

1. The dishonest parties should not learn too much:
   (a) The only leakage about the input of an honest party should come from
         the result of the evaluated function (**Input privacy**).
   (b) A dishonest party should be able to evaluate a function on honest inputs
         only as agreed by the corresponding honest party (**Input agreement**).
2. The honest parties learn the correct result (**Result integrity**).

The distinction between input privacy and input agreement separates the
task of input protection for honest parties into (a) protecting the honest input
during the protocol flow (without bothering about the output of the function);
and (b) ensuring that function outputs are released only as agreed to by the
owners of private inputs. This distinction helps to address automated verification
problems when the public output of the protocol depends on the private input
of parties. For example, automating privacy proofs for electronic voting protocols is known to be problematic, because care should be taken to separate the
legitimate (e.g. the result of the election) from the illegitimate information flow
[29,30]. This is also a problem for automating simulation-based proofs, where
an ideal functionality models exactly what can be leaked by the protocol, and a
simulator needs to be found that shows the protocol not to leak more [11–13].
Our separation of this property into (a) and (b) is a new way of addressing this
problem, and is making more explicit the properties that are achieved, without
requiring a simulator as in [11–13] or additional honest parties as in [29,30].

These security properties can be formalized in a general setting, but for
brevity we present them in relation to the models of Sects. 3 and 4, and leave

their generalization as future work. In this setting, a specification of a two-party computation protocol is given by a triple $(\mathcal{A}, \mathcal{B}, \mathcal{E})$, where $\mathcal{E}$ is an equational theory containing $\mathcal{E}_{GC}$ from Sect. 3, $\mathcal{A}$ is a sender process with free variables $x_{\mathcal{F}}, x_{\mathcal{A}}$, $\mathcal{B}$ is a receiver process with free variables $x_{\mathcal{F}}, x_{\mathcal{B}}$, and these processes are enriched with events $\mathcal{A}_{in}, \mathcal{B}_{in}, \mathcal{A}_{res}, \mathcal{B}_{res}$ presented in Sect. 4.

5.1   Result Integrity

Result integrity should ensure that the final result obtained by an honest party $\mathcal{P} \in \{\mathcal{A}, \mathcal{B}\}$ after a session of the protocol is consistent with the function that $\mathcal{P}$ expects to be evaluated, with the input of $\mathcal{P}$ in this session, and with the input of the other party, that has responded to this session, or has initiated it. Formally, the events $\mathcal{A}_{res}(x_{\mathcal{F}}, x_{\mathcal{A}}, x_c, x_{res})$ and $\mathcal{B}_{res}(x_{\mathcal{F}}, x_{ga}, x_{\mathcal{B}}, x_{res})$ capture the views of $\mathcal{A}$ and $\mathcal{B}$ after a session of the protocol has ended, recording all the relevant data, in particular the result obtained by the respective party, and the committed (resp. garbled) input of the other party. Therefore, we can specify the requirement of result integrity by the correspondence assertions $\Phi_{int}^{\mathcal{A}}$ and $\Phi_{int}^{\mathcal{B}}$ presented in Definition 1.

Definition 1 (Result Integrity). *Let $(\mathcal{A}, \mathcal{B}, \mathcal{E})$ be a specification of a two-party computation protocol. We define the correspondence assertions $\Phi_{int}^{\mathcal{A}}$ and $\Phi_{int}^{\mathcal{B}}$ as follows:*

$$\Phi_{int}^{\mathcal{A}} \doteq ev : \mathcal{A}_{res}(x, y, z, w) \rightsquigarrow z = com(z_1, z_2) \wedge w = eval(x, y, z_1)$$
$$\Phi_{int}^{\mathcal{B}} \doteq ev : \mathcal{B}_{res}(x, y, z, w) \rightsquigarrow y = gw(y_1, y_2, a) \wedge w = eval(x, y_1, z)$$

We say that $(\mathcal{A}, \mathcal{B}, \mathcal{E})$ satisfies result integrity if

$$! \, (\, in(c, x_{\mathcal{F}}); in(c, x_{\mathcal{A}}); \mathcal{A}(x_{\mathcal{F}}, x_{\mathcal{A}}) \,) \models_{\mathcal{E}} \Phi_{int}^{\mathcal{A}} \quad and$$
$$! \, (\, in(c, x_{\mathcal{F}}); in(c, x_{\mathcal{B}}); \mathcal{B}(x_{\mathcal{F}}, x_{\mathcal{B}}) \,) \models_{\mathcal{E}} \Phi_{int}^{\mathcal{B}}$$

The specification lets the attacker execute any number of sessions of an honest party $\mathcal{A}$ or $\mathcal{B}$, with any function $x_{\mathcal{F}}$ and any values $x_{\mathcal{A}}, x_{\mathcal{B}}$ as inputs, and requires the correspondence assertions $\Phi_{int}^{\mathcal{A}}$ and $\Phi_{int}^{\mathcal{B}}$ to be satisfied by this process. In turn, $\Phi_{int}^{\mathcal{A}}$ and $\Phi_{int}^{\mathcal{B}}$ require that for any occurence of the event $\mathcal{A}_{res}$ or $\mathcal{B}_{res}$, the result obtained by the respective honest party, recorded in the variable w, correctly reflects the function and relevant messages of the corresponding session, recorded in variables x, y, z. Note that the variables z_1, z_2, y_1, y_2 in $\Phi_{int}^{\mathcal{A}}, \Phi_{int}^{\mathcal{B}}$ are existentially quantified implicitly. This allows the specified property to hold for any message choices in the protocol, as long as the desired constraints are satisfied.

5.2   Input Agreement

Input agreement should ensure that the function outputs obtained by a dishonest party after executing a session of the protocol are consistent with the expectation of an honest party when it releases its private inputs. Specifically, consider the case where an honest party $\mathcal{A}$ supplied an input $T_{\mathcal{A}}$ in order to compute a function $T_{\mathcal{F}}$. Then, the other party should only be able to obtain $eval(T_{\mathcal{F}}, T_{\mathcal{A}}, T_{\mathcal{B}})$, where $T_{\mathcal{B}}$ is its own input when playing the role of $\mathcal{B}$ in the corresponding protocol session. In particular, the other party should not be able to obtain $eval(T_{\mathcal{F}}, T_{\mathcal{A}}, T'_{\mathcal{B}})$, for a different input $T'_{\mathcal{B}}$, or $eval(T'_{\mathcal{F}}, T_{\mathcal{A}}, T_{\mathcal{B}})$, for different function $T'_{\mathcal{F}}$. Similar guarantees should hold for an honest party $\mathcal{B}$.

We formally define these requirements as correspondence assertions. The fact that the attacker knows a particular function output can be expressed by the formula $att ::eval(x, y, z)$. To express the constraints associated with this formula, we rely on events $\mathcal{A}_{in}(x_{\mathcal{F}}, x_{\mathcal{A}}, x_c)$ and $\mathcal{B}_{in}(x_{\mathcal{F}}, x_{ga}, x_{\mathcal{B}})$, that record the parameters of each honest party in a started protocol session. In particular, the event $\mathcal{A}_{in}$ records the commited input of $\mathcal{B}$, received by $\mathcal{A}$, and $\mathcal{B}_{in}$ records the garbled input of $\mathcal{A}$, received by $\mathcal{B}$. Therefore, these events fully determine the result that each party (and in particular a dishonest party) should obtain from the respective protocol session. Then, in Definition 2 we require that to any function output $eval(x, y, z)$ obtained by the attacker, there corresponds an initial event recording the agreement of the respective honest party $\mathcal{A}$ or $\mathcal{B}$.

Definition 2 (Input Agreement). *Let $(\mathcal{A}, \mathcal{B}, \mathcal{E})$ be a specification of a two-party computation protocol. We define the correspondence assertions $\Phi_{agr}^{\mathcal{A}}$ and $\Phi_{agr}^{\mathcal{B}}$ as follows:*

$$\Phi_{agr}^{\mathcal{A}} \doteq att : eval(x, y, z) \rightsquigarrow (\ ev : \mathcal{A}_{in}(x, y, z_1) \wedge z_1 = com(z, z_2)\ ) \vee att : y$$
$$\Phi_{agr}^{\mathcal{B}} \doteq att : eval(x, y, z) \rightsquigarrow (\ ev : \mathcal{B}_{in}(x, y_1, z) \wedge y_1 = gw(y, y_2, a)\ ) \vee att : z$$

We say that a specification $(\mathcal{A}, \mathcal{B}, \mathcal{E})$ of a two-party computation protocol satisfies input agreement *if:*

$$!\ (\ in(c, x_{\mathcal{F}}); new\ i_{\mathcal{A}}; \mathcal{A}(x_{\mathcal{F}}, i_{\mathcal{A}})\ ) \models_{\mathcal{E}} \Phi_{agr}^{\mathcal{A}} \quad and$$
$$!\ (\ in(c, x_{\mathcal{F}}); new\ i_{\mathcal{B}}; \mathcal{B}(x_{\mathcal{F}}, i_{\mathcal{B}})\ ) \models_{\mathcal{E}} \Phi_{agr}^{\mathcal{B}}$$

Note, however, that this property cannot be achieved if the input of the honest party is known to the attacker, who can obtain $eval(x, y, z)$ from x, y, z, by simply evaluating the function. Therefore, input agreement as defined here makes sense only for honest input values that are not available to the attacker. This is captured by the disjunction in the correspondence assertions $\Phi_{agr}^{\mathcal{A}}$ and $\Phi_{agr}^{\mathcal{B}}$ of Definition 2, and by the fact that inputs $i_{\mathcal{A}}, i_{\mathcal{B}}$ of honest parties in the test processes $\mathcal{A}(x_{\mathcal{F}}, i_{\mathcal{A}}), \mathcal{B}(x_{\mathcal{F}}, i_{\mathcal{B}})$ are locally generated for each session.

5.3   Input Privacy

Traditionally, e.g. for verifying strong secrecy [31] or vote privacy [29,30], the privacy of an input x in a process $\mathcal{P}(x)$ is defined as a property of indistinguishability between two of its instances, say $\mathcal{P}(a_1)$ and $\mathcal{P}(a_2)$. In our case, we have to make the indistinguishability notion robust in order to take into account information flow that is inherent from the functionality of the protocol. In fact, we will require that the only leakage about the input of an honest party comes from the evaluated function. In other words, if the output of the function is withheld from the attacker, *no* leakage should occur about the honest inputs. This amounts to a standard requirement of strong secrecy, which can be formalized as an observational equivalence.

It remains to formalize what it means for the output of the function to be withheld from the attacker. The attacker might be able to compute the output by combining data gathered throughout the protocol (for example, an attacker playing the role of $\mathcal{B}$ in Yao's protocol can evaluate the function output from the received garbled data). In such cases, it is not clear what data can be legitimately withheld from the attacker when defining input privacy. Instead, we will enrich the equational theory such that, for honest inputs, all corresponding function outputs are equivalent, i.e. the attacker cannot observe the difference between them. Therefore, rather than suppressing the function output in the protocol specification, we suppress the attacker's ability to gain information from this output. The enriched equational theory relies on special function symbols α and β that will decorate the private inputs of an honest party $\mathcal{A}$, respectively $\mathcal{B}$. The additional rewrite rules for *eval* declare function evaluations of these inputs to be equivalent, relying on the constants α_0, β_0.

Definition 3. *Let $\mathcal{E}$ be an equational theory. Consider the function symbols α, β and the constants α_0, β_0. We define the equational theories $\mathcal{E}_\alpha = \mathcal{E} \cup \{eval(x, \alpha(y), z) \to eval(x, \alpha_0, z)\}$ and $\mathcal{E}_\beta = \mathcal{E} \cup \{eval(x, y, \beta(z)) \to eval(x, y, \beta_0)\}$*

The specification in Definition 4 considers two versions of a process: for any number of sessions, and any choice of terms x^0, x^1 for each session, in the first version an honest party $\mathcal{A}$, respectively $\mathcal{B}$, inputs $\alpha(x^0)$, respectively $\beta(x^0)$; in the second version the party inputs $\alpha(x^1)$, respectively $\beta(x^1)$. We say that the protocol satisfies input privacy if these two versions are in observational equivalence, i.e. indistinguishable for the attacker.

Definition 4 (Input Privacy). *Let $(\mathcal{A}, \mathcal{B}, \mathcal{E})$ be a specification of a two-party computation protocol and $\mathcal{E}_\alpha, \mathcal{E}_\beta$ be the equational theories from Definition 3. Let $\mathcal{C}_{in}[\_]$ be the process context $in(c, x_\mathcal{F}); in(c, x^0); in(c, x^1); [\_]$. We say that $(\mathcal{A}, \mathcal{B}, \mathcal{E})$ satisfies input privacy if*

$$! \, \mathcal{C}_{in}[\, \mathcal{A}(x_\mathcal{F}, \alpha(x^0)) \,] \sim_{\mathcal{E}_\alpha} ! \, \mathcal{C}_{in}[\, \mathcal{A}(x_\mathcal{F}, \alpha(x^1)) \,] \quad and$$
$$! \, \mathcal{C}_{in}[\, \mathcal{B}(x_\mathcal{F}, \beta(x^0)) \,] \sim_{\mathcal{E}_\beta} ! \, \mathcal{C}_{in}[\, \mathcal{B}(x_\mathcal{F}, \beta(x^1)) \,]$$

Note that $\alpha(x^0)$ and $\alpha(x^1)$ remain distinct terms with respect to $\mathcal{E}_\alpha$ when considered in any context other than in terms of the form $eval(y, \alpha(x^0), z)$, $eval(y, \alpha(x^1), z)$; and similarly for $\mathcal{E}_\beta$. That is why, if there is a privacy weakness in the protocol, the attacker will be able to spot the difference between the two experiments in Definition 4, for either $\mathcal{A}$ or $\mathcal{B}$.

6   Conclusion and Related Work

The ProVerif code for the models introduced in this paper is available online and in the associated research report [25]. ProVerif returns within seconds positive results for all queries, and we also perform reachability tests to ensure that all parties can execute the protocol correctly. Our models and results differ from related work in several aspects, and also open new research questions:

The model of Backes et al. [14] considers multi-party computation functionalities abstractly, allowing to reason about their use in larger protocols, without necessarily representing the cryptographic primitives that realize the functionality. Their framework comes equipped with a computational soundness result and is applied to the case study of an auction protocol [32]. A property of robust safety, which can be related to our property of result integrity, is verified automatically relying on type-checking.

Dahl and Damgård [13] propose a computationally sound formal framework for two-party computation protocols in applied pi-calculus and use ProVerif to verify an oblivious transfer protocol based on homomorphic encryption [28]. In order to use ProVerif, they have to find a simulator and to additionally transform the processes manually. On the other hand, we do not require a simulator and our models can be given as input directly to automated tools. Our case study is also different, allowing to evaluate any given function, relying on garbled circuits and on oblivious transfer as a sub-protocol. However, we do not provide a soundness result, and the relation of our models to simulation-based security remains an open question. In that direction, we can also explore extensions of our models into a general framework allowing the verification of other protocols, for two or multiple parties, and relying on various cryptographic primitives.

Delaune et al. [11] and Böhl and Unruh [12] study definitions of simulation-based security in applied pi-calculus, showing their application to the analysis of several protocols. Although quite general, their frameworks are not easily amenable to automation. As in [13], the authors of [12] have to perform a significant amount of manual proof before applying ProVerif. Earlier computationally sound symbolic models for simulation-based security are yet more complex [9,10,33]. Our paper proposes a different approach: rather than directly expressing simulation-based security in formal models, we propose several security notions whose conjunction should be sufficient for secure two-party computation, while it remains to be seen under what conditions they imply simulation-based security. This methodology promises not only better automation, but also a better understanding of what security properties are achieved. In turn, this may aid the design of new protocols, where some of the properties can be relaxed.

A formal model for oblivious transfer in applied pi-calculus is presented by Dahl and Damgård [13]. Their specification is a process modeling a particular protocol, whereas we propose a more abstract equational theory. However, our theory only models oblivious transfer of garbled values; automated verification modulo a more general equational theory for oblivious transfer remains for future work. Conversely, the model of Goubault et al. [34] aims to capture formally the probabilistic aspect of some oblivious transfer protocols.

Acknowledgement. We thank the reviewers for their valuable comments.

References

1. Yao, A.: Protocols for secure computations (extended abstract). In: FOCS, pp. 160–164. IEEE Computer Society (1982)
2. Yao, A.: How to generate and exchange secrets (extended abstract). In: FOCS, pp. 162–167. IEEE Computer Society (1986)
3. Lindell, Y., Pinkas, B.: An efficient protocol for secure two-party computation in the presence of malicious adversaries. In: Naor [35], pp. 52–78
4. Jarecki, S., Shmatikov, V.: Efficient two-party secure computation on committed inputs. In: Naor [35], pp. 97–114
5. Canetti, R.: Universally composable security: A new paradigm for cryptographic protocols. In: FOCS, pp. 136–145. IEEE Computer Society (2001)
6. Lindell, Y., Pinkas, B.: A proof of security of Yao's protocol for two-party computation. J. Cryptol. **22**(2), 161–188 (2009)
7. Abadi, M., Blanchet, B., Comon-Lundh, H.: Models and proofs of protocol security: a progress report. In: Bouajjani, A., Maler, O. (eds.) CAV 2009. LNCS, vol. 5643, pp. 35–49. Springer, Heidelberg (2009)
8. Cortier, V., Kremer, S. (eds.): Formal Models and Techniques for Analyzing Security Protocols. Cryptology and Information Security Series. IOS Press, Amsterdam (2011)
9. Canetti, R., Herzog, J.: Universally composable symbolic security analysis. J. Cryptol. **24**(1), 83–147 (2011)
10. Backes, M., Pfitzmann, B., Waidner, M.: A composable cryptographic library with nested operations. In: Proceedings of the 10th ACM Conference on Computer and Communications Security, CCS 2003, Washington, DC, USA, 27–30 October 2003 (2003)
11. Delaune, S., Kremer, S., Pereira, O.: Simulation based security in the applied pi calculus. In: Kannan, R., Narayan Kumar, K. (eds.), FSTTCS. LIPIcs, vol. 4, pp. 169–180 (2009)
12. Böhl, F., Unruh, D.: Symbolic universal composability. In: 2013 IEEE 26th Computer Security Foundations Symposium, New Orleans, LA, USA, 26–28 June 2013, pp. 257–271. IEEE (2013)
13. Dahl, M., Damgård, I.: Universally composable symbolic analysis for two-party protocols based on homomorphic encryption. In: Nguyen, P.Q., Oswald, E. (eds.) EUROCRYPT 2014. LNCS, vol. 8441, pp. 695–712. Springer, Heidelberg (2014)
14. Backes, M., Maffei, M., Mohammadi, E.: Computationally sound abstraction and verification of secure multi-party computations. In: Lodaya, K., Mahajan, M. (eds.) FSTTCS. LIPIcs, vol. 8, pp. 352–363 (2010)
15. Rabin, M.O.: How to exchange secrets with oblivious transfer. IACR Cryptol. ePrint Arch. **2005**, 187 (2005)
16. Even, S., Goldreich, O., Lempel, A.: A randomized protocol for signing contracts. Commun. ACM **28**(6), 637–647 (1985)
17. Huang, Y., Katz, J., Evans, D.: Efficient secure two-party computation using symmetric cut-and-choose. In: Canetti, R., Garay, J.A. (eds.) CRYPTO 2013, Part II. LNCS, vol. 8043, pp. 18–35. Springer, Heidelberg (2013)
18. Goldreich, O., Micali, S., Wigderson, A.: How to play any mental game or a completeness theorem for protocols with honest majority. In: Aho, A.V. (eds.) STOC, pp. 218–229. ACM (1987)
19. Abadi, M., Fournet, C.: Mobile values, new names, and secure communication. In: Proceedings of the 28th ACM Symposium on Principles of Programming Languages (POPL 2001), pp. 104–115, January 2001

20. Blanchet, B.: An efficient cryptographic protocol verifier based on prolog rules. In: Computer Security Foundations Workshop (CSFW 2001) (2001)
21. Blanchet, B.: Automatic verification of correspondences for security protocols. J. Comput. Secur. **17**(4), 363–434 (2009)
22. Blanchet, B., Abadi, M., Fournet, C.: Automated verification of selected equivalences for security protocols. J. Log. Algebr. Program. **75**(1), 3–51 (2008)
23. Ryan, M., Smyth, B.: Applied pi calculus. In: Cortier, V., Kremer, S. (eds.) Formal Models and Techniques for Analyzing Security Protocols. Cryptology and Information Security Series. IOS Press (2011)
24. Dershowitz, N., Jouannaud, J.-P.: Rewrite systems. In: Handbook of Theoretical Computer Science, Volume B: Formal Models and Sematics (B), pp. 243–320. MIT Press (1990)
25. Bursuc, S.: Secure two-party computation in applied pi-calculus: models and verification. Cryptology ePrint Archive, Report 2015/782 (2015). http://eprint.iacr.org/
26. Cortier, V., Delaune, S.: A method for proving observational equivalence. In: Computer Security Foundations Symposium (CSF), Port Jefferson, New York, USA, 8–10 July 2009, pp. 266–276. IEEE Computer Society (2009)
27. Lindell, Y., Pinkas, B.: Secure two-party computation via cut-and-choose oblivious transfer. J. Cryptol. **25**(4), 680–722 (2012)
28. Damgård, I., Nielsen, J.B., Orlandi, C.: Essentially optimal universally composable oblivious transfer. In: Lee, P.J., Cheon, J.H. (eds.) ICISC 2008. LNCS, vol. 5461, pp. 318–335. Springer, Heidelberg (2009)
29. Delaune, S., Kremer, S., Ryan, M.: Verifying privacy-type properties of electronic voting protocols. J. Comput. Secur. **17**(4), 435–487 (2009)
30. Backes, M., Hriţcu, C., Maffei, M.: Automated verification of remote electronic voting protocols in the applied pi-calculus. In: Computer Security Foundations Symposium (CSF), pp. 195–209. IEEE Computer Society (2008)
31. Blanchet, B.: Automatic proof of strong secrecy for security protocols. In: 2004 IEEE Symposium on Security and Privacy (S&P 2004), 9–12 May 2004, Berkeley, CA, USA, p. 86. IEEE Computer Society (2004)
32. Bogetoft, P., Christensen, D.L., Damgård, I., Geisler, M., Jakobsen, T., Krøigaard, M., Nielsen, J.D., Nielsen, J.B., Nielsen, K., Pagter, J., Schwartzbach, M., Toft, T.: Secure multiparty computation goes live. In: Dingledine, R., Golle, P. (eds.) FC 2009. LNCS, vol. 5628, pp. 325–343. Springer, Heidelberg (2009)
33. Backes, M., Pfitzmann, B., Waidner, M.: The reactive simulatability (RSIM) framework for asynchronous systems. Inf. Comput. **205**(12), 1685–1720 (2007)
34. Goubault-Larrecq, J., Palamidessi, C., Troina, A.: A probabilistic applied pi–calculus. In: Shao, Z. (ed.) APLAS 2007. LNCS, vol. 4807, pp. 175–190. Springer, Heidelberg (2007)
35. Naor, M. (ed.): EUROCRYPT 2007. LNCS, vol. 4515, pp. 52–78. Springer, Heidelberg (2007)

Multiparty Testing Preorders

Rocco De Nicola[1] and Hernán Melgratti[2](✉)

[1] IMT, Institute for Advanced Studies, Lucca, Italy
rocco.denicola@imtlucca.it
[2] FCEyN, University of Buenos Aires, Buenos Aires, Argentina
hmelgra@dc.uba.ar

Abstract. Variants of the must testing approach have been successfully applied in Service Oriented Computing for analysing the compliance between (contracts exposed by) clients and servers or, more
generally, between two peers. It has however been argued that multiparty scenarios call for more permissive notions of compliance because
partners usually do not have full coordination capabilities. We propose
two new testing preorders, which are obtained by restricting the set of
potential observers. For the first preorder, called uncoordinated, we allow
only sets of parallel observers that use different parts of the interface of
a given service and have no possibility of intercommunication. For the
second preorder, that we call independent, we instead rely on parallel
observers that perceive as silent all the actions that are not in the interface of interest. We have that the uncoordinated preorder is coarser than
the classical must testing preorder and finer than the independent one.
We also provide a characterisation in terms of decorated traces for both
preorders: the uncoordinated preorder is defined in terms of must-sets
and Mazurkiewicz traces while the independent one is described in terms
of must-sets and classes of filtered traces that only contain designated
visible actions.

1 Introduction

A desired property of communication-centered systems is the graceful termination of the partners involved in a multiparty interaction, i.e., every possible
interaction among a set of communicating partners ends successfully, in the sense
that there are no messages waiting forever to be sent, or sent messages which
are never received. The theories of session types [8,16] and of contracts [3,5,6,9]
are commonly used to ensure such kind of properties. The key idea behind both
approaches is to associate to each process a type (or *contract*) that gives an
abstract description of its external, visible behaviour and to use type checking
to verify correctness of behaviours.

Services are often specified by sequential nondeterministic CCS processes [12]
describing the communications offered by peers, built-up from invoke and accept
activities, which are abstractly represented as input and output actions that take
place over a set of channels or names, and internal τ actions. Basic actions can

© Springer International Publishing Switzerland 2016
P. Ganty and M. Loreti (Eds.): TGC 2015, LNCS 9533, pp. 16–31, 2016.
DOI: 10.1007/978-3-319-28766-9_2

be composed sequentially (prefix operator "."$)$ or as alternatives (non deterministic choice "+") and no operator for parallel composition is used for describing services.It is assumed that all possible interleavings are made explicit in the description of a service and communication is used only for modelling the interaction among different peers.

Services come equipped with a notion of *compliance* that characterises all valid clients of a service, i.e., those clients that are guaranteed to terminate after any possible interaction with the service. Compliance has been characterised by using a variant of the *must testing* approach [7], which allows comparing processes according to the ability of external observers to distinguishing them. Processes that are must-equivalent are characterised by the set of tests or observers that they are able to pass; an observer is just a process that runs in parallel with the tested service. Two processes p and q are related via the must preorder ($p \sqsubseteq_{\mathsf{must}} q$) if q passes all tests that are passed by p. Consequently, p and q are equivalent ($p \approx_{\mathsf{must}} q$) if they pass exactly the same tests.

If one considers a multiparty setting, each service may interact with several partners and its interface is often (logically) partitioned by allowing each partner to communicate only through dedicated parts of the interface. Moreover, in many cases, the peers of a specific service do not communicate with each other. In these situations, the classical testing approach to process equivalences or preorders turns out to be too demanding.

Consider the following scenario involving three partners: an organisation (the broker) that sells goods produced by a different company (the producer) to a specific customer (the client). The behaviour of the broker can be described with the following process:

$$B = req.\overline{order}.\overline{inv}.$$

The broker accepts requests on channel req and then places an order to the producer with the message $\overline{order}$ and sends an invoice to the customer with the message $\overline{inv}$. In this scenario, the broker uses the channels req and inv to interact with the customer, while the interaction with the producer is over the channel $order$. Moreover, the customer and the producer do not know each other and are completely independent. Hence, the order in which messages $\overline{order}$ and $\overline{inv}$ are sent is completely irrelevant for them. They would be equally happy with a broker defined as follows:

$$B' = req.\overline{inv}.\overline{order}.$$

Nevertheless, these two different implementations are not considered mustequivalent.

The main goal of this paper is to introduce alternative, less discriminating, preorders that take into account the distributed nature of the peers and thus the limited coordination and interaction capabilities of the different players. A first preorder, called *uncoordinated must preorder*, is obtained by assuming that all clients of a given service do interact with it via disjoint sets of ports, i.e. they use different parts of its interface, have no possibility of intercommunication, and all of them terminate successfully in every possible interaction.

However, even without communication among clients, some inter-dependency among them is still possible, e.g. because one of them does not behave as expected and thus blocks the other. Indeed, the uncoordinated must preorder differentiates B from B' when the observer cannot communicate over the port *order*. We, thus, introduce a second preorder, called *independent must preorder*, that avoids inter-dependencies among clients actions and, thanks to its limited discriminating power, guarantees increased acceptability of offered services.

The two preorders are defined as usual in terms of the outcomes of experiments by specific sets of observers. For defining the uncoordinated must preorder, we allow only sets of parallel observers that cannot intercommunicate and do challenge services via disjoint parts of their interface. For defining the independent must preorder, we instead rely on parallel observers that, again, cannot intercommunicate but in addition perceive as silent all the actions that are not in the interface of their interest. This is instrumental to permit all observers to perform independent tests. As expected, we have that the uncoordinated preorder is coarser than the classical must testing preorder and finer than the independent one.

Just like for classical testing preorders, we provide a characterisation for both new preorders in terms of decorated traces, which avoids dealing with universal quantifications over the set of observers for relating any two processes. The alternative characterisations make it even more evident that our preorders permit action reordering. Indeed, the uncoordinated preorder is defined in terms of Mazurkiewicz traces [11] while the independent one is described in terms of classes of traces quotiented via specific sets of visible actions. We would like to remark that our two preorders are different from those defined in [4, 13, 14], which also permit action reordering by relying on buffered communication. Additional details will be provided in Sect. 6.

Synopsis. The remainder of this paper is organised as follows. In Sect. 2 we recall the basics of the classical must testing approach. In Sects. 3 and 4 we present the theory of uncoordinated and independent must testing preorders and their characterisation in terms of traces. In Sect. 5 we show that the uncoordinated preorder is coarser than the must testing preorder but finer than the independent one. Finally, we discuss some related work and future developments in Sect. 6.

2   Processes and Testing Preorders

Let $\mathcal{N}$ be a countable set of action names, ranged over by $a, b, \ldots$. As usual, we write co-names in $\overline{\mathcal{N}}$ as $\overline{a}, \overline{b}, \ldots$ and assume $\overline{\overline{a}} = a$. We will use α, β to range over $\mathsf{Act} = (\mathcal{N} \cup \overline{\mathcal{N}})$. Moreover, we consider a distinguished internal action τ, not in Act, and use μ to range over $\mathsf{Act} \cup \{\tau\}$. We fix the language of defining services as the sequential fragment of CCS extended with a *success* operator, as specified by the following grammar.

$$p, q ::= \mathbf{0} \mid \mathbf{1} \mid \mu.p \mid p + q \mid X \mid \mathbf{rec}_X.p$$

The process **0** stands for the terminated process, **1** for the process that reports success and then terminates, and $\mu.p$ for a service that executes μ and then continues as p. Alternative behaviours are specified by terms of the form $p + q$, while recursive ones are introduced by terms like $\mathbf{rec}_X.p$. We sometimes omit trailing **0** and write, e.g., $a.b + c$ instead of $a.b.\mathbf{0} + c.\mathbf{0}$. We write $\mathbf{n}(p)$ for the set of names $a \in \mathcal{N}$ such that either a or $\bar{a}$ occur in p.

The operational semantics of processes is given in terms of a labelled transition system (LTS) $p \xrightarrow{\lambda} q$ with $\lambda \in \mathsf{Act} \cup \{\tau, \checkmark\}$, where $\checkmark$ signals the successful termination of an execution.

Definition 1 (Transition Relation). *The transition relation on processes, noted $\xrightarrow{\lambda}$, is the least relation satisfying the following rules*

$$
\mathbf{1} \xrightarrow{\checkmark} \mathbf{0} \qquad \mu.p \xrightarrow{\mu} p \qquad \frac{p \xrightarrow{\lambda} p'}{p + q \xrightarrow{\lambda} p'} \qquad \frac{q \xrightarrow{\lambda} q'}{p + q \xrightarrow{\lambda} q'} \qquad \frac{p[\mathbf{rec}_X.p/X] \xrightarrow{\lambda} p'}{\mathbf{rec}_X.p \xrightarrow{\lambda} p'} \qquad \square
$$

Multiparty applications, named *configurations*, are built by composing processes concurrently. Formally, configurations are given by the following grammar.

$$
c, d ::= p \mid c \| d
$$

We sometimes write $\Pi_{i \in 0..n} p_i$ for the parallel composition $p_0 \| \ldots \| p_n$. The operational semantics of configurations, which accounts for the communication between peers, is obtained by extending the rules in Definition 1 with the following ones:

$$
\frac{c \xrightarrow{\mu} c'}{c \| d \xrightarrow{\mu} c' \| d} \qquad \frac{d \xrightarrow{\mu} d'}{c \| d \xrightarrow{\mu} c \| d'} \qquad \frac{c \xrightarrow{\alpha} c' \quad d \xrightarrow{\bar{\alpha}} d'}{c \| d \xrightarrow{\tau} c' \| d'} \qquad \frac{c \xrightarrow{\checkmark} c' \quad d \xrightarrow{\checkmark} d'}{c \| d \xrightarrow{\checkmark} c' \| d'}
$$

All rules are standard apart for the last one that is not present in [7]. This rule states that the concurrent composition of processes can report success only when all processes in the composition do so.

We write $c \xrightarrow{\lambda}$ when there exists c' s.t. $c \xrightarrow{\lambda} c'$; $\Rightarrow$ for the reflexive and transitive closure of $\xrightarrow{\tau}$. Moreover, we write $c \xRightarrow{\lambda} c'$ when $\lambda \in \mathsf{Act} \cup \{\checkmark\}$ and $c \Rightarrow \xrightarrow{\lambda} \Rightarrow$; $c \xRightarrow{\lambda_0 \ldots \lambda_n} c'$ when $c \xRightarrow{\lambda_0} \ldots \xRightarrow{\lambda_n} c'$; and, finally, $c \xRightarrow{s}$ when $s \in (\mathsf{Act} \cup \{\checkmark\})^*$ and there exists c' s.t. $c \xRightarrow{s} c'$. We use $\mathsf{str}(c)$ and $\mathsf{init}(c)$ to denote the sets of strings and enabled actions of c, defined as follows

$$
\mathsf{str}(c) = \{s \in (\mathsf{Act} \cup \{\checkmark\})^* \mid c \xRightarrow{s}\} \qquad\qquad \mathsf{init}(c) = \{\lambda \in \mathsf{Act} \cup \{\checkmark\} \mid c \xRightarrow{\lambda}\}
$$

As behavioural semantics, we will consider the must preorder of [7]. We take all possible configurations obtained from processes and from groups of $\mathcal{O}$ of *observers*, ranged over by $o, o_0, o_1, \ldots, o', \ldots$. It is worth noting that, to recover the standard framework of [7], it is sufficient to use only sequential observers, and to allow only to them to use action $\checkmark$.

Definition 2 (Must).

– *A sequence of transitions* $p_0 \parallel o_0 \xrightarrow{\tau} \ldots \xrightarrow{\tau} p_k \parallel o_k \xrightarrow{\tau} \ldots$ *is a maximal computation if either it is infinite or the last term* $p_n \parallel o_n$ *is such that* $p_n \parallel o_n \not\xrightarrow{\tau}$.
– p must o *iff for each maximal computation* $p \parallel o = p_0 \parallel o_0 \xrightarrow{\tau} \ldots \xrightarrow{\tau} p_k \parallel o_k \xrightarrow{\tau} \ldots$ *there exists* $n \geq 0$ *such that* $o_n \xrightarrow{\checkmark}$. □

We say that a computation $c_o \xrightarrow{\mu_0} \ldots c_i \xrightarrow{\mu_i} \ldots \xrightarrow{\mu_n} c_{n+1}$ is unsuccessful when $c_j \not\xrightarrow{}$ for all $0 \leq j \leq n+1$, we say it successful otherwise.

The notion of passing a test represents the fact that a set of partners (observers) can successfully interact with the process under test. It is then natural to compare processes according to their capacity to satisfy set of partners.

Definition 3 (Must Preorder).

– $p \sqsubseteq_{\mathsf{must}} q$ *iff* $\forall o \in \mathcal{O} : p$ must o *implies* q must o.
– *We write* $p \approx_{\mathsf{must}} q$ *when both* $p \sqsubseteq_{\mathsf{must}} q$ *and* $q \sqsubseteq_{\mathsf{must}} p$. □

2.1 Semantic Characterisation

The must testing preorder has been characterised in [7] in terms of the sequences of actions that a process may perform and the possible sets of actions that it may perform after executing a particular sequence of actions. This characterisation relies on a few auxiliary predicates and functions that are presented below. A process p *diverges*, written $p \Uparrow$, when it exhibits an infinite, internal computation $p \xrightarrow{\tau} p_0 \xrightarrow{\tau} p_1 \xrightarrow{\tau} \ldots$. We say p *converges*, written $p \Downarrow$, otherwise. For $s \in \mathsf{Act}^*$, the convergence predicate is inductively defined by the following rules:

– $p \Downarrow \varepsilon$ if $p \Downarrow$.
– $p \Downarrow \alpha.s$ if $p \Downarrow$ and $p \xRightarrow{\alpha} p'$ implies $p' \Downarrow s$.

The *residual* of a process p (or a set of processes P) after the execution of $s \in \mathsf{Act}^*$ is given by the following equations

– $(p \text{ after } s) = \{p' \mid p \xRightarrow{s} p'\}$.
– $(P \text{ after } s) = \bigcup_{p \in P}(p \text{ after } s)$.

Definition 4 (Must-set). *A* must-set *of process* p *(or set of processes* P*) is* $L \subseteq \mathsf{Act}$, *with* L *finite and such that*

– p MUST L *iff* $\forall p'$ *s.t.* $p \Longrightarrow p'$, $\exists \alpha \in L$ *such that* $p' \xRightarrow{\alpha}$.
– P MUST L *iff* $\forall p \in P.p$ MUST L. □

Then, the must testing preorder can be characterised in terms of strings and must-sets as follows.

Definition 5. $p \preceq_{\mathsf{must}} q$ *if for every* $s \in \mathsf{Act}^*$, *for all finite* $L \subseteq \mathsf{Act}$, *if* $p \Downarrow s$ *then*

– $q \Downarrow s$.
– $(p \text{ after } s)$ MUST L *implies* $(q \text{ after } s)$ MUST L. □

Theorem 1 ([7]). $\sqsubseteq_{\mathsf{must}} = \preceq_{\mathsf{must}}$.

3   A Testing Preorder with Uncoordinated Observers

The must testing preorder is defined in terms of the tests that each process is able to pass. Remarkably, the classical setting can be formulated by considering only sequential tests (see the characterisation of minimal tests in [7]). Each sequential test is a unique, centralised process that handles all the interaction with the service under test and, therefore, has a complete view of the externally observable behaviour of the service. For this reason, we refer to the classical must testing preorder as a *centralised preorder*. Multiparty interactions are generally structured in such a way that pairs of partners communicate through dedicated channels, for example, partner links in service oriented models or buffers in communicating machines [1]. Conceptually, the interface (i.e., the set of channels) of a service is partitioned and a given service interacts with each partner by using only specific sets of channels in its interface. In addition, there are common scenarios in which partners do not know each other and cannot directly communicate. As a consequence, clients of a service cannot establish causal dependencies among actions that take place over different parts of the service interface. These constraints reduce the discriminating power of partners and call for coarser equivalences that equate processes that cannot be distinguished by independent sets of sequential processes that are interested only in specific interactions.

Example 1. Consider the classical scenario for planning a trip. A user U interacts with a broker B, which is responsible for booking flights provided by a service F and hotel rooms available at service H. The expected interaction can be described as follows: U makes a booking request by sending a message req to B (we will just describe the interaction and abstract away from data details such as trip destination, departure dates and duration). Depending on the request, B may contact service F (for booking just a flight ticket), H (for booking rooms) or both. Service B uses channels $reqF$ and $reqH$ to respectively contact F and H (for the sake of simplicity, we assume that any request to F and H will be granted). Then, the expected behaviour of B can be described with the following process:

$$B_0 \stackrel{def}{=} req.(\tau.\overline{reqF} + \tau.\overline{reqH} + \tau.\overline{reqH}.\overline{reqF})$$

In this process, the third branch represents B's choice to contact first H and then F. Nevertheless, the other partners (U, F and H) are not affected in any way by this choice, thus they would be equally happy with alternative definitions such as:

$$B_1 \stackrel{def}{=} req.(\tau.\overline{reqF} + \tau.\overline{reqH} + \tau.\overline{reqF}.\overline{reqH})$$
$$B_2 \stackrel{def}{=} req.(\tau.\overline{reqF} + \tau.\overline{reqH} + \tau.\overline{reqH}.\overline{reqF} + \tau.\overline{reqF}.\overline{reqH})$$

Unfortunately, B_0, B_1 and B_2 are distinguished by the must testing equivalence. It suffices to consider $o_0 = \overline{req}.(\tau.\mathbf{1} + reqF.(\tau.\mathbf{1} + reqH.\mathbf{0}))$ for showing that $B_0 \not\sqsubseteq_{\mathsf{must}} B_1$ and that $B_0 \not\sqsubseteq_{\mathsf{must}} B_2$, and use $o_1 = \overline{req}.(\tau.\mathbf{1} + reqH.(\tau.\mathbf{1} + reqF.\mathbf{0}))$ for proving that $B_1 \not\sqsubseteq_{\mathsf{must}} B_2$.   □

This rest of this section is devoted to the study of a preorder that is coarser than the classical must preorder and relates processes that cannot be distinguished by distributed contexts. A (trace-based) alternative characterisation of the new preorder will also be introduced. We start by defining uncoordinated observers.

Definition 6 (Uncoordinated Observer). *A process* $\Pi_{i \in 0..n} o_i = o_0 \parallel \cdots \parallel o_n$ *is an* Uncoordinated observer *if* $\mathbf{n}(o_i) \cap \mathbf{n}(o_j) = \emptyset$ *for all* $i \neq j$. □

Obviously, the condition $\mathbf{n}(o_i) \cap \mathbf{n}(o_j) = \emptyset$ forbids the direct communication between the sequential components of an uncoordinated observer. As a consequence, an uncoordinated observer cannot impose a total order between actions that are controlled by different components of the observer. Indeed, the executions of such an observer are the interleavings of the executions of all sequential components $\{o_i\}_{i \in 0..n}$ (this property is formally stated in Sect. 3.1, Lemma 1). We remark that a configuration does report success (i.e., perform action $\checkmark$) only when all sequential processes in the composition do report success; an uncoordinated observer reports success when all its components report success simultaneously.

The uncoordinated must testing preorder is obtained by restricting the set of observers to consider just uncoordinated observers over a suitable partition of the interface of a process. We will say $\mathbb{I} = \{I_i\}_{i \in 0...n}$ is an interface whenever $\mathbb{I}$ is a partition of Act and $\forall \alpha \in$ Act, $\alpha \in I_i$ implies $\overline{\alpha} \in I_i$. In the remainder of this paper, we usually will write only the relevant part of an interface. For instance, we will write $\{\{a\}, \{b\}\}$ for any interface $\{I_0, I_1\}$ such that $a \in I_0$ and $b \in I_1$, if only action a and b are of interest.

Definition 7 (Uncoordinated must Preorder $\sqsubseteq_{\mathsf{unc}}^{\mathbb{I}}$). *Let* $\mathbb{I} = \{I_i\}_{i \in 0...n}$ *be an interface.*

- *We say* $p \sqsubseteq_{\mathsf{unc}}^{\mathbb{I}} q$ *iff for all* $\Pi_{i \in 0..n} o_i$ *such that* $\mathbf{n}(o_i) \subseteq I_i$, p must $\Pi_{i \in 0..n} o_i$ *implies* q must $\Pi_{i \in 0..n} o_i$.
- *We write* $p \approx_{\mathsf{unc}}^{\mathbb{I}} q$ *when both* $p \sqsubseteq_{\mathsf{unc}}^{\mathbb{I}} q$ *and* $q \sqsubseteq_{\mathsf{unc}}^{\mathbb{I}} p$. □

Example 2. Consider the scenario presented in Example 1 and the following interface $\mathbb{I} = \{\{req\}, \{reqF\}, \{reqH\}\}$ for the process B that thus interacts with each of the other partners by using a dedicated part of its interface. It can be shown that the three definitions for B in Example 1 are equivalent when considering the uncoordinated must testing preorder, i.e., $B_0 \approx_{\mathsf{unc}}^{\mathbb{I}} B_1 \approx_{\mathsf{unc}}^{\mathbb{I}} B_2$. The actual proof, which uses the (trace-based) alternative characterisation of the preorder, is deferred to Example 3. □

3.1   Semantic Characterisation

We now address the problem of characterising the uncoordinated must testing preorder in terms of traces and must-sets. In order to do that, we shift from strings to Mazurkiewicz traces [10]. A *Mazurkiewicz trace* is a set of strings, obtained by permuting independent symbols. Traces represent concurrent computations, in which commuting letters stand for actions that execute independently of one another and non-commuting symbols represent causally dependent actions. We start by summarising the basics of the theory of traces; the interested reader is referred to [10] for further details.

Let $D \subseteq \mathsf{Act} \times \mathsf{Act}$ be a finite, equivalence relation, called the *dependency relation*, that relates the actions that cannot be commuted. Thus if $(\alpha, \beta) \in D$, the two actions have to be considered causally dependent. Symmetrically, $I_D = (\mathsf{Act} \times \mathsf{Act}) \setminus D$ stands for the *independency* relation with $(\alpha, \beta) \in I_D$ meaning that α and β are concurrent.

The trace equivalence induced by the dependency relation D is the least congruence $\equiv_D$ in Act such that for all $\alpha, \beta \in \mathsf{Act} : (\alpha, \beta) \in I_D \implies \alpha\beta \equiv_D \beta\alpha$.

The equivalence classes of $\equiv_D$, denoted by $[s]_D$, are the (Mazurkiewicz) *traces*, namely the strings quotiented via $\equiv_D$. The trace monoid, denoted as $\mathbb{M}(D)$, is the quotient monoid $\mathbb{M}(D) = \mathsf{Act}^*/_{\equiv_D}$ whose elements are the traces induced by D. We remark that no action can commute with $\checkmark$ because I_D is defined over $\mathsf{Act} \times \mathsf{Act}$.

Let $\mathbb{I}$ be an interface, the *dependency relation induced by* $\mathbb{I}$ is $D = \bigcup_{I \in \mathbb{I}} I \times I$. The alternative characterisation of the uncoordinated preorder is defined in terms of equivalence classes of traces. Hence, we extend the transition relation and the notions of convergence and residuals to equivalence classes of strings:

- $q \xrightarrow{[s]_D} q'$ if and only if $\exists s' \subset [s]_D$ such that $q \xrightarrow{s'} q'$
- $p \Downarrow [s]_D$ if $\forall s' \in [s]_D . p \Downarrow s'$
- $(p \text{ after } [s]_D) = \{p' \mid p \xrightarrow{[s]_D} p'\}$

Now we can characterise the behaviour of an uncoordinated observer. We formally state that an uncoordinated observer reaches the same processes after executing any of the sequences of actions in an equivalence class. This result is instrumental for proving the alternative characterisation of the uncoordinated preorder.

Lemma 1. *Let $o = \Pi_{i \in 0..n} o_i$ be an observer for the interface $\mathbb{I} = \{I_i\}_{i \in 0..n}$ and D the dependency relation induced by $\mathbb{I}$. Then, for all $s \in \mathsf{Act}^*$ and $s' \in [s]_D$ we have $o \xrightarrow{s} o'$ iff $o \xrightarrow{s'} o'$.*

Corollary 1. *Let $o = \Pi_{i \in 0..n} o_i$ be an observer for the interface $\mathbb{I} = \{I_i\}_{i \in 0..n}$ and D the dependency relation induced by $\mathbb{I}$. Then, $\forall s \in \mathsf{Act}^*, s' \in [s]_D,$*

1. $s \in \mathsf{str}(o)$ *implies* $s' \in \mathsf{str}(o)$.
2. $o \Downarrow s$ *implies* $o \Downarrow s'$.
3. $(o \text{ after } s)$ MUST L *implies* $(o \text{ after } s')$ MUST L.
4. *If there exists an unsuccessful computation $o \xrightarrow{s}$, then there exists an unsuccessful computation $o \xrightarrow{s'}$.*

The alternative characterisation for the uncoordinated preorder mimics the definition of the classical one, but relies on Mazurkiewicz traces. In the definition below, the condition $L \subseteq I$, with $I \in \mathbb{I}$, captures the idea that each observation is relative to a specific part of the interface.

Definition 8. *Let $\mathbb{I}$ be an interface and D the dependency relation induced by $\mathbb{I}$. Then, $p \preceq^{\mathbb{I}}_{\text{unc}} q$ if for every $s \in \text{Act}^*$, for any part $I \in \mathbb{I}$, for all finite $L \subseteq I$, if $p \Downarrow [s]_D$ then*

1. $q \Downarrow [s]_D$
2. $(p \text{ after } [s]_D) \text{ MUST } L$ implies $(q \text{ after } [s]_D) \text{ MUST } L$ □

Theorem 2. $\sqsubseteq^{\mathbb{I}}_{\text{unc}} = \preceq^{\mathbb{I}}_{\text{unc}}$.

In the following we will write $L^I_{p,[s]_D}$ for the smallest set such that if $(p \text{ after } [s]_D) \text{ MUST } L$ and $L \subseteq I$ then $L^I_{p,[s]_D} \subseteq L$.

Example 3. We take advantage of the alternative characterisation of the unco-ordinated preorder to show that the three processes for the broker in Example 1 are equivalent when considering $\mathbb{I} = \{\{req\}, \{reqF\}, \{reqH\}\}$. Actually, we will only consider $B_0 \approx^{\mathbb{I}}_{\text{unc}} B_1$, being that the proofs for $B_0 \approx^{\mathbb{I}}_{\text{unc}} B_2$ and $B_1 \approx^{\mathbb{I}}_{\text{unc}} B_2$ are analogous.

Firstly, we have to consider that $B_0 \Downarrow s$ and $B_1 \Downarrow s$ for any s because B_0 and B_1 do not have infinite computations. The relation between must-sets are described in the two tables below. The first table shows the sets $(B_0 \text{ after } [s]_D)$ and $L^I_{B_0,[s]_D}$. Note that $[s]_D$ in the first column will be represented by any string $s' \in [s]_D$. Moreover, we write "$-$" in the tree last columns whenever $L^I_{B_0,[s]_D}$ does not exist. The second table does the same for B_1. In the tables, we let B'_0 stand for $\tau.\overline{reqF} + \tau.\overline{reqH} + \tau.\overline{reqH}.\overline{reqF}$ and B'_1 stand for $\tau.\overline{reqF} + \tau.\overline{reqH} + \tau.\overline{reqF}.\overline{reqH}$.

$[s]_D$	$B_0 \text{ after } [s]_D$	$L^{\{req\}}_{B_0,[s]_D}$	$L^{\{reqH\}}_{B_0,[s]_D}$	$L^{\{reqF\}}_{B_0,[s]_D}$
ϵ	B_0	$\{req\}$	$-$	$-$
req	$\{B'_0, \overline{reqF}, \overline{reqH}, \overline{reqH}.\overline{reqF}\}$	$-$	$-$	$-$
$req.\overline{reqF}$	$\{0\}$	$-$	$-$	$-$
$req.\overline{reqH}$	$\{0, \overline{reqF}\}$	$-$	$-$	$-$
$req.\overline{reqF}.\overline{reqH}$	$\{0\}$	$-$	$-$	$-$
other	$\emptyset$	$\emptyset$	$\emptyset$	$\emptyset$

$[s]_D$	$B_1 \text{ after } [s]_D$	$L^{\{req\}}_{B_0,[s]_D}$	$L^{\{reqH\}}_{B_0,[s]_D}$	$L^{\{reqF\}}_{B_0,[s]_D}$
ϵ	B_1	$\{req\}$	$-$	$-$
req	$\{B'_1, \overline{reqF}, \overline{reqH}, \overline{reqF}.\overline{reqH}\}$	$-$	$-$	$-$
$req.\overline{reqF}$	$\{0, \overline{reqH}\}$	$-$	$-$	$-$
$req.\overline{reqH}$	$\{0\}$	$-$	$-$	$-$
$req.\overline{reqF}.\overline{reqH}$	$\{0\}$	$-$	$-$	$-$
other	$\emptyset$	$\emptyset$	$\emptyset$	$\emptyset$

By inspecting the tables, we can check that for any possible trace $[s]_D$ and $I \in \mathbb{I}$, it holds that $L^I_{B_0,[s]_D} = L^I_{B_1,[s]_D}$. Consequently, $(B_0$ after $[s]_D)$ MUST L iff $(B_1$ after $[s]_D)$ MUST L and thus we have $B_0 \approx^{\mathbb{I}}_{\mathsf{unc}} B_1$.

We now present two additional examples that help us in understanding the discriminating capability of the uncoordinated preorder, its differences with the classical must preorder and its adequacy for modelling process conformance.

The first of these examples shows that a process that does not communicate its internal choices to all of its clients is useless in a distributed context.

Example 4. Consider the process $p = \tau.a + \tau.b$ that is intended to be used by two partners with the following interface: $\mathbb{I} = \{\{a\}, \{b\}\}$. We show that this process is less useful than 0 in an uncoordinated context, i.e., $\tau.a + \tau.b \sqsubseteq^{\mathbb{I}}_{\mathsf{unc}} 0$. It is immediate to see that p and 0 strongly converge for any $s \in \mathsf{Act}^*$, then the minimal sets $L^{\{a\}}_{p,[s]_D}$, $L^{\{b\}}_{p,[s]_D}$, $L^{\{a\}}_{0,[s]_D}$ and $L^{\{b\}}_{0,[s]_D}$ presented in the tables below are sufficient for proving our claim.

$[s]_D$	p after $[s]_D$	$L^{\{a\}}_{p,[s]_D}$	$L^{\{b\}}_{p,[s]_D}$
ϵ	p, a, b	$-$	$-$
a	$\{0\}$	$-$	$-$
b	$\{0\}$	$-$	$-$
other	$\emptyset$	$\emptyset$	$\emptyset$

$[s]_D$	0 after $[s]_D$	$L^{\{a\}}_{0,[s]_D}$	$L^{\{b\}}_{0,[s]_D}$
ϵ	0	$-$	$-$
a	$\emptyset$	$\emptyset$	$\emptyset$
b	$\emptyset$	$\emptyset$	$\emptyset$
other	$\emptyset$	$\emptyset$	$\emptyset$

Note that differently from the classical must preorder, the uncoordinated preorder does not consider the must-set $\{a, b\}$ to distinguish p from 0 because this set involves channels in different parts of the interface. The key point here is that each internal reduction of p is observed just by one part of the interface: the choice of branch a is only observed by one client and the choice of b is observed by the other one. Since uncoordinated observers do not intercommunicate, they can only report success simultaneously if they can do it independently from the interactions with the tested process, but such observers are exactly the ones that 0 can pass.

Like in the classical must preorder, we have that $0 \not\sqsubseteq^{\mathbb{I}}_{\mathsf{unc}} \tau.a + \tau.b$. This is witnessed by the observer $o = \overline{a}.\mathbf{0} + \tau.\mathbf{1} \parallel \mathbf{1}$ that is passed by 0 but not by $\tau.a + \tau.b$.   □

The second example shows that the uncoordinated preorder falls somehow short with respect to the target we set in the introduction of allowing servers to swap actions that are targeted to different clients.

Example 5. Consider the interface $\mathbb{I} = \{\{a\}, \{b\}\}$ and the two pairs of processes

- $a.b + a + b$ and $b.a + a + b$
- $a.b$ and $b.a$

By inspecting traces and must-sets in the two tables below, where we use p and q to denote $a.b + a + b$ and $b.a + a + b$

$[s]_D$	p after $[s]_D$	$L_{p,[s]_D}^{\{a\}}$	$L_{p,[s]_D}^{\{b\}}$
ϵ	$\{p\}$	$\{a\}$	$\{b\}$
a	$\{b,0\}$	$-$	$-$
b	$\{0\}$	$-$	$-$
ab	$\{0\}$	$-$	$-$
other	$\emptyset$	$\emptyset$	$\emptyset$

$[s]_D$	q after $[s]_D$	$L_{q,[s]_D}^{\{a\}}$	$L_{q,[s]_D}^{\{b\}}$
ϵ	$\{p\}$	$\{a\}$	$\{b\}$
a	$\{0\}$	$-$	$-$
b	$\{a,0\}$	$-$	$-$
ab	$\{0\}$	$-$	$-$
other	$\emptyset$	$\emptyset$	$\emptyset$

It is easy to see that

$$a.b + a + b \approx_{\mathrm{unc}}^{\mathbb{I}} b.a + a + b$$

However, by using $o = \overline{a}.1 \parallel 1$ and $o' = 1 \parallel \overline{b}.1$ as observers, it can be shown that

$$a.b \not\sqsubseteq_{\mathrm{unc}}^{\mathbb{I}} b.a \qquad \text{and} \qquad b.a \not\sqsubseteq_{\mathrm{unc}}^{\mathbb{I}} a.b$$

Note that $o = \overline{a}.1 \parallel 1$ actually interacts with the process under test by using just one part of the interface and relies on the fact that the remaining part of the interface stays idle. Thanks to this ability, uncoordinated observers have still a limited power to track some dependencies among actions on different parts of the interface.

The preorder presented in the next section limits further the discriminating power of observers and allows us to equate processes $a.b$ and $b.a$.   □

4   A Testing Preorder with Independent Observers

In this section we explore a notion of equivalence equating processes that can freely permute actions over different parts of their interface. As for the uncoordinated observers, the targeted scenario is that of a service with a partitioned interface interacting with two or more independent partners by using separate sets of ports. In addition, each component of an observer cannot exploit any knowledge about the design choices made by the other components, i.e., each of them has a local view of the behaviour of the process that ignores all actions controlled by the remaining components. Local views are characterised in terms of a projection operator defined as follows.

Definition 9 (Projection). *Let $V \subseteq \mathcal{N}$ be a set of observable ports. We write $p \upharpoonright V$ for the process obtained by hiding all actions of p over channels that are not in V. Formally,*

$$\frac{p \xrightarrow{\alpha} p' \quad \alpha \in V \cup \overline{V}}{p \upharpoonright V \xrightarrow{\alpha} p' \upharpoonright V} \qquad\qquad \frac{p \xrightarrow{\alpha} p' \quad \alpha \notin V \cup \overline{V}}{p \upharpoonright V \xrightarrow{\tau} p' \upharpoonright V}$$

□

Definition 10 (Independent(must) Preorder $\sqsubseteq_{\mathrm{ind}}^{\mathbb{I}}$). *Let $\mathbb{I} = \{I_i\}_{i \in 0..n}$ be an interface.*

$- p \sqsubseteq^{\mathbb{I}}_{\mathsf{ind}} q$ *iff for all* $\Pi_{i \in 0..n} o_i$ *such that* $\mathbf{n}(o_i) \subseteq I_i$, $p \upharpoonright I_i$ must o_i *implies* $q \upharpoonright I_i$ must o_i. □

Note that $a.b$ and $b.a$ cannot be distinguished anymore by the observer $o = \bar{a}.\mathbf{1} \parallel \mathbf{1}$ used in the previous section to prove $a.b \not\sqsubseteq^{\{\{a\},\{b\}\}}_{\mathsf{unc}} b.a$ (Example 5), because $a.b \upharpoonright \{a\}$ must $\bar{a}.\mathbf{1}$, $b.a \upharpoonright \{a\}$ must $\bar{a}.\mathbf{1}$, $a.b \upharpoonright \{b\}$ must $\mathbf{1}$ and $b.a \upharpoonright \{b\}$ must $\mathbf{1}$. Indeed, later (Example 6) we will see that:

$$a.b \approx^{\{\{a\},\{b\}\}}_{\mathsf{ind}} b.a$$

4.1   Semantic Characterisation

In this section we address the characterisation of the independent preorder in terms of traces. We start by introducing an equivalence notion of traces that ignores hidden actions.

Definition 11 (Filtered Traces). *Let* $I \subseteq \mathsf{Act}$. *Two strings* $s_1, s_2 \in \mathsf{Act}^*$ *are* equivalent up-to I, *written* $s_1 \overset{\bullet}{\equiv}_I s_2$, *if there exist* $s_1', s_2' \in (\mathsf{Act} \setminus I)^*$ *s.t.* $s_1 s_1' \equiv_D s_2 s_2'$ *where* D *is the dependency relation induced by* $\{I, \mathsf{Act} \setminus I\}$. *We write* $[[s]]_I$ *for the equivalence class of* s. □

Basically, two traces are equivalent up-to I when they coincide after the removal of hidden actions. Note that the set $s' \in [[s]]_I \cap I^*$ has a unique element, which is the string obtained by removing from s all actions that are not in I. We write $s \upharpoonright I$ to denote that element. As for the distributed preorder, we extend the notions of reduction, convergence and residuals to equivalence classes of strings.

$- q \overset{[[s]]_I}{\Longrightarrow} q'$ if and only if $\exists t \in [[s]]_I$ such that $q \overset{t}{\Longrightarrow} q'$
$- p \Downarrow [[s]]_I$ if and only if $\forall t \in [[s]]_I . p \Downarrow t$
$- (p$ after $[[s]]_I) = \{p' \mid p \overset{[[s]]_I}{\Longrightarrow} p'\}$

The following auxiliary result establishes properties relating reductions, hiding and filtered traces, which will be useful in the proof of the correspondence theorem.

Lemma 2.

1. $p \overset{s}{\Longrightarrow} p'$ *implies* $p \upharpoonright I \overset{s \upharpoonright I}{\Longrightarrow} p' \upharpoonright I$.
2. $p \upharpoonright I \overset{s}{\Longrightarrow} p' \upharpoonright I$ *implies* $\exists t \in [[s]]_I$ *and* $p \overset{t}{\Longrightarrow} p'$.
3. $p \upharpoonright [[s]]_I$ *implies* $p \upharpoonright I \upharpoonright s \upharpoonright I$.
4. $(p$ after $[[s]]_I)$ MUST L *iff* $(p \upharpoonright I$ after $s \upharpoonright I)$ MUST $L \cap I$.

The alternative characterisation for the independent preorder is given in terms of filtered traces.

Definition 12. *Let* $p \preceq^{\mathbb{I}}_{\mathsf{ind}} q$ *if for every* $I \in \mathbb{I}$, *for every* $s \in I^*$, *and for all finite* $L \subseteq I$, *if* $p \Downarrow [[s]]_I$ *then*

1. $q \Downarrow [[s]]_I$
2. $(p \text{ after } [[s]]_I) \text{ MUST } L \cup (\text{Act}\backslash I) \text{ implies } (q \text{ after } [[s]]_I) \text{ MUST } L \cup (\text{Act}\backslash I)$

We would like to draw attention to condition 2 above; it only considers must-sets that always include all the actions in $(\text{Act}\backslash I)$ to avoid the possibility of distinguishing reachable states because of actions that are not in I. Consider that this condition could be formulated as follows: for all finite $L \subseteq \text{Act}$,

$(p \text{ after } [[s]]_I) \text{ MUST } L \text{ implies } \exists L' \text{ s.t } (q \text{ after } [[s]]_I) \text{ MUST } L' \text{ and } L \cap I = L' \cap I$ that makes evident that only the actions from the observable part of the interface are relevant.

Theorem 3. $\sqsubseteq^I_{\text{ind}} = \preceq^I_{\text{ind}}$.

Example 6. Consider the processes $p = a.b$ and $q = b.a$ and the interface $\mathbb{I} = \{\{a\}, \{b\}\}$. The table below shows the analysis for the part of the interface $\{a\}$.

$[[s]]_{\{a\}}$	$p \text{ after } [[s]]_{\{a\}}$	$L^{\{a\}}_{p,[[s]]_I}$	$q \text{ after } [[s]]_{\{a\}}$	$L^{\{a\}}_{q,[[s]]_I}$
ϵ	$\{p\}$	$\{a\}$	$\{q, a\}$	$\{a\}$
a	$\{0, b\}$	$-$	$\{0\}$	$-$
other	$\emptyset$	$\emptyset$	$\emptyset$	$\emptyset$

When analysing the sets $(p \text{ after } [[\epsilon]]_{\{a\}}) = \{p\}$ and $(q \text{ after } [[\epsilon]]_{\{a\}}) = \{q, a\}$, we ignore the fact that q starts with a hidden action b; the only relevant residuals are those performing a. With a similar analysis we conclude that the condition on must-sets also holds for set $\{b\}$. Hence, $a.b \approx^I_{\text{ind}} b.a$ holds. □

The following example illustrates also the fact that independent observers are unable to track causal dependencies between choices made in different parts of the interface.

Example 7. Let $p_1 = a.c + b.d$ and $p_2 = a.d + b.c$ be two alternative implementations for a service with interface $\mathbb{I} = \{\{a, b\}, \{c, d\}\}$. These two implementations are distinguished by the uncoordinated preorder $(p_1 \not\approx^{\{\{a,b\},\{c,d\}\}}_{\text{unc}} p_2)$ because of the observers $o_1 = \bar{a}.1 \parallel \bar{c}.1$ $(p_1 \not\sqsubseteq^{\{\{a,b\},\{c,d\}\}}_{\text{unc}} p_2)$ and $o_2 = \bar{b}.1 \parallel \bar{c}.1$ $(p_2 \not\sqsubseteq^{\{\{a,b\},\{c,d\}\}}_{\text{unc}} p_1)$.

They are instead equated by the independent preorder, $p_1 \approx^I_{\text{ind}} p_2$, indeed, if only the part of the interface $\{a, b\}$ is of interest, we have that p_1 and p_2 are equivalent because they exhibit the same interactions over channels a and b. Similarly, without any a priori knowledge of the choices made for $\{a, b\}$, the behaviour observed over $\{c, d\}$ can be described by the non-deterministic choice $\tau.c + \tau.d$, and hence, p_1 and p_2 are indistinguishable also over $\{c, d\}$.

We use the alternative characterisation to prove our claim. As usual, $p_1 \Downarrow s$ and $p_2 \Downarrow s$ for any s. The tables below show coincidence of the must-sets. We would only like to remark that $ac \in [[a]]_{\{a,b\}}$ and, consequently, $p_1 \text{ after } [[a]]_{\{a,b\}}$ contains also process 0.

$[[s]]_{\{a,b\}}$	p_1 after $[[s]]_{\{a,b\}}$	$L^{\{a,b\}}_{p_1,[[s]]_I}$	p_2 after $[[s]]_{\{a,b\}}$	$L^{\{a,b\}}_{p_2,[[s]]_I}$
ϵ	p_1	$\{a,b\}$	p_2	$\{a,b\}$
a	$\{c,0\}$	$-$	$\{d,0\}$	$-$
b	$\{d,0\}$	$-$	$\{c,0\}$	$-$
other	$\emptyset$	$\emptyset$	$\emptyset$	$\emptyset$

$[[s]]_{\{c,d\}}$	p_1 after $[[s]]_{\{a,b\}}$	$L^{\{c,d\}}_{p_1,[[s]]_I}$	p_2 after $[[s]]_{\{a,b\}}$	$L^{\{c,d\}}_{p_2,[[s]]_I}$
ϵ	p_1	$\{c,d\}$	p_2	$\{c,d\}$
c	$\{0\}$	$-$	$\{0\}$	$-$
d	$\{0\}$	$-$	$\{0\}$	$-$
other	$\emptyset$	$\emptyset$	$\emptyset$	$\emptyset$

$\square$

5 Relating Must, Uncoordinated and Independent Preorders

In this section, we formally study the relationships between the classical must preorder and the two preorders we have introduced. We start by showing that a refinement of an interface induces a coarser preorder, e.g., splitting the observation among more uncoordinated observers decreases the discriminating power of the tests. We say that an interface $\mathbb{I}'$ is a *refinement* of another interface $\mathbb{I}$ when the partition $\mathbb{I}'$ is finer than the partition $\mathbb{I}$.

Lemma 3. *If $\mathbb{I}$ is an interface and $\mathbb{I}'$ a refinement of $\mathbb{I}$, we have that $p \sqsubseteq^{\mathbb{I}}_{unc} q$ implies $p \sqsubseteq^{\mathbb{I}'}_{unc} q$.*

This result allows us to conclude that the uncoordinated preorder is coarser than the classical must testing preorder. It suffices to note that the preorder associated to the maximal element of the partition lattice, i.e., the trivial partition $\mathbb{I} = \{Act\}$, corresponds to $\sqsubseteq_{must}$.

Proposition 1. *If $\mathbb{I}$ is an interface, we have that $p \sqsubseteq_{must} q$ implies $p \sqsubseteq^{\mathbb{I}}_{unc} q$.*

The converse of Lemma 3 and Proposition 1 do not hold. Consider the processes $p = a.b + a + b$ and $q = b.a + a + b$. It has been shown, in Example 5, that we have $p \sqsubseteq^{\{\{a\},\{b\}\}}_{unc} q$. Nonetheless, it is easy to check that $p \not\sqsubseteq_{must} q$ (i.e., $p \sqsubseteq^{\{Act\}}_{unc} q$) by using $o = \bar{b}.(\tau.1 + \bar{a}.0)$ as observer.

   We also have that the independent preorder is coarser than the uncoordinated one.

Proposition 2. *Let $\mathbb{I}$ be an interface. Then, $p \sqsubseteq^{\mathbb{I}}_{unc} q$ implies $p \sqsubseteq^{\mathbb{I}}_{ind} q$.*

The converse does not hold, i.e., $p \sqsubseteq^{\mathbb{I}}_{ind} q$ does not imply $q \sqsubseteq^{\mathbb{I}}_{unc} p$. Indeed, we have that $a.b \sqsubseteq^{\{\{a\},\{b\}\}}_{ind} b.a$ (Example 6) but $a.b \not\sqsubseteq^{\{\{a\},\{b\}\}}_{unc} b.a$ (Example 5).

6   Conclusions and Related Works

In this paper we have explored two different relaxations of the must preorder aiming at defining new behavioural relations that, in the framework of Service Oriented Computing, are more suitable to study compliance between contracts exposed by clients and servers interacting via synchronous binary communication primitives in multiparty sessions.

The first variant of the must preorder, that we called *uncoordinated preorder*, corresponds to multiparty contexts without runtime communication between peers but with the possibility of one peer blocking another by not performing the expected action. The second variant we introduced is called *independent preorder* and accounts for partners that are completely independent. Indeed, from a viewpoint of a client, actions by other clients are considered as fully unobservable.

We have shown that the discriminating power of the induced equivalences decreases as observers become weaker; and thus that the *independent preorder* is coarser than the *uncoordinated preorder* which in turn is coarser than the *classical must preorder*. As future work we plan to consider different "real life" scenarios and to assess the impact of the different assumptions at the basis of the two new preorders and the identifications/orderings they induce. We plan also to perform further studies to get a fuller account, possibly via axiomatisations, of their discriminating power. In the near future, we will also consider the impact of our testing framework on calculi based on asynchronous interactions.

We would like now to briefly consider related works. Several variants of must preorder, contract compliance and sub-contract relation have been developed in the literature to deal with different aspects of services compositions, such as buffered asynchronous communication [4,13,14], fairness [15], peer-interaction [2], or others. We wold like to stress that these approaches deal with aspects that are orthogonal to the discriminating power of the distributed tests analysed in this work. Our preorders have some similarities with those relying on buffered communications in that both aim at guaranteeing the possibility of reordering actions performed by independent peers. Nevertheless, our work considers a model with synchronous communication and, hence, message reordering is not obtained by swapping buffered messages. As mentioned above, we have left the study of distributed tests under asynchronous communication as a future work. However, we would like to remark that the uncoordinated and the independent preorders are different from those in [4,13,14] that permit explicit action reordering. The paradigmatic example is the equivalence $a.c + b.d \approx_{\mathsf{ind}}^{\{a,b\},\{c,d\}} a.d + b.c$, which does not hold for any of the preorders with buffered communication. The main reason is that in the works based on reordering buffered messages, the local causal dependence (e.g., between a and c in the example above) is taken into account.

Acknowledgments. We would like to thank Maria Grazia Buscemi with whom we started investigating this topic. We have also to thank the anonymous reviewers of CONCUR and TGC 2015 for their careful reading of our manuscript and their many insightful comments and suggestions. This research has been partially supported by UBACyT 20020130200092BA and by the MIUR PRIN project CINA.

References

1. Basu, S., Bultan, T., Ouederni, M.: Deciding choreography realizability. In: ACM SIGPLAN Notices, vol. 47, pp. 191–202. ACM (2012)
2. Bernardi, G., Hennessy, M.: Mutually testing processes. In: D'Argenio, P.R., Melgratti, H. (eds.) CONCUR 2013 – Concurrency Theory. LNCS, vol. 8052, pp. 61–75. Springer, Heidelberg (2013)
3. Bravetti, M., Zavattaro, G.: Towards a unifying theory for choreography conformance and contract compliance. In: Lumpe, M., Vanderperren, W. (eds.) SC 2007. LNCS, vol. 4829, pp. 34–50. Springer, Heidelberg (2007)
4. Bravetti, M., Zavattaro, G.: A foundational theory of contracts for multi-party service composition. Fundam. Informaticae **89**(4), 451–478 (2008)
5. Castagna, G., Gesbert, N., Padovani, L.: A theory of contracts for web services. In: POPL, pp. 261–272 (2008)
6. Castagna, G., Gesbert, N., Padovani, L.: A theory of contracts for web services. ACM Trans. Program. Lang. Syst. **31**(5), 1–61 (2009)
7. De Nicola, R., Hennessy, M.: Testing equivalences for processes. Theor. Comput. Sci. **34**, 83–133 (1984)
8. Honda, K., Vasconcelos, V.T., Kubo, M.: Language primitives and type discipline for structured communication-based programming. In: Hankin, C. (ed.) ESOP 1998. LNCS, vol. 1381, pp. 122–138. Springer, Heidelberg (1998)
9. Laneve, C., Padovani, L.: The *Must* preorder revisited. In: Caires, L., Vasconcelos, V.T. (eds.) CONCUR 2007. LNCS, vol. 4703, pp. 212–225. Springer, Heidelberg (2007)
10. Mazurkiewicz, A.: Trace theory. In: Brauer, W., Reisig, W., Rozenberg, G. (eds.) Petri Nets: Applications and Relationships to Other Models of Concurrency. LNCS, vol. 255, pp. 278–324. Springer, Heidelberg (1986)
11. Mazurkiewicz, A.W.: Introduction to trace theory. The Book of Traces pp. 3–41 (1995)
12. Milner, R.: Communication and Concurrency. Prentice Hall International, Hertfordshire (1989)
13. Mostrous, D., Yoshida, N., Honda, K.: Global principal typing in partially commutative asynchronous sessions. In: Castagna, G. (ed.) ESOP 2009. LNCS, vol. 5502, pp. 316–332. Springer, Heidelberg (2009)
14. Padovani, L.: Contract-based discovery of web services modulo simple orchestrators. Theoret. Comput. Sci. **411**(37), 3328–3347 (2010)
15. Padovani, L.: Fair subtyping for multi-party session types. In: De Meuter, W., Roman, G.-C. (eds.) COORDINATION 2011. LNCS, vol. 6721, pp. 127–141. Springer, Heidelberg (2011)
16. Takeuchi, K., Honda, K., Kubo, M.: An interaction-based language and its typing system. In: Halatsis, C., Philokyprou, G., Maritsas, D., Theodoridis, S. (eds.) PARLE 1994. LNCS, vol. 817, pp. 398–413. Springer, Heidelberg (1994)

Data Tracking in Parameterized Systems

Giorgio Delzanno[(⊠)]

DIBRIS, University of Genova, Genoa, Italy
giorgio.delzanno@unige.it

Abstract. We study parameterized verification problems for concurrent systems with data enriched with a permission model for invoking remote services. Processes are modelled via register automata. Communication is achieved by rendez-vous with value passing. Permissions are represented as graphs with an additional conflict relation to specify incompatible access rights. The resulting model is inspired by communication architectures underlying operating systems for mobile devices. We consider decision problems involving permission violations and data tracking formulated for an arbitrary number of processes and use reductions to well structured transition systems to obtain decidable fragments of the model.

1 Introduction

Resource control is a very difficult task in presence of interprocess communication. An interesting example comes from Android applications, whose underlying communication model is based on RPC. In Android processes use special messages, called intents, to start new activities. Intents can contain data that can thus be trasmitted from the caller to the callee. Consider for instance the example in [9]. Assume that processes of type A (Activities in Android) have permissions, statically declared in the Manifest, to retrieve user contact details and to start new instances of process of type B. Furthermore, assume that, upon reception of a start intent, a process of type B extracts the data and send them to a third party. Process interaction does not directly violate the permissions declared in the Manifest. However data exchanged by process instances can lead to leakage of private information.

In this paper we study the problem of resource control from the perspective of parameterized verification, i.e., formal verification of concurrent systems composed by an arbitrary number of components. We model processes as communicating register automata, i.e., automata with a local memory defined by a finite set of registers. Registers are used to store identifiers, an abstract representation of resources. Rendez-vous communication with value passing is used to model remote service invocations and data flows between components. To control access to remote services, we define a permission model using two additional components: a permission graph, whose edges are indicated $A \rightharpoonup B$, where A and B are process types, and a conflict relation $A \notmid B$ again defined on process types.

© Springer International Publishing Switzerland 2016
P. Ganty and M. Loreti (Eds.): TGC 2015, LNCS 9533, pp. 32–46, 2016.
DOI: 10.1007/978-3-319-28766-9_3

For instance, we represent the above mentioned example in Fig. 1 where component C and I have both a single register r_1 and a single loop with label $\mathbf{s}(c,1)$ and $\mathbf{r}(i,\downarrow 1)$, respectively. The permission graph contains the edges $C \rightharpoonup A \rightharpoonup B \rightharpoonup I$. C is a process that handles the contents of a device, and I represents a potential intruder. We assume here that $C \nmid I$.

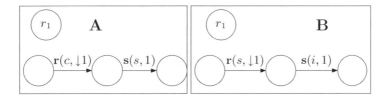

Fig. 1. Register automata for components A and B.

We consider verification problems that capture two types of design errors: permission violations, i.e., a process instance invokes a service without rights, and conflict detection, i.e., during a computation an identifier is transferred from a process of type A to a process of type B such that A and B are incompatible. Since processes are designed to operate in an open environment, it is particularly interesting to consider verification problems in which the number of concurrent processes in the initial configuration is not fixed a priori, i.e., parameterized verification. In the paper we first show that, despite of the fact that permission graphs are statically defined on finitely many process types, parameterized verification of permission violations and conflict detection is undecidable in general. We then consider fragments of the model by restricting the interplay between registers and message fields, and show that it is possible to obtain non trivial fragments for which we can give decision procedures for both properties. For properties that require data tracking, the proof consists of two steps: we first extend the operational semantics with predicates that encode footprints of data exchanged by processes. The additional information represent an unbounded memory containing footprints that share information with the current state. The alphabet used to represent the memory is infinite. We then show that the resulting semantics can be represented symbolically via a low level language based on rewriting and constraints [11] and infer decidability results from those obtained in that setting. In the general case of $r > 1$ registers, the link with rewriting and constraints can be exploited to apply a symbolic backward reachability engine [10] as a possibly non terminating procedure to verify absence of violations and conflicts for any number of component instances.

2   Process Model

We model a concurrent system using a collection of interacting processes. Each process is described by an automaton with operations over a finite set of registers.

Data are identifiers viewed as handlers to more complex resources. Communication is achieved via rendez-vous, an abstraction of synchronization, message passing and remote procedure calls. We assume here that send and receptions are executed without delays. A process can transmit part of its current data to other nodes by inserting the current value of some of its registers inside messages. Messages carry both a type and a finite tuple of data. A receiver can either compare the data contained inside messages with the current values of its registers, can store data in the registers or simply ignore some of the fields in the message payload.

Let us first describe the set of actions. We use $r \geq 0$ and $f \geq 0$ to denote resp. the number of registers in each node and the number of data fields available in each message and consider a finite alphabet Σ of message types.

The set of actions $\mathcal{A}$ is defined as follows. Local actions are defined by labels $\mathbf{l}(m)$ where $m \in \Sigma$. Send actions are defined by labels $\mathbf{s}(m, \overline{p})$, where $m \in \Sigma$, $\overline{p} = p_1, \ldots, p_f$ and $p_i \in [1..r]$ for $i \in [1..f]$. The action $\mathbf{s}(m, \overline{p})$ corresponds to a message or remote procedure call of type m whose i-th field contains the value of the register p_i of the sending node. For instance, in $\mathbf{s}(req, 1, 1)$ the current value of the register 1 of the sender is copied in the first two fields of the message.

The set of field actions Op^r is defined as $\{?k, \downarrow k, * \mid k \in [1..r]\}$. When used at position i of a reception action, $?k$ tests whether the content of the k-th register is equal to the i-th field of the message, $\downarrow k$ is used to store the field into the k-th register, and $*$ is used to ignore the field. Reception actions are defined by labels $\mathbf{r}(m, \overline{\alpha})$, $\overline{\alpha} = \alpha_1, \ldots, \alpha_f$, where $m \in \Sigma$, $\alpha_i \in Op^r$ for $i \in [1..f]$.

As an example, for $r = 2$ and $f = 3$, $\mathbf{r}(req, ?2, *, \downarrow 1)$ specifies the reception of a message of type req in which the first field is tested for equality against the current value of the second register, the second field is ignored, and the third field is assigned to the first register.

Definition 1. *A process definition over Σ is a tuple $D = \langle Q, R, q_0 \rangle$ where: Q is a finite set of control states, $q_0 \in Q$ is an initial control state, and $R \subseteq Q \times \mathcal{A} \times Q$.*

We use $\mathcal{D} = \{D_1, \ldots, D_n\}$ to denote a set of process definitions such that $D_i = \langle Q_i, R_i, q_0^i \rangle$, and $\mathcal{Q} = Q_1 \cup \ldots \cup Q_n \cup \{error\}$ to denote the set of all control states. We assume here that $Q_i \cap Q_j = \emptyset$ and that $error \notin Q_i$ for all i, j.

In the rest of the paper, we will use definitions as process types, i.e., we will say that a process has type D if its behaviour is defined by the automata D.

Definition 2. *Process Definitions with Permissions (PDP) are defined by a graph $\mathcal{G} = (\mathcal{D}, \rightharpoonup)$, where $\mathcal{D}$ is a set of process definitions, and $\rightharpoonup \subseteq \mathcal{D} \times \mathcal{D}$ is a set of permission edges. $D_1 \rightharpoonup D_2$ is used to denote $\langle D_1, D_2 \rangle \in \rightharpoonup$.*

The permission graph defines a dependency relation between process definitions. Namely, if $D_1 \rightharpoonup D_2$, then a process of type D_1 has the permission to use services provided by a process of type D_2.

2.1 Operational Semantics

We now move to the definition of an operational semantics for our model. First of all, values of registers are taken from a denumerable set of identifiers Id.

A configuration γ is a tuple $\langle V, L \rangle$, where $V = \{n_1, \ldots, n_k\}$ is a set of process instances for $k \geq 0$, $L : V \rightarrow \mathcal{D} \times \mathcal{Q} \times Id^r$ is a labeling function that associates a definition, a control state (taken from the union of control states of all definitions), and values to registers of each process. We use Γ to denote the infinite set of all configurations (the set is infinite since it contains configurations with any number of process instances).

Terminology For a process $v \in V$, we denote by $L_D(v)$, $L_Q(v)$ and $L_M(v)$ the three projections of $L(v)$. With an abuse of a notation, we use the same notation to extract the projections relative to a given node v from a configuration γ, i.e., $L_D(\gamma, v) = L_D(v)$ is the definition (or type) associated to node v in γ; $L_Q(\gamma, v) = L_Q(v)$ is the current state of node v in γ; and $L_M(\gamma, v, i) = L_M(v)[i]$ is the current value of register i of node v in γ. Finally, the configuration γ is said to be initial if (1) all nodes are in their initial control states, i.e., for all $v \in V$, $L_Q(v) = q_0$ if $L_D(v) = \langle Q, R, q_0 \rangle$; (2) for all nodes, all registers contain different values, i.e., for all $u, v \in V$ and all $i, j \in [1..r]$, if $u \neq v$ or $i \neq j$ then $L_M(v)[i] \neq L_M(v)[j]$. We use $\Gamma_0 \subseteq \Gamma$ to denote the infinite subset of initial configurations.

For a configuration $\gamma = \langle V, L \rangle$, $u, v \in V$, $\overline{p} = p_1, \ldots, p_f$ and an action $A = \mathbf{s}(m, \overline{p})$, let $S(v, u, A) \subseteq \mathcal{Q} \times Id^r$ be the set of the possible labels that can take u on reception of the message m sent by v, i.e., we have $(q', M) \in S(v, u, A)$, where M is an r-tuple of identifiers, if and only if there exists a receive action of the form $\langle L_Q(u), \mathbf{r}(m, \overline{\alpha}), q' \rangle$ where $\overline{\alpha} = \alpha_1, \ldots, \alpha_f$ verifying the following condition: For all $i \in [1..f]$, (1) if $\alpha_i = ?j$, then $L_M(u)[j] = L_M(v)[p_i]$; (2) if $\alpha_i = \downarrow j$ then $M[j] = L_M(v)[p_i]$, otherwise $M[j] = L_M(u)[j]$.

Given $\mathcal{G} = \langle \mathcal{D}, \rightharpoonup \rangle$, we define the transition system $TS_{\mathcal{G}} = \langle \Gamma, \Rightarrow \rangle$, where $\Rightarrow \subseteq \Gamma \times \Gamma$. Specifically, for $\gamma = \langle V, L \rangle$ and $\gamma' = \langle V, L' \rangle \in \Gamma$, $A = \mathbf{s}(m, \overline{p})$ we have $\gamma \Rightarrow \gamma'$ if and only if (1) for all $u \in V$, $L_D(\gamma', u) = L_D(\gamma, u)$, and (2) one of the following conditions holds:

- there exist $u, v \in V$ $u \neq v$ s.t. $\langle L_Q(\gamma, v), A, L_Q(\gamma', v) \rangle \in R$, $L_M(\gamma', v) = L_M(\gamma, v)$ $\langle L_Q(\gamma', u), L_M(\gamma', u) \rangle \in S(v, u, A)$, $L_D(\gamma, v) \rightharpoonup L_D(\gamma, u)$, $L_Q(\gamma', u') = L_Q(\gamma, u')$ and $L_M(\gamma', u') = L_M(\gamma, u')$ for $u' \in V$ s.t. $u' \neq u, v$.
- there exist $v, u \in V$ $v \neq u$, $q_1, q_2 \in \mathcal{Q}$, and $M \in Id^r$ s.t. $\langle L_Q(\gamma, v), A, q_1 \rangle \in R$, $\langle q_2, M \rangle \in S(v, u, A)$, $L_D(\gamma, v) \not\rightharpoonup L_D(\gamma, u)$, $L_Q(\gamma', v) = error$, $L_M(\gamma', v) = L_M(\gamma, v)$, $L_Q(\gamma', u') = L_Q(\gamma, u')$, $L_M(\gamma', u') = L_M(\gamma, u')$, for $u' \in V$ (including u) s.t. $u' \neq u$.
- there exist $v \in V$, $\langle L_Q(\gamma, v), \mathbf{l}(a), L_Q(\gamma', v) \rangle \in R$ and $L_Q(\gamma', u) = L_Q(\gamma, u)$, $L_M(\gamma', u) = L_M(\gamma, u)$ for $u \in V$ s.t. $u \neq v$.

We use $\overset{*}{\Rightarrow}$ to denote the reflexive and transitive closure of $\Rightarrow$.

Finally, given $\mathcal{G} = \langle \mathcal{D}, \rightharpoonup \rangle$ with $TS_{\mathcal{G}} = \langle \Gamma, \Rightarrow \rangle$, the set of reachable configurations is defined as follows: $Reach(\mathcal{G}) = \{\gamma \in \Gamma \mid \exists \gamma_0 \in \Gamma_0 \text{ s.t. } \gamma_0 \overset{*}{\Rightarrow} \gamma\}$. We observe that the number of nodes in V does not change during a computation, i.e., all successors of a given configuration γ_0 have the same set of nodes V. However, assuming that $\mathcal{D} \neq \emptyset$, the set of initial configuration Γ_0 is infinite by construction and contains all possible combinations (of any number) of instances of process with types in $\mathcal{D}$. Therefore, $Reach(\mathcal{G})$ is always infinite when $\mathcal{D} \neq \emptyset$.

Detection of Permission Violations. Given a PDP $\mathcal{G} = \langle \mathcal{D}, \rightharpoonup \rangle$, our goal is to decide whether there exists an initial configuration containing any number of process instances of any type from which it is possible to reach a configuration exposing a permission violation, i.e., containing a process with *error* control state. The formal definition of the decision problem is given below.

Definition 3. *Given a PDP $\mathcal{G} = \langle \mathcal{D}, \rightharpoonup \rangle$ s.t. $\mathcal{D} \neq \emptyset$, with $TS_\mathcal{G} = \langle \Gamma, \Rightarrow \rangle$, the problem $VD(r, f)$ is defined as follows: $\exists \gamma \in Reach(\mathcal{G})$ with nodes in V and $\exists v \in V$ such that $L_Q(\gamma, v) = error$?*

As remarked in the previous section, Γ_0 is an infinite set of configurations. Hence for fixed r, f $VD(r, f)$ cannot be solved directly by using a reduction to a finite-state system. Intuitively, we need to guess an adequate number of processes in the initial configuration to expose a violation. We will show that in general this is not possible in algorithmic way.

Data Tracking. We are also interested in tracking data exchanged by different processes during a computation and data can generate violations of permissions that are invisible to the $\rightharpoonup$ dependency relation. More specifically, we first introduce a symmetric relation $\notmid \subseteq \mathcal{D} \times \mathcal{D}$ to specify (a priori) potential conflicts between permissions associated to process types (i.e. definitions in $\mathcal{D}$). We now consider the extended model PDP with conflicts (PDPC), defined as $\mathcal{G} = \langle \mathcal{D}, \rightharpoonup, \notmid \rangle$. For instance, if processes of type D_1, D_2 can access internet services of type D_3 cannot, then we assume that $D_1 \notmid D_3$ and $D_2 \notmid D_3$.

We now move to the second decision problem that we consider in the paper.

Definition 4. *Given PDPC $\mathcal{G} = \langle \mathcal{D}, \rightharpoonup, \notmid \rangle$ with $TS_\mathcal{G} = \langle \Gamma, \Rightarrow \rangle$, the problem $CD(r, f)$ is defined as follows: $\exists \gamma_1, \gamma_2 \in Reach(\mathcal{G})$ with nodes in V, $\exists u, v \in V$, and $\exists$ registers i, j such that $\gamma_1 \overset{*}{\Rightarrow} \gamma_2$, $L_M(\gamma_1, u, i) = L_M(\gamma_2, v, j)$, and $L_D(\gamma_1, u) \notmid L_D(\gamma_2, v)$?*

Finally, we say that a PDP [resp. a PDPC] is violation-free [resp. conflict-free] if and only if there are no violations of the above mentioned types. As for VD, in the CD decision problem there are no restrictions a priori on the number of component instances in the initial configuration. From a computational perspective, this feature is a major obstacle for algorithmic solutions to the problem.

3   Violation Detection

In this section we prove that violation detection is undecidable for $r \geq 2, f = 1$. This property is due to the special parameterized formulation of the problem. The possibility of choosing an initial configuration of arbitrary size can be exploited to set up a network configuration in which a special node plays the role of controller linked to a finite but arbitrary sequence of nodes that encode unitary elements of a memory (e.g. a counter or the tape of a Turing machine). Elements of the memory are linked via identifiers stored in registers. By setting up a specific set of process definitions and an adequate permission relation, it is possible to reduce the halting problem of a counter machine to violation detection. The statement is proved formally in the rest of the section.

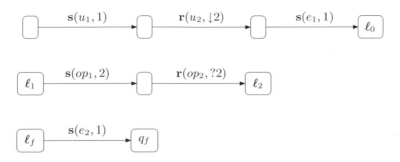

Fig. 2. Process of type C: we use op_1 and op_2 to denote messages needed for completing an entire simulation step of instruction op; op is a label in $\{incN, zeroN, nzeroN, decN\}$ for a counter N, .

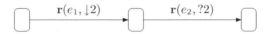

Fig. 3. Component of type E.

Theorem 1. *The $VD(2,1)$ problem is undecidable.*

We exhibit a reduction from the termination problem for two counter machines. Counter machines are sequential programs that manipulate a finite set of counters with values over natural numbers. We consider here instructions such as inc_i, dec_i, *if* $zero_i$ $goto_j$, *if* $notzero_i$ $goto_j$ for $i \in [1, \ldots, r]$ (number of counters) and $j \in [1 \ldots k]$ (instructions) and programs P with instructions $I_1, \ldots, I_k$. For the encoding, we need process definitions C, U and E whose permission graph is as follows: $C \rightharpoonup U, U \rightharpoonup C, C \rightharpoonup E$. An instance I_C of process definition C is used to keep track of the current instruction of P (program counter). Furthermore, in the initialization phase I_C has the following tasks: synchronization with a process of type E used in the last step of the simulation, construction of a linked list, connected to I_C whose elements are instances of type U. Processes of type C and U have two registers, id and $next$ for simplicity. Register id is used as identifier of each process instance. Register $next$ is used as pointer to the first/next process instance (the next cell in the list). Instances of type U simulate the unit of a counter c_i, its state denotes a zero or one value for c_i. The types of the elements in the list are chosen non-deterministically. In other words we represent the current values of all counters in a single list.

To create a list of finite but arbitrary length, we just need to first propagate a request message through U cells. U cells can non-deterministically decide to stop propagation and return their identifier to a process of type C. In this phase, upon reception, a process instance stores the identifier in the second register, the "next pointer" and sends its own identifier to another instance. Several lists can be constructed in parallel starting from different initial states. The acknowledgment phases is then needed to build a well formed list in which each node has the identifier of the next cell. Observe that, due to the non-determinism

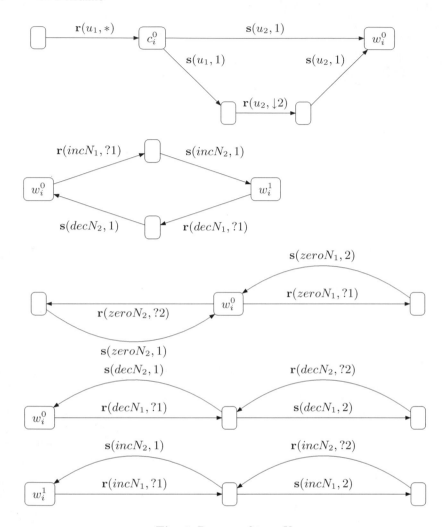

Fig. 4. Process of type U.

of rendez-vous, a well formed lists can have elements taken from other lists constructed in the first phase. An alternative algorithm can be obtained by constructing a list backwards, i.e., propagating the "next pointer" sending id to a node that directly stores in its second register. We adopt the first algorithm so as to use process of type C as initiator and coordinator of all the phases and to show the power of data to isolate special topologies in a fully connected set of processes. When the list is ready, I_C synchronizes, via handshaking, with one instance I_E of a process of type E. The simulation of the program P can now start. The list denotes value k for counter c_i if it contains k instances of process U with an internal state that encode a single unit for the counter c_i. Process U is such that, upon reception of an operation request, it can either execute it locally

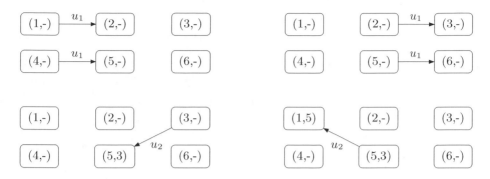

Fig. 5. Example of list construction in which the second phase is used to fix the "next" pointers.

(e.g. increment of a zero cell) or forward the request to the next cell and wait for an answer (in state w). Simulation of an increment on counter C_i propagates the request to set to one the internal state of a cell of type c_i with value zero in the list. Simulation of a decrement on counter C_i propagates the request to set to zero the internal state of a cell of type c_i with value one in the list. Simulation of a zero-test on counter C_i propagates the test on on the value of the cell to the whole list. An acknowledgment is sent back to the sender if all cells are zero. For a non-zero test the first non-zero cell sends an acknowledgement back to the sender (Fig. 5).

The last phase of the simulation starts when the simulation of the counter machine terminates, i.e., I_C has a control state that corresponds to the halt location of P. I_C then sends a special request pv to the first U cell in the list. Upon reception of the pv request, the cell tries to call an action of the I_E instance, generating a permission violation. The definition of process C, E and U are given in Figs. 2, 3 and 4, respectively.

By construction, the counter machine P terminates if and only if there exists an initial configuration from which we can generate a configuration with well-formed lists, and enough memory cells, that can simulate a complete execution of the program P. Formally, P reaches location ℓ_f if an only if there exists an initial configuration γ_0 s.t. $\gamma_0 \Rightarrow^* \gamma_1$ and $L_Q(\gamma_1, u) = \ell_f$ for some node u. From the previous property and following from the interaction between C and E processes, it follows that P reaches location ℓ_f if and only if there exists an initial configuration γ_0 s.t. $\gamma_0 \Rightarrow^* \gamma_1$ and $L_Q(\gamma_1, u) = error$ for some node u. Therefore halting of P is reduced to violation detection in the application $\mathcal{D} = \langle C, E, U \rangle$.

When processes do not exchange data, i.e., $r = 0$ or $f = 0$, it is possible to decide violation detection by using algorithms for deciding the coverability problem in Petri Nets (see appendix for main definitions). Formally, the following property holds.

Theorem 2. *The $VD(r, f)$ problem is decidable if either $r = 0$ or $f = 0$.*

Proof. Let $\mathcal{D} = \{C_1, \ldots, C_n\}$ with $C_i = \langle Q_i, \Sigma_i, \delta_i, q_0^i \rangle$ for $i : 1, \ldots, n$. The reduction is defined as follows. The set P of places is defined as $P = \{err\} \cup$

$(\bigcup_{i=1}^{n} Q_i)$. The transitions are defined as follows. For $i \in \{n\}$ and every rule $r = \langle q, a, q' \rangle \in \delta_i$, we define a transition $t_r = \langle Pre, Post \rangle$ s.t. $Pre = \{q\}$ and $Post = \{q'\}$. For $i, j \in \{n\}$ and every pair of rules $r_1 = \langle q_1, \mathbf{s}(a), q'_1 \rangle \in \delta_i$, $r_2 = \langle q_2, \mathbf{r}(a), q'_2 \rangle \in \delta_j$ s.t. $C_i \rightharpoonup C_j$, we define a transition $t_r = \langle Pre, Post \rangle$ s.t. $Pre = \{q_1, q_2\}$ and $Post = \{q'_1, q'_2\}$. For $i, j \in \{n\}$ and every pair of rules $r_1 = \langle q_1, \mathbf{s}(a), q'_1 \rangle \in \delta_i$, $r_2 = \langle q_2, \mathbf{r}(a), q'_2 \rangle \in \delta_j$ s.t. $C_i \not\rightharpoonup C_j$, we define a transition $t_r = \langle Pre, Post \rangle$ s.t. $Pre = \{q_1, q_2\}$ and $Post = \{err, q_2\}$.

Given a configuration $\gamma = \langle q_1, \ldots, q_n \rangle$ we define the associated marking M_γ that contains as many occurrences of state q as those in γ. By construction of our reduction, we obtain that γ_0 reaches configuration γ_1 iff $M_{\gamma_0} \rhd M_{\gamma_1}$. To represent an arbitrary initial configuration, we add a transition that non-deterministically adds token to places that represent initial states of processes. Furthermore, to separate initialization and normal operations we can simply use and additional place ok and use it to block process interactions during the initialization phase. Namely, $it_i = \langle Pre, Post \rangle$ s.t. $Pre = \{init\}$ and $Post = \{init, q_0^i\}$ for any i. Furthermore, $it_{i+1} = \langle Pre, Post \rangle$ s.t. $Pre = \{init\}$ and $Post = \{ok\}$. All the other rules are modified in order to add ok to their pre-set. As a corollary, we have that the safety property holds for $\mathcal{D}$ iff coverability holds for the Petri net P and the two markings $M_{\gamma_0} = \{init\}$ and $M_{err} = \{e\}$. Following from properties of Petri Nets, we obtain that the safety problem is decidable for $VD(0,0)$.

In the rest of the paper we will focus our attention on conflict detection and derive other decidability results for violation detection as a side-effect of more general results obtained for processes and messages with data.

4   Conflict Detection

In this section we move to the analysis of the conflict detection problem. We first observe that conflict detection is undecidable for $r > 1$. The proof is similar to the encoding of counter machines used for the undecidability of violation detection. Instead of generating a permission violation as a last step of the simulation the controller C sends its identifier to a special process of type D s.t. C and D are in conflict. This way, a conflict is detected starting from some initial configuration if and only if the counter machine program terminates. We show that both violation and conflict detection are decidable for $r = f = 1$.

The decidability proof consists of two steps. We first extend the transition system of a PDPC by adding a sort of external memory in which to keep track of footprints of identifiers. Footprints are represented via a collection of predicates that mark all types of processes in which an identifier has been stored. It is important to remark that footprints share data with current configurations, i.e., the alphabet used to define footprints is infinite as for configurations. To deal with the conflict detection problem, we may need infinite set of footprints since the problem is parametric in the initial configuration. By extending the transition relation with historical information we can reduce conflict detection to a reachability problem formulated over the predicates in the history. It is important to notice that for this kind of problem we just need a monotonically increasing external memory. The second step of the proof consists in reducing the reachability problem for the transition system with history to coverability in a formalism called MSR(C) that is a special class of multiset rewriting with constraints. The desired result follows then by observing that, for $r = 1$, the resulting encoding produces only rewriting rules with monadic predicates. We can then apply the decision procedure based on the theory of well-structured transition systems defined in [11] to solve algorithmically the CD problem. We start from defining the extended operational semantics.

4.1   Transition System with History

Given $\mathcal{D}$, let us consider the set of unary predicates $P_{\mathcal{D}} = \{h_C | C \in \mathcal{D}\}$. We use the formula $h_C(id)$ to denote a footprint for the identifier $id \in Id$. Let $F_{\mathcal{D}} = \{h_C(id) | id \in Id, \ h_C \in P\}$ be the set of all footprints associated to $\mathcal{D}$. We use $H_{\mathcal{D}}$ to denote all possible multisets of footprints in $F_{\mathcal{D}}$, i.e., $H_{\mathcal{D}} = F_{\mathcal{D}}^{\oplus}$. For a configuration γ, let $fp(\gamma)$ be the multiset of footprints such that $h_C(id) \in fp(\gamma)$ iff the identifier id occurs in some register of a process of type C in γ. As an example, for γ with nodes n_1, n_2, n_3 of type A, B, C with values in the two registers resp. $(1, 2)$, $(2, 3)$, and $(3, 4)$, $fp(\gamma) = \{h_A(1), h_A(2), h_B(2), h_B(3), h_C(3), h_C(4)\}$.

Extended configurations are tuples of the form $\gamma[h]$, where γ is a configuration and $h \in H_{\mathcal{D}}$. An initial configuration is defined then as $\gamma_0[h_0]$, where $h_0 = fp(\gamma_0)$, i.e., h_0 contains the footprints for each identifier in γ_0.

The extended transition relation $\Rightarrow_h \subseteq \Gamma \times H_{\mathcal{D}}$ is built on top of $\Rightarrow$ as follows:

- $\gamma[h] \Rightarrow_h \gamma'[h]$ if $\gamma \Rightarrow \gamma'$ via an application of a local rule;
- $\gamma[h] \Rightarrow_h \gamma'[h \oplus fps(\gamma')]$ if $\gamma \Rightarrow \gamma'$ via an application of a rendez-vous step, where $fps(\gamma')$ is the multiset of footprints in $fp(\gamma')$ generated by store operations after a reception, i.e., $h_C(id) \in fps(\gamma')$ iff $h_C(id) \in fp(\gamma')$ and id is stored in a register of a process of type C during the rendez-vous, for some C and identifier id.

We use $\overset{*}{\Rightarrow}_h$ to denote the reflexive and transitive closure of $\Rightarrow_h$.

The CD problem can now be formulated by considering the history of a computation. Namely, CD amounts to checking whether there exists an initial configuration $\gamma_0[h_0]$ (of arbitrary shape) from which it is possible to reach a configuration $\gamma[h]$ such that h contains at least two footprints $h_C(i)$ and $h_D(i)$ for some process type C, D s.t. $C \natural D$. It is important to observe that we just need unary predicates to represent footprints for identifiers.

4.2   Encoding into MSR(Id)

An encoding of the problem into coverability of a model inspired by Petri nets with identifiers called MSR(C) in which the constraint system consists of equalities. In the encoding we model both the behavior of an application as well as footprints of data exchanged by instances of processes. Footprints are represented via monadic predicates. Each predicate keeps track of the history of a given identifier during its lifetime, namely every type of process in which the identifier has been stored during execution. The history can then be queried in search for conflicts. MSR($\mathcal{C}$) is a formal model for concurrent systems based on a combination of rewriting and constraints. A constraint system $\mathcal{C}$ is defined by formulas with free variables in V, an interpretation domain $\mathcal{D}$, and a satisfiability relation $\models$ for formulas in $\mathcal{C}$ interpreted over $\mathcal{D}$. We use $\mathcal{D} \models_\sigma \varphi$ to denote satisfiability of φ via a substitution $\sigma : Var(\varphi) \to \mathcal{D}$, where $Var(\varphi)$ is the set of free variables in φ. For a fixed set of predicates P, an atomic formula with variables has the form $p(x_1, \ldots, x_n)$ where $p \in P$ and $x_1, \ldots, x_n \in V$. A rewriting rule has the form $M \to M' : \varphi$, where M and M' are multiset of atomic formulas with variables over P and V, and φ is a constraint formula over variables $Var(M \oplus M')$ occurring in $M \oplus M'$. We use $M = A_1, \ldots, A_n$ to denote a multiset of atoms.

MSR(Id) is the instance obtained by considering the constraint system Id defined as follows. Constraint formulas are defined by the grammar $\varphi ::= \varphi_1, \varphi_2 | x = y | x < y$ for variables $x, y \in V$. Here φ_1, φ_2 denotes a conjunction of formulas φ_1 and φ_2. The interpretation domain is defined over an infinite and ordered set of identifiers $\langle Id, =, < \rangle$. For substitution $\sigma : V \to Id$, $x = y$ is interpreted as $\sigma(x) = \sigma(y)$, $x < y$ is interpreted as $\sigma(x) < \sigma(y)$, and φ_1, φ_2 is interpreted as $\sigma(\varphi_1) \land \sigma(\varphi_2)$. A constraint φ is satisfied by a substitution σ if $\sigma(\varphi)$ evaluates to $true$. An instance $M\sigma \to M'\sigma$ of a rule $M \to M' : \varphi$ is defined by taking a substitution $\sigma : Var(M \oplus M') \to Id$ such that $\sigma(\varphi)$ is satisfied in the interpretation Id.

As an example, consider the rule $p(x, y), q(x) \to p(x, y), q(x), q(u) : x < u$ The intuition is that processes $p(x, y)$ and $q(z)$ synchronize when $x = z$ and generate a new instance $q(u)$ with $x < u$. By associating natural numbers to identifiers, $p(1, 2), q(1) \to p(1, 2), q(1), q(4)$ and $p(3, 10), q(3) \to p(3, 10), q(3), q(8)$ are two instances of the considered rule. We use $Inst(\Delta)$ to indicate the infinite set of instances of a set Δ of MSR rules.

A configuration is a multiset N of atoms of the form $p(d_1, \ldots, d_n)$ with $d_i \in Id$ for $i : 1, \ldots, n$. For a set Δ of rules and a configuration N, a rewriting step is defined by the relation $\triangleright$ s.t. $N = (M \oplus Q) \triangleright (M' \oplus Q) = N'$ for $(M \to M') \in Inst(\Delta)$. A computation is a sequence of configurations $N_1 \ldots N_m \ldots$ s.t. $N_i \triangleright N_{i+1}$ for $i \geq 0$. For a set of rules Δ, an initial configuration N_0, and a zerary predicate p_f, the coverability problem, COV, consists in checking whether there exists a computation from N_0 to a configuration N_1 s.t. $p_f \in N_1$.

We now encode the $CD(r, f)$ problem as a coverability instance in monadic MSR(Id). Let $\mathcal{D} = \{C_1, \ldots, C_n\}$ with $C_i = \langle Q_i, R_i, q_0^i \rangle$ for $i : 1, \ldots, n$. We define the set $P = \{init, max, ok\} \cup \{h_C | C \in \mathcal{D}\} \cup (\bigcup_{i=1}^n Q_i)$ of monadic predicates. Predicates $init$ and ok are used to separate the initialization phase from the simulation steps. Predicates h_C define footprints for data. In order to represent an arbitrary initial configuration we define MSR(Id) rules that non-deterministically add predicates with distinct identifiers. The rules are defined as follows:

- $init \to init, max(x) : true$ where max is used to generate fresh identifiers;
- for each initial state q_0 of process $C \in \mathcal{D}$ with $\bar{x} = x_1, \ldots, x_n$,

$$init, max(x) \rightarrow init, max(y), q_0(\overline{x}), h_C(x_1), \dots, h_C(x_n) : \phi,$$

with $\phi = y > x_1 > x_2 \dots x_n > x$, injects a node with initial state q_0 and registers initialized to fresh values $x_1, \dots, x_n$. The value stored in max is reset to a value greater than the last value seen so far.

- The initialization is non-deterministically terminated by the rule $init, max(x) \rightarrow ok : true$. Inserting ok marks the beginning of the simulation phase.

The simulation of process rules is defined by the following rules.

Local For $i \in \{n\}$ and every rule $r = \langle q, \mathbf{l}(a), q' \rangle \in R_i$, we define a rewriting rule

$$ok, q(x_1, \dots, x_n) \rightarrow ok, q'(x'_1, \dots, x'_n) : x'_1 = x_1, \dots, x'_n = x_n$$

where $x_1, \dots, x_n$ denote the current values of the registers, and q/q' is the current/next state.

Rendez-vous. For $i, j \in \{n\}$ and every pair of rules $r_1 = \langle q_1, \mathbf{s}(a, p_1, \dots, p_f), q'_1 \rangle \in R_i$, $r_2 = \langle q_2, \mathbf{r}(a, \alpha_1, \dots, \alpha_f), q'_2 \rangle \in R_j$ s.t. q_1 is the state of a process of type A, q_2 is the state of a process of type B, $A \rightharpoonup B$, we define a rule

$$ok, q_1(x_1, \dots, x_r), q_2(y_1, \dots, y_r) \rightarrow ok, q'_1(x'_1, \dots, x'_r), q'_2(y'_1, \dots, y'_r) \oplus M_f : \varphi$$

where φ is the constraint $\varphi_1, \dots, \varphi_f, \psi_1, \psi_2$ defined as follows: for $i : 1, \dots, f$, if $\alpha_i =?p_j$, then φ_i is the equality $y_i = x_j$ (each guard must be satisfied); if $\alpha_i =\downarrow p_j$, then φ_i is the equality $y'_i = x_j$ (assignment to register i) and M_f contains predicate $h_B(x_j)$ encoding a footprint; if $\alpha_i = *$, then $\varphi_i = true$. Furthermore, $\psi = (\wedge_{i=1}^r x'_i = x_i) \wedge (\wedge_{i=1, \alpha_i \neq \downarrow k, k \geq 1}^r y'_i = y_i)$ to denote that values of registers remain unchanged unless modified by some store operations in the receiver process.

Violation. For $i, j \in \{n\}$ and every pair of rules $r_1 = \langle q_1, \mathbf{s}(a, p_1, \dots, p_f), q'_1 \rangle \in R_i$, $r_2 = \langle q_2, \mathbf{r}(a, \alpha_1, \dots, \alpha_f), q'_2 \rangle \in R_j$ s.t. q_1 is the state of a process of type A, q_2 is the state of a process of type B, $A \not\rightharpoonup B$, we define a rule:

$$ok, q_1(x_1, \dots, x_r), q_2(y_1, \dots, y_r) \rightarrow ok, err(x'_1, \dots, x'_r), q'_2(y'_1, \dots, y'_r) : \varphi$$

where φ is the constraint $\varphi_1, \dots, \varphi_f, \psi$ defined as follows: for $i : 1, \dots, f$, if $\alpha_i =?p_j$, then φ_i is the equality $y_i = x_j$ (each guard must be satisfied), if $\alpha_i =\downarrow p_j$ or $\alpha_i = *$, then $\varphi_i = true$; Furthermore, $\psi = \wedge_{i=1}^r x'_i = x_i, y'_i = y_i$ to denote that values of registers remain unchanged.

Finally, for each pair $C \not\downarrow D$ we define a rule $h_C(x), h_D(x) \rightarrow conflict$ to detect conflicts over data that have been stored in incompatible processes.

By construction of our reduction, we obtain that $\gamma_0[h_0]$ reaches configuration $\gamma[h]$ iff $init \triangleright N_\gamma \oplus h$, where N_γ is the multiset that contains ok, and, for each node u of type A in γ, a formula $q(\overline{v})$ where $q = L_Q(\gamma, u)$, and $\overline{v} = L_M(\gamma, u)$.

In the above construction we use the monadic predicate $h_C(x)$ to maintain footprints of identifier x received by an instance of a process of type C. The last rule is used to detect conflicts between two footprints for the same identifier. Footprints work as records of an infinite memory that associates to every identifier all processes visited during an execution. We need here infinite memory since our decision problems consider any possible initial configuration.

Theorem 3. *The $CD(1,1)$ problem is decidable.*

Proof. For $r = 1$, the rewriting rules resulting from the encoding of the $CD(1,1)$ problem into MSR(Id) consist of monadic predicates only. By construction, the problem $CD(1,1)$ is satisfied if and only if from the MSR(Id) configuration *init* it is possible to reach a configuration N s.t. *conflict* belongs to N. This is an instance of the coverability problem for MSR(Id) that is decidable for monadic rewriting rules as shown in [11].

Besides decidability, the encoding can still be applied to obtain a possibly non terminating procedure for solving conflict detection for $r > 2$. The procedure is based on the symbolic backward reachability procedure for MSR(C) specifications described in [11].

Theorem 4. *The $VD(1,1)$ problem is decidable.*

Proof. We use the same reduction to MSR(Id) used for conflict-detection and add rules of the form $err(x_1, \ldots, x_n) \rightarrow err : true$ to detect error states in individual processes. By construction, it follows that $VD(1,1)$ holds if and only if from the configuration *init* we can reach a configuration N s.t. $err \in N$.

5   Conclusions and Related Work

We have presented a framework for reasoning about abstract models of concurrent systems in which interaction is regulated by a statically defined permission model. In this setting we have studied computational issues of two fundamental problems: detecting permission violations and conflicts due to value passing. The problems are formulated in sucha a way to capture properties for concurrent systems with an arbitrary number of components. Our model is inspired by the automata-based model of distributed systems proposed in [13–15] to study of robustness of broadcast communication in unreliable networks with different types of topology and different types of dynamic reconfigurations. Verification of broadcast protocols in fully connected networks in which nodes and messages range over a finite set of states has been considered, e.g., in [4,16–18,24]. Differently from the above mentioned works, the focus of the present paper is the analysis of process interaction, via rendez-vous and value passing, controlled by permission models and of its interplay with data. Parameterized verification of provenance in distributed applications has been considered in [20] where regular languages are used as a formal tool to symbolically analyze the provenance of messages taken from a finite alphabet. In the present paper we consider messages from an infinite alphabet and use transition systems with histories that share information in common with the current state. The use of predicates to observe the history of data shares similarities with approaches based on the use of policy automata and type systems. Type systems have been defined in abstract languages that model Android applications in [2,9] based on the history expressions introduced in [5,6]. Policy automata are automata with management of names that can be used to specify policies for accessing resources. They can be analyzed by using model checking algorithms for BPAs [7]. Concerning validation of updates of access control policies, parameterized reasoning via constraint and SMT solvers has been considered, e.g., in [3,21,22,25]. Register Automata and History-Register Automata have also been used to model programs with dynamic allocation in [26,27]. To our knowledge, the use of history predicates that share information with the current state and the application of well-structured transition systems to verify data tracking in parameterized concurrent systems are two novel ideas. From a technical point of view, our results are obtained via reductions to low level concurrency models like Petri nets and rewriting systems in which it is possible to manipulate data taken from an infinite ordered domain of identifiers like MSR(Id) [1,8,11]. MSR(Id) is also strictly related to ν-nets [23] that provide fresh name generation and equality constraints. The relation between MSR(Id) and ν-nets is studied in [12]. As shown in [1], the MSR(Id) model is strictly more expressive than Petri Nets and it has the same expressive power of Datanets [19], an extension of Petri Nets with ordered data.

References

1. Abdulla, P.A., Delzanno, G., Van Begin, L.: A classification of the expressive power of well-structured transition systems. Inf. Comput. **209**(3), 248–279 (2011)
2. Armando, A., Costa, G., Merlo, A.: Formal modeling and reasoning about the android security framework. In: Palamidessi, C., Ryan, M.D. (eds.) TGC 2012. LNCS, vol. 8191, pp. 64–81. Springer, Heidelberg (2013)
3. Armando, A., Ranise, S.: Scalable automated symbolic analysis of administrative role-based access control policies by SMT solving. J. Comput. Secur. **20**(4), 309–352 (2012)
4. Arons, T., Pnueli, A., Ruah, S., Xu, J., Zuck, L.D.: Parameterized verification with automatically computed inductive assertions. In: Berry, G., Comon, H., Finkel, A. (eds.) CAV 2001. LNCS, vol. 2102, pp. 221–234. Springer, Heidelberg (2001)
5. Bartoletti, M., Degano, P., Ferrari, G.-L., Zunino, R.: Types and effects for resource usage analysis. In: Seidl, H. (ed.) FOSSACS 2007. LNCS, vol. 4423, pp. 32–47. Springer, Heidelberg (2007)
6. Bartoletti, M., Degano, P., Ferrari, G.L., Zunino, R.: Local policies for resource usage analysis. ACM TOPLAS, vol. 31(6) (2009)
7. Bartoletti, M., Degano, P., Ferrari, G.L., Zunino, R.: Model checking usage policies. MSCS **25**(3), 710–763 (2015)
8. Bozzano, M.: A Logic-Based Approach to Model Checking of Parameterized and Infinite-State Systems, Ph.D. thesis, DISI, University of Genova, June 2002
9. Bugliesi, M., Calzavara, S., Spanò, A.: Lintent: towards security type-checking of android applications. In: Beyer, D., Boreale, M. (eds.) FORTE 2013 and FMOODS 2013. LNCS, vol. 7892, pp. 289–304. Springer, Heidelberg (2013)
10. Delzanno, G.: An overview of MSR(C): A CLP-based framework for the symbolic verification of parameterized concurrent systems. ENTCS **76**, 65–82 (2002)
11. Delzanno, G.: Constraint-based automatic verification of abstract models of multithreaded programs. TPLP **7**(1–2), 67–91 (2007)
12. Delzanno, G., Rosa-Velardo, F.: On the coverability and reachability languages of monotonic extensions of petri nets. Theor. Comput. Sci. **467**, 12–29 (2013)

13. Delzanno, G., Sangnier, A., Traverso, R., Zavattaro, G.: On the complexity of parameterized reachability in reconfigurable broadcast networks. In: FSTTCS 2012, pp. 289–300 (2012)
14. Delzanno, G., Sangnier, A., Zavattaro, G.: Parameterized verification of ad hoc networks. In: Gastin, P., Laroussinie, F. (eds.) CONCUR 2010. LNCS, vol. 6269, pp. 313–327. Springer, Heidelberg (2010)
15. Delzanno, G., Sangnier, A., Zavattaro, G.: On the Power of Cliques in the Parameterized Verification of Ad Hoc Networks. In: Hofmann, M. (ed.) FOSSACS 2011. LNCS, vol. 6604, pp. 441–455. Springer, Heidelberg (2011)
16. Emerson, E.A., Namjoshi, K.S.: On model checking for non-deterministic infinite-state systems. In: LICS, pp. 70–80 (1998)
17. Esparza, J., Finkel, A., Mayr, R.: On the verification of broadcast protocols. In: LICS 1999, pp. 352–359 (1999)
18. German, S.M., Sistla, A.P.: Reasoning about systems with many processes. J. ACM **39**(3), 675–735 (1992)
19. Lazic, R., Newcomb, T., Ouaknine, J., Roscoe, A.W., Worrell, J.: Nets with tokens which carry data. Fundam. Inform. **88**(3), 251–274 (2008)
20. Majumdar, R., Meyer, R., Wang, Z.: Provenance verification. In: RP, pp. 21–22 (2013)
21. Ranise, S.: Symbolic backward reachability with effectively propositional logic - applications to security policy analysis. FMSD **42**(1), 24–45 (2013)
22. Ranise, S., Traverso, R.: ALPS: an action language for policy specification and automated safety analysis. In: Mauw, S., Jensen, C.D. (eds.) STM 2014. LNCS, vol. 8743, pp. 146–161. Springer, Heidelberg (2014)
23. Rosa-Velardo, F., de Frutos-Escrig, D.: Decidability results for restricted models of petri nets with name creation and replication. In: Franceschinis, G., Wolf, K. (eds.) PETRI NETS 2009. LNCS, vol. 5606, pp. 63–82. Springer, Heidelberg (2009)
24. Schnoebelen, P.: Revisiting ackermann-hardness for lossy counter machines and reset petri nets. In: Hliněný, P., Kučera, A. (eds.) MFCS 2010. LNCS, vol. 6281, pp. 616–628. Springer, Heidelberg (2010)
25. Stoller, S.D., Yang, P., Gofman, M.I., Ramakrishnan, C.R.: Symbolic reachability analysis for parameterized administrative role-based access control. Comput. Secur. **30**(2–3), 148–164 (2011)
26. Tzevelekos, N.: Fresh-register automata. In: POPL 2011, pp. 295–306 (2011)
27. Tzevelekos, N., Grigore, R.: History-register automata. In: Pfenning, F. (ed.) FOSSACS 2013 (ETAPS 2013). LNCS, vol. 7794, pp. 17–33. Springer, Heidelberg (2013)

Modular Monitor Extensions for Information Flow Security in JavaScript

José Fragoso Santos[1]([⊠]), Tamara Rezk[2], and Ana Almeida Matos[3]

[1] Imperial College London, London, UK
jose.fragoso.santos@imperial.ac.uk
[2] Inria, Sophia Antipolis, France
tamara.rezk@inria.fr
[3] SQIG-Instituto de Telecomunicações, University of Lisbon, Lisbon, Portugal
ana.matos@ist.utl.pt

Abstract. Client-side JavaScript programs often interact with the web page into which they are included, as well as with the browser itself, through APIs such as the DOM API, the XMLHttpRequest API, and the W3C Geolocation API. Precise reasoning about JavaScript security must therefore take API invocation into account. However, the continuous emergence of new APIs, and the heterogeneity of their forms and features, renders API behavior a moving target that is particularly hard to capture. To tackle this problem, we propose a methodology for modularly extending sound JavaScript information flow monitors with a generic API. Hence, to verify whether an extended monitor complies with the proposed noninterference property requires only to prove that the API satisfies a predefined set of conditions. In order to illustrate the practicality of our methodology, we show how an information flow monitor-inlining compiler can take into account the invocation of arbitrary APIs, without changing the code or the proofs of the original compiler. We provide an implementation of such a compiler with an extension for handling a fragment of the DOM Core Level 1 API. Furthermore, our implementation supports the addition of monitor extensions for new APIs at runtime.

1 Introduction

Isolation properties guarantee protection for trusted JavaScript code from malicious code. The noninterference property [9] provides the mathematical foundations for reasoning precisely about isolation. In particular, noninterference properties guarantee absence of flows from confidential/untrusted resources to public/trusted ones.

Although JavaScript can be used as a general-purpose programming language, many JavaScript programs are designed to be executed in a browser in the context of a web page. Such programs often interact with the web page in which they are included, as well as with the browser itself, through Application Programming Interfaces (APIs). Some APIs are fully implemented in JavaScript,

P. Ganty and M. Loreti (Eds.): TGC 2015, LNCS 9533, pp. 47–62, 2016.
DOI: 10.1007/978-3-319-28766-9_4

whereas others are built with a mix of different technologies, which can be exploited to conceal sophisticated security violations. Thus, understanding the behavior of client-side web applications, as well as proving their compliance with a given security policy, requires cross-language reasoning. The size, complexity, and number of commonly used APIs poses an important challenge to any attempt at formally reasoning about the security of JavaScript programs [13]. To tackle this problem, we propose a methodology for extending JavaScript monitored semantics. This methodology allows us to verify whether a monitor complies with the proposed noninterference property in a modular way. Thus, we make it possible to prove that a security monitor is still noninterferent when extending it with a new API, without having to revisit the whole model. Generally, an API can be viewed as a particular set of specifications that a program can follow to make use of the resources provided by another particular application. For client-side JavaScript programs, this definition of API applies both to: (1) interfaces of services that are provided to the program by the environment in which it executes, namely the web browser (for instance, the DOM, the XMLHttpRequest, and the W3C Geolocation APIs); (2) interfaces of JavaScript libraries that are explicitly included by the programmer (for instance, jQuery, Prototype.js, and Google Maps Image API). In the context of this work, the main difference between these two types of APIs is that in the former case their semantics escapes the JavaScript semantics, whereas in the latter it does not. The methodology proposed here was designed as a generic way of extending security monitors to deal with the first type of APIs. Nevertheless, we can also apply it to the second type whenever we want to execute the library's code in the original JavaScript semantics instead of the monitored semantics.

Example 1 (Running example: A Queue API). Consider the following API for creating and manipulating priority queues. The API is available to the programmer through the global variable *queueAPI*, and variable *queueObj* is bound to a concrete queue:

> *queueAPI.queue()* : creates a new priority queue;
> *queueObj.push(el, priority)* : adds a new element to the queue;
> *queueObj.pop()* : pops the element with the highest priority.

The method calls from this API cannot be verified by the JavaScript monitor, as we are assuming that the code of the methods is not available to the JavaScript engine. Furthermore, the specification of the queue API may not obey the JavaScript semantics and hence prevention of the security leaks may need different constraints.

In order to extend a JavaScript security monitor to control the behavior of this API, one has to define what we call an *API Register* to set the security constraints associated to the corresponding API method calls on *queueAPI* and *queueObj*. API method calls should be implemented as interception points of the monitor semantics and the API Register should then make the invocation of these methods if the security constraints are satisfied.

The following questions then arise: What constraints must we impose on the new API register in order to preserve the noninterference guarantees of the JavaScript monitor? Is it possible to modularly prove noninterference of the extended monitor without revisiting the whole set of constraints, including those of the JavaScript monitor?

There are two main approaches for implementing a monitored JavaScript semantics: either one modifies a JavaScript engine so that it also implements the security monitor (as in [15]), or one inlines the monitor in the original program (as in [8,10,16]). Both these approaches suffer from the problem of requiring ad-hoc security mechanisms for all targeted APIs. We show how to extend an information flow monitor-inlining compiler so that it also takes into account the invocation of APIs. Our extensible compiler requires each API to be associated with a set of JavaScript methods that we call its *IFlow Signature*, which describes how to handle the information flows triggered by its invocation. We provide a prototype of the compiler, which is available online [20]. A user can easily extend it by loading new IFlow signatures. Using the compiler, we give realistic examples of how to prevent common security violations that arise from the interaction between JavaScript and the DOM API. In a nutshell, the benefit of our approach is that it allows us to separate the proof of security for each API from the proof of security for the core language. This separation is, to the best of our knowledge, new and useful as new APIs are continuously emerging.

The contributions of the paper are: (1) a methodology for extending JavaScript monitors with API monitoring (Sect. 3.2), (2) the design of an extensible information flow monitor-inlining compiler that follows our methodology (Sect. 4), (3) an implementation [20] of a JavaScript information flow monitor-inlining compiler (Sect. 5) that handles an important subset of the DOM API and is extensible with new APIs by means of IFlow Signatures.

2   Related Work

We refer the reader to a recent survey [7] on web scripts security and to [19] for a complete survey on information flow enforcement mechanisms up to 2003, while focusing here on the most closely related work on dynamic mechanisms for enforcing noninterference.

Flow-sensitive monitors for enforcing noninterference can be divided into *purely dynamic monitors* [3–5] and *hybrid monitors* [12,22]. While hybrid monitors use static analysis to reason about untaken execution paths, purely dynamic monitors do not rely on any kind of static analysis. There are three main strategies in designing sound purely dynamic information flow monitors. The *no-sensitive-upgrade* (NSU) strategy [3] forbids the update of public resources inside private contexts. The *permissive-upgrade* strategy [4] allows sensitive upgrades, but forbids programs to branch depending on values upgraded in private contexts. Finally, the *multiple facet* strategy [5] makes use of values that appear differently to observers at different security levels. Here, we show how to extend information flow monitors that follow the NSU discipline.

Hedin and Sabelfeld [15] are the first to propose a runtime monitor for enforcing noninterference for JavaScript. The technique that we present for extending security monitors can be applied to this monitor, which is purely dynamic and follows the NSU discipline. In [14], the authors implement their monitor as an extended JavaScript interpreter. Their implementation makes use of the informal concepts of shallow and deep information flow models in order to cater for the invocation of built-in libraries and DOM API methods. However, these concepts are not formalised. In fact, our definition of monitored API can be seen as a formalisation of the notion of deep information flow model for libraries.

Both Chudnov and Naumann [8] and Magazinius et al. [16] propose the inlining of information flow monitors for simple imperative languages. In [10], we present a compiler that inlines a purely dynamic information flow monitor for a realistic subset of JavaScript. In the implementation presented in this paper we extend the inlining compiler of [10] with the DOM API, applying the methodology proposed here.

Taly et al. [21] study API confinement. They provide a static analysis designed to verify whether an API may leak its confidential resources. Unlike us, they only target APIs implemented in JavaScript, whose code is available for either runtime or static analysis.

Russo et al. [18] present an information flow monitor for a WHILE language with primitives for manipulating DOM-like trees and prove it sound. They do not model references. In [2], we present an information flow monitor for a simple language that models a core of the DOM API based on the work of Gardner et al. [11]. In contrast to [18], we can handle references and live collections. Here, we apply the techniques of [2] to develop monitor extensions for a fragment of the DOM Core Level 1 API [17]. Recent work [23] presents an information flow monitor for JavaScript extended with the DOM API that also considers event handling loops. To the best of our knowledge, no prior work proposes a generic methodology to extend JavaScript monitors and inlining compilers with arbitrary web APIs.

3 Modular Extensions for JavaScript Monitors

In this section we show how to extend a noninterferent monitor so that it takes into account the invocation of web APIs, while preserving the noninterference property.

3.1 Noninterferent JavaScript Monitors

JavaScript Memory Model. In JavaScript [1], objects can be seen as partial functions mapping strings to values. The strings in the domain of an object are called its properties. Memories are mappings from references to objects. In the following, we assume that memories include a reference to a special object called the *global object* pointed to by a fixed reference $\#glob$, that binds global variables. In this presentation, objects, properties, memories, references and values, are ranged over by o, p, μ, r and v, respectively.

We use the notation $[p_0 \mapsto v_0, \ldots, p_n \mapsto v_n]$ for the partial function that maps p_i to v_i where $i = 0, \ldots n$, and $f[p_0 \mapsto v_0, \ldots, p_n \mapsto v_n]$ for the function that coincides with f everywhere except in $p_0, \ldots, p_n$, which are otherwise mapped to $v_0, \ldots, v_n$ respectively. Furthermore, we denote by $\mathsf{dom}(f)$ the domain of a function f, and by $f|_P$ the restriction of f to P (when $P \subseteq \mathsf{dom}(f)$). Finally, we write $f(r)(p)$ instead of $(f(r))(p)$, the application of the image of r by function f to p.

Sequences are denoted by stacking an arrow as in $\overrightarrow{v}$, and ϵ denotes the empty sequence. The length of $\overrightarrow{v}$ is given by $|\overrightarrow{v}|$ and $\cdot$ denotes concatenation of sequences.

Security Setting. Information flow policies such as noninterference are specified over security labelings that assign security levels, taken from a given security lattice, to the observable resources of a program. In the following, we use a fixed lattice $\mathcal{L}$ of security levels ranged over by σ. We denote by $\leq$ its order relation, by $\sigma_0 \sqcup \sigma_1$ the least upper bound between levels σ_0 and σ_1, and by $\sqcup \overrightarrow{\sigma}$ the least upper bound of all levels in the sequence $\overrightarrow{\sigma}$. In the examples, we consider two security levels $\{H, L\}$ such that $L < H$, meaning that resources labeled with *high* level H are more confidential than those labeled with *low* level L.

In our setting, a security labeling is as a pair $\langle \Gamma, \Sigma \rangle$, where Γ maps references, followed by properties, to security levels, and Σ maps references to security levels. Then, given an object o pointed to by a reference r, if defined, $\Gamma(r)(p)$ corresponds to the security levels associated with o's property p, and $\Sigma(r)$ with o's domain. The latter, also referred to as o's *structure security level*, controls the observability of the existence of properties [15].

We say that memory μ is well-labeled by $\langle \Gamma, \Sigma \rangle$ if $\mathsf{dom}(\Gamma) = \mathsf{dom}(\Sigma) \subseteq \mathsf{dom}(\mu)$ and for every reference $r \in \mathsf{dom}(\Gamma)$, $\mathsf{dom}(\Gamma(r)) \subseteq \mathsf{dom}(\mu(r))$.

Security Monitor. JavaScript programs are statements, that include expressions, ranged over by s and e, respectively. We model an information flow monitor as a small-step semantics relation $\rightarrow_{\mathsf{IF}}$ between configurations of the form $\langle \mu, s, \overrightarrow{\sigma_{\mathsf{pc}}}, \Gamma, \Sigma, \overrightarrow{\sigma} \rangle$ composed of (1) a memory μ (2) a statement s, that is to execute, (3) a sequence of security levels $\overrightarrow{\sigma_{\mathsf{pc}}}$, matching the expressions on which the original program branched to reach the current context, (4) a security labeling $\langle \Gamma, \Sigma \rangle$, and (5) a sequence of security levels $\overrightarrow{\sigma}$ matching the reading effects of the subexpressions of the expression being computed.

The *reading effect* [19] of an expression is defined as the least upper bound on the security levels of the resources on which the value to which it evaluates depends. Additionally, we assume that the reading effect of an expression is always higher than or equal to the level of the context in which it is evaluated, $\sqcup \overrightarrow{\sigma_{\mathsf{pc}}}$.

Low-equality. In order to account for a non-deterministic memory allocator, we rely on a partial injective function which relates observable references that point to the same resource in different executions of the same program [6]. The β relation is extended to relate observable values via the β-*equality*, which is denoted $\sim_\beta$: two objects are β-equal if they have the same domain and all their corresponding properties are β-equal; primitive values and parsed functions are β-equal if syntactically equal; and, two references r_0 and r_1 are β-equal if the latter is the image by β of the former.

Two memories μ_0 and μ_1 are said to be *low-equal* with respect to labelings $\langle \Gamma_0, \Sigma_0 \rangle$ and $\langle \Gamma_1, \Sigma_1 \rangle$, a security level σ, and a partial injective function β, written $\mu_0, \Gamma_0, \Sigma_0 \approx_{\beta,\sigma} \mu_1, \Gamma_1, \Sigma_1$, if μ_0 and μ_1 are well-labeled by $\langle \Gamma_0, \Sigma_0 \rangle$ and $\langle \Gamma_1, \Sigma_1 \rangle$ respectively, and for all references $r_0, r_1 \in \mathsf{dom}(\beta)$, such that $r_1 = \beta(r_0)$, the following hold:

1. The observable domains (i.e. set of observable properties) of the objects pointed by r_0, r_1, coincide: $P_\sigma = \{p \in \mathsf{dom}(\mu_0(r_0)) \mid \Gamma_0(r_0)(p) \leq \sigma\} = \{p \in \mathsf{dom}(\mu_1(r_1)) \mid \Gamma_1(r_1)(p) \leq \sigma\}$;
2. The objects pointed by r_0, r_1 coincide in their observable domain: $\mu_0(r_0)|_P \sim_\beta \mu_1(r_1)|_P$;
3. If the structure security level of either object pointed by r_0, r_1 is observable ($\Sigma_0(r_0) \leq \sigma$ or $\Sigma_1(r_1) \leq \sigma$), then their domains and structure security levels coincide: $\mathsf{dom}(\mu_0(r_0)) = \mathsf{dom}(\mu_1(r_1))$ and $\Sigma_0(r_0) = \Sigma_1(r_1)$.

We extend informally the definition of low-equality to sequences of labeled values and to program continuations (the interested reader can find the formal definitions in [20]). Two sequences of labeled values are low-equal with respect to a given security level σ, denoted $\overrightarrow{v_0}, \overrightarrow{\sigma_0} \approx_{\beta,\sigma} \overrightarrow{v_1}, \overrightarrow{\sigma_1}$ if for each position of both sequences, either the two values in that position are low-equal, or the levels that are associated with both of them are not observable. Low-equality between program continuations $s_0, \overrightarrow{\sigma_{pc0}}, \overrightarrow{\sigma_0} \approx_{\beta,\sigma} s_1, \overrightarrow{\sigma_{pc1}}, \overrightarrow{\sigma_1}$ relaxes syntactic equality between programs in order to relate the intermediate states of the execution of the same original program in two low-equal memories, as illustrated by the following example.

Example 2 (Low-equal program continuations). Consider the program $x = y$, an initial labeling $\langle \Gamma, \Sigma \rangle$ such that $\Gamma(\#glob)(x) = \Gamma(\#glob)(y) = H$, and two memories μ_0 and μ_1 such that $\mu_i = [\#glob \mapsto [x \mapsto undefined, y \mapsto i]]$, for $i \in \{0, 1\}$. The execution of one computation step of this program in μ_0 and μ_1 yields the programs $x = 0$ and $x = 1$. Since the reading effects associated with the values 0 and 1 are both H, the expressions $x = 0$ and $x = 1$ are low-equal. Formally: $x = 0, \langle L \rangle, \langle H \rangle \approx_{\mathsf{id}, L} x = 1, \langle L \rangle, \langle H \rangle$ (where id is the identity function).

Finally, two monitor configurations $\langle \mu_i, s_i, \overrightarrow{\sigma_{pci}}, \Gamma_i, \Sigma_i, \overrightarrow{\sigma_i} \rangle$ with $i = 0, 1$ are said to be *low-equal* w.r.t a level σ and function β, written $\langle \mu_0, s_0, \overrightarrow{\sigma_{pc0}}, \Gamma_0, \Sigma_0, \overrightarrow{\sigma_0} \rangle \approx_{\beta,\sigma} \langle \mu_1, s_1, \overrightarrow{\sigma_{pc1}}, \Gamma_1, \Sigma_1, \overrightarrow{\sigma_1} \rangle$, if $\mu_0, \Gamma_0, \Sigma_0 \approx_{\beta,\sigma} \mu_1, \Gamma_1, \Sigma_1$ and $s_0, \overrightarrow{\sigma_{pc0}}, \overrightarrow{\sigma_0} \approx_{\beta,\sigma} s_1, \overrightarrow{\sigma_{pc1}}, \overrightarrow{\sigma_1}$.

Noninterferent Monitor. In the remaining of the paper, we consider only *noninterferent* JavaScript monitors. As usual, a monitor $\rightarrow_{\mathsf{IF}}$ is noninterferent, written $\mathbf{NI_{mon}}(\rightarrow_{\mathsf{IF}})$, if its application on two low-equal configurations produces two low-equal configurations.

Definition 1 (Monitor Noninterference). *A monitor $\rightarrow_{\mathsf{IF}}$ is said to be noninterferent, written $\mathbf{NI_{mon}}(\rightarrow_{\mathsf{IF}})$, if for every programs s_0, s_1, memories μ_0, μ_1,* and labeling $\langle \Gamma, \Sigma \rangle$, such that μ_0, μ_1 are well-labeled by $\langle \Gamma, \Sigma \rangle$ and, for all security levels σ, if there exists β such that $\langle \mu_0, s_0, \epsilon, \Gamma, \Sigma, \epsilon \rangle \approx_{\beta, \sigma} \langle \mu_1, s_1, \epsilon, \Gamma, \Sigma, \epsilon \rangle$ and $\langle \mu_i, s_i, \epsilon, \Gamma, \Sigma, \epsilon \rangle \rightarrow_{\mathsf{IF}}^* \langle \mu_i', v_i', \epsilon, \Gamma', \Sigma', \sigma' \rangle$ for $i = 0, 1$ then there is an extension β' of β such that $\langle \mu_0', v_0', \epsilon, \Gamma', \Sigma', \sigma' \rangle \approx_{\beta, \sigma} \langle \mu_1', v_1', \epsilon, \Gamma', \Sigma', \sigma' \rangle$.

3.2 API Extensions to JavaScript Monitors

API Relation. Even if the execution of certain APIs escapes the JavaScript semantics, the interaction between JavaScript programs and these APIs is mediated via special API objects that exist in the JavaScript memory. In the following, we assume that (1) the state of the API can be fully encoded in a JavaScript memory and (2) the behavior of each API method only depends on its state. An API is thus modeled as a semantic relation $\Downarrow_{\mathsf{API}}^{\mathsf{JS}}$ of the form $\langle \mu, \overrightarrow{v} \rangle \Downarrow_{\mathsf{API}}^{\mathsf{JS}} \langle \mu', v' \rangle$ where μ is the JavaScript memory in which the API is executed, μ' is the resulting memory, the sequence of values $\overrightarrow{v}$ corresponds to the arguments of the API invocation, and v' is the value to which the API invocation evaluates. Accordingly, a *monitored API relation*, $\Downarrow_{\mathsf{API}}$, has the form

$$\langle \mu, \Gamma, \Sigma, \overrightarrow{v}, \overrightarrow{\sigma} \rangle \ \Downarrow_{\mathsf{API}} \ \langle \mu', \Gamma', \Sigma', v, \sigma \rangle$$

which adds to the original API configuration the initial and final labelings $\langle \Gamma, \Sigma \rangle$ and $\langle \Gamma', \Sigma' \rangle$ (respectively), the sequence of security levels $\overrightarrow{\sigma}$ that is associated with the arguments of the API invocation, and their corresponding reading effect σ.

API Register. The bridge between API invocations and the corresponding monitored API semantics is performed by a *API register*, denoted by $\mathcal{R}_{\mathsf{API}}$. We define an API register as a function that, given a memory and a sequence of values, returns a monitored API relation.

Example 3 (Queue API Register). In order for an extended monitor to take into account the methods of the Queue API from Example 1, the API Register must be extended to handle invocations of the Queue API methods. In the following, $\Downarrow_{QU}$, $\Downarrow_{PU}$, and $\Downarrow_{PO}$ are the API relations corresponding to each one of the methods of the Queue API:

$$\mathcal{R}_Q(\mu, \langle r, m, \ldots \rangle) = \begin{cases} \Downarrow_{QU} & \text{if } m = \text{``queue''} \wedge \$q \in \mathsf{dom}(\mu(r)) \\ \Downarrow_{PU} & \text{if } m = \text{``push''} \wedge \$q \in \mathsf{dom}(\mu(r)) \\ \Downarrow_{PO} & \text{if } m = \text{``pop''} \wedge \$q \in \mathsf{dom}(\mu(r)) \end{cases}$$

The idea is to "mark" the Queue API object (the one bound to variable *queueAPI*) as well as the concrete queue objects, with a special property (in this case, $\$q$).

Monitor-Extending Constructor. We now define a monitor-extending constructor $\mathcal{E}$ that, given a monitored small-step semantics $\rightarrow_{\mathsf{IF}}$, a partial function Intercept mapping statements to sequences of values, and an API register $\mathcal{R}_{\mathsf{API}}$, produces a new monitored small-step semantics $\mathcal{E}(\rightarrow_{\mathsf{IF}}, \mathsf{Intercept}, \mathcal{R}_{\mathsf{API}})$. The new

NON-INTERCEPTED PROGRAM CONSTRUCT

$$\frac{s \notin \mathsf{Intercept} \qquad \langle \mu, s, \overrightarrow{\sigma_{\mathsf{pc}}}, \Gamma, \Sigma, \overrightarrow{\sigma} \rangle \to_{\mathsf{IF}} \langle \mu', s', \overrightarrow{\sigma_{\mathsf{pc}}}', \Gamma', \Sigma', \overrightarrow{\sigma}' \rangle}{\langle \mu, s, \overrightarrow{\sigma_{\mathsf{pc}}}, \Gamma, \Sigma, \overrightarrow{\sigma} \rangle \; \mathcal{E}(\to_{\mathsf{IF}}, \mathsf{Intercept}, \mathcal{R}_{\mathsf{API}}) \; \langle \mu', s', \overrightarrow{\sigma_{\mathsf{pc}}}', \Gamma', \Sigma', \overrightarrow{\sigma}' \rangle}$$

INTERCEPTED PROGRAM CONSTRUCT - STANDARD EXECUTION

$$\frac{s \in \mathsf{Intercept} \qquad (\mu, \mathsf{SubExpressions}[[s]]) \notin \mathrm{dom}(\mathcal{R}_{\mathsf{API}})}{\langle \mu, s, \overrightarrow{\sigma_{\mathsf{pc}}}, \Gamma, \Sigma, \overrightarrow{\sigma} \rangle \to_{\mathsf{IF}} \langle \mu', s', \overrightarrow{\sigma_{\mathsf{pc}}}', \Gamma', \Sigma', \overrightarrow{\sigma_{\mathsf{pc}}}' \rangle}{\langle \mu, s, \overrightarrow{\sigma_{\mathsf{pc}}}, \Gamma, \Sigma, \overrightarrow{\sigma} \rangle \; \mathcal{E}(\to_{\mathsf{IF}}, \mathsf{Intercept}, \mathcal{R}_{\mathsf{API}}) \; \langle \mu', s', \overrightarrow{\sigma_{\mathsf{pc}}}', \Gamma', \Sigma', \overrightarrow{\sigma}' \rangle}$$

INTERCEPTED PROGRAM CONSTRUCT - API EXECUTION

$$\frac{\begin{array}{c} s \in \mathsf{Intercept} \qquad (\mu, \mathsf{SubExpressions}[[s]]) \in \mathrm{dom}(\mathcal{R}_{\mathsf{API}}) \qquad |\mathsf{SubExpressions}[[s]]| = n + 1 \\ \overrightarrow{\sigma} = \overrightarrow{\sigma}' \cdot \langle \sigma_0, \ldots, \sigma_n \rangle \qquad \Downarrow_{\mathsf{API}} = \mathcal{R}_{\mathsf{API}}(\mu, \mathsf{SubExpressions}[[s]]) \\ \langle \mu, \Gamma, \Sigma, \mathsf{SubExpressions}[[s]], \langle \sigma_0, \ldots, \sigma_n \rangle \rangle \Downarrow_{\mathsf{API}} \langle \mu', \Gamma', \Sigma', v', \sigma' \rangle \end{array}}{\langle \mu, s, \overrightarrow{\sigma_{\mathsf{pc}}}, \Gamma, \Sigma, \overrightarrow{\sigma} \rangle \; \mathcal{E}(\to_{\mathsf{IF}}, \mathsf{Intercept}, \mathcal{R}_{\mathsf{API}}) \; \langle \mu', v', \overrightarrow{\sigma_{\mathsf{pc}}}', \Gamma', \Sigma', \overrightarrow{\sigma}' \cdot \sigma' \rangle}$$

Fig. 1. Definition of the monitor-extending constructor $\mathcal{E}$.

extended semantics handles the invocation of APIs by applying the API relation that is returned by $\mathcal{R}_{\mathsf{API}}$. API invocation is triggered by *interception points*, statements containing expression redexes (expressions that only have values as subexpressions) and that are in the set Intercept. Then, if the sequence of values to which its subexpressions evaluate is in the domain of the API register $\mathcal{R}_{\mathsf{API}}$, their image by $\mathcal{R}_{\mathsf{API}}$ is the semantic relation that models the API to be executed.

The definition of $\mathcal{E}$, given in Fig. 1, makes use of a syntactic function, SubExpressions, defined on JavaScript statements, such that SubExpressions$[[s]]$ corresponds to the sequence comprising all the subexpressions of s in the order by which they are evaluated. Rules [NON-INTERCEPTED PROGRAM CONSTRUCT] and [INTERCEPTED PROGRAM CONSTRUCT - STANDARD EXECUTION] model the case in which the new small-step semantics behaves according to the original semantics $\to_{\mathsf{IF}}$. Rule [INTERCEPTED PROGRAM CONSTRUCT - API EXECUTION] models the case in which an API is executed. The semantics rule retrieves the semantics relation that models the API to execute (using the API register) and then executes the API. After executing the API, the sequence of values of its subexpressions is replaced with the value to which the API call evaluates. Analogously, the sequence of levels of its subexpressions is replaced with the reading effect of the API call.

3.3 Sufficient Conditions for Noninterferent API Extensions

We identify sufficient conditions to be satisfied by API relations in order for the new extended monitored semantics $\mathcal{E}(\to_{\mathsf{IF}}, \mathsf{Intercept}, \mathcal{R}_{\mathsf{API}})$ to be noninterferent, assuming that the original monitor $\to_{\mathsf{IF}}$ is noninterferent.

The first condition requires that the API relation is *confined*, as formalized in Definition 2. An API relation is *confined* if it only creates/updates resources whose levels are higher than or equal to the least upper bound on the levels of its arguments. This constraint is needed because the choice of which API to execute may depend on all of its arguments.

Definition 2 (Confined API Relation/Register). *An API relation* $\Downarrow_{\mathsf{API}}$ *is confined if, for every memory* μ *well-labeled by a labeling* $\langle \Gamma, \Sigma \rangle$*, every sequence of argument values* $\overrightarrow{v}$ *and corresponding sequence of security levels* $\overrightarrow{\sigma}$*, if* $\langle \mu, \langle \Gamma, \Sigma \rangle, \overrightarrow{v}, \overrightarrow{\sigma} \rangle \Downarrow_{\mathsf{API}} \langle \mu', \langle \Gamma', \Sigma' \rangle, v', \sigma' \rangle$ *for some memory* μ'*, labeling* $\langle \Gamma', \Sigma' \rangle$*, value* v'*, and level* σ'*; then, for all security levels* $\hat{\sigma}$*:*

$$\sqcup \overrightarrow{\sigma} \not\preceq \hat{\sigma} \quad \Rightarrow \quad \mu, \Gamma, \Sigma \approx_{\mathsf{id}, \hat{\sigma}} \mu', \Gamma', \Sigma' \; \wedge \; \sigma' \not\preceq \hat{\sigma}$$

Furthermore, we say that the API Register function $\mathcal{R}_{\mathsf{API}}$ *is confined, written* **Conf**$(\mathcal{R}_{\mathsf{API}})$*, if all the API relations in its range are confined, and if for every memories* μ *and* μ'*, labelings* $\langle \Gamma, \Sigma \rangle$ *and* $\langle \Gamma', \Sigma' \rangle$*, sequence of values* $\overrightarrow{v}$*, security level* σ*, and function* β*, such that* $\mu, \Gamma, \Sigma \approx_{\beta, \sigma} \mu', \Gamma', \Sigma'$*, then* $\mathcal{R}_{\mathsf{API}}(\mu, \overrightarrow{v}) = \mathcal{R}_{\mathsf{API}}(\mu', \beta(\overrightarrow{v}))$*.*

The second condition requires that the API relation is *noninterferent*, as formalized in Definition 3. In order to relate the outputs of the API Register in two low-equal memories, we extend the notion of low-equality to API registers. Informally, two API registers are said to be low-equal if, whenever they are given as input two low-equal memories and two low-equal sequences of values, they output the same noninterferent API relation. Then, an API relation is *noninterferent* if whenever it is executed on two low-equal memories, it produces two low-equal memories and two low-equal values.

Definition 3 (Noninterferent API Relation/Register). *An API relation* $\Downarrow_{\mathsf{API}}$ *is said to be noninterferent, written* **NI**$(\Downarrow_{\mathsf{API}})$*, if for every two memories* μ_0 *and* μ_1 *respectively well-labeled by* $\langle \Gamma_0, \Sigma_0 \rangle$ *and* $\langle \Gamma_1, \Sigma_1 \rangle$*, any two sequences of values* $\overrightarrow{v_0}$ *and* $\overrightarrow{v_1}$*, respectively labeled by two sequences of security levels* $\overrightarrow{\sigma_0}$ *and* $\overrightarrow{\sigma_1}$*, and any security level* σ *for which there exists a function* β *such that* $\overrightarrow{v_0}, \overrightarrow{\sigma_0} \approx_{\beta, \sigma} \overrightarrow{v_1}, \overrightarrow{\sigma_1}$ *and* $\mu_0, \Gamma_0, \Sigma_0 \approx_{\beta, \sigma} \mu_1, \Gamma_1, \Sigma_1$*, if:*

$$\langle \mu_0, \Gamma_0, \Sigma_0, \overrightarrow{v_0}, \overrightarrow{\sigma_0} \rangle \Downarrow_{\mathsf{API}} \langle \mu'_0, \Gamma'_0, \Sigma'_0, v'_0, \sigma'_0 \rangle \; \wedge \; \langle \mu_1, \Gamma_1, \Sigma_1, \overrightarrow{v_1}, \overrightarrow{\sigma_1} \rangle \Downarrow_{\mathsf{API}} \langle \mu'_1, \Gamma'_1, \Sigma'_1, v'_1, \sigma'_1 \rangle$$

then: $\mu'_0, \Gamma'_0, \Sigma'_0 \approx_{\beta', \sigma} \mu'_1, \Gamma'_1, \Sigma'_1$ *and* $\langle v'_0 \rangle, \langle \sigma'_0 \rangle \approx_{\beta', \sigma} \langle v'_1 \rangle, \langle \sigma'_1 \rangle$ *for some* β' *that extends* β*. Furthermore, we say that the API Register function* $\mathcal{R}_{\mathsf{API}}$ *is noninterferent, written* **NI**$(\mathcal{R}_{\mathsf{API}})$*, if all the API relations in its range are noninterferent.*

Example 4 (Noninterferent JavaScript program using the Queue API). Assume that the APIs given in Example 1 are noninterferent and consider the following program that starts by computing two objects o0 and o1:

```
1  q = queueAPI.createQueue();
2  if (h) { q.push(o1, 1); }
3  q.push(o0, 0); l = q.pop();
```

If this program starts with memories μ_i $(i \in \{0, 1\})$ using labeling $\langle \Gamma, \Sigma \rangle$ and assuming that in both executions the invocations of all the external APIs go through (i.e. the execution is never blocked), then it must terminate with memories μ'_i labeled by Γ', Σ:

$$\mu_i = \begin{bmatrix} (\#glob,o0)\mapsto r_0,(\#glob,o1)\mapsto r_1, \\ (\#glob,h)\mapsto i \end{bmatrix}$$

$$\mu'_i = \begin{bmatrix} (\#glob,o0)\mapsto r_0,(\#glob,o1)\mapsto r_1, \\ (\#glob,h)\mapsto i,(\#glob,l)\mapsto r_i,(\#glob,q)\mapsto r_q \end{bmatrix}$$

$$\Gamma = \begin{bmatrix} (\#glob,h)\mapsto H,(\#glob,l)\mapsto L, \\ (\#glob,o0)\mapsto L,(\#glob,o1)\mapsto L \end{bmatrix}$$

$$\Gamma' = \begin{bmatrix} (\#glob,h)\mapsto H,(\#glob,l)\mapsto H, \\ (\#glob,o0)\mapsto L,(\#glob,o1)\mapsto L \end{bmatrix}$$

Since initial memories are low-equal, $\mu_0,\Gamma,\Sigma \approx_{\mathrm{id},L} \mu_1,\Gamma,\Sigma$, we use the hypothesis that all three API relations are noninterferent to conclude that the memories yielded by the invocation of the API relations in lines 1, 2 and 3 are also low-equal. Furthermore, in the execution that maps h to 1, the value of 1 clearly depends on the value of h, from which we conclude that it is also the case in the execution that maps h to 0.

Our main result states that if the API relation is confined and noninterferent, then the extension of the noninterferent JavaScript monitor with the API monitor is noninterferent.

Theorem 1 (Security). *For every monitored semantics $\to_{\mathsf{IF}}$, API register $\mathcal{R}_{\mathsf{API}}$ and set of interception points* Intercept:

$$\mathbf{NI_{mon}}(\to_{\mathsf{IF}}) \wedge \mathbf{NI}(\mathcal{R}_{\mathsf{API}}) \wedge \mathbf{Conf}(\mathcal{R}_{\mathsf{API}}) \;\Rightarrow\; \mathbf{NI_{mon}}(\mathcal{E}(\to_{\mathsf{IF}}, \mathsf{Intercept}, \mathcal{R}_{\mathsf{API}}))$$

4 A Meta-Compiler for Securing Web APIs

We now propose a way of extending an information flow monitor inlining compiler to take into account the execution of arbitrary APIs.

Input compilers. We assume available two inlining compilers specified by compilation functions $\mathcal{C}_e$ and $\mathcal{C}_s$ for compiling JavaScript expressions and statements, respectively. Function $\mathcal{C}_s$ makes use of function $\mathcal{C}_e$. The compilers $\mathcal{C}_e/\mathcal{C}_s$ map every expression e/statement s to a pair $\langle s', i\rangle$, where:

1. statement s' simulates the execution of e/s in the monitored semantics;
2. index i is such that, after the execution of s', (1) the compiler variable $\$\hat{v}_i$ stores the value to which e/s evaluates in the original semantics and (2) the compiler variable $\$\hat{l}_i$ stores its corresponding reading effect.

We assume that the inlining compiler works by pairing up each variable/property with a new one, called its *shadow* variable/property [8,16], that holds its corresponding security level. Since the compiled program has to handle security levels, we include them in the set of program values, which means adding them to the syntax of the language as such, as well as adding two new binary operators corresponding to $\leq$ (the order relation) and $\sqcup$ (the least upper bound). Besides adding to every object o an additional shadow property $\$l_p$ for every property p in its domain, the inlined monitoring code is also assumed to extend o with a special property $\$struct$ that stores its structure security level.

Example 5 (Instrumented Labeling). Given an object $o = [p \mapsto v_0, q \mapsto v_1]$ pointed to by r_o and a labeling $\langle \Gamma, \Sigma\rangle$, such that $\Gamma(r_o) = [p \mapsto H, q \mapsto L]$ and $\Sigma(r_o) = L$, the instrumented counterpart of o labeled by $\langle \Gamma, \Sigma\rangle$ is $\hat{o} = [p \mapsto v_0, q \mapsto v_1, \$l_p \mapsto H, \$l_q \mapsto L, \$struct \mapsto L]$.

$$\mathsf{SubExpressions}[[e]] = \langle e_0, \ldots, e_n \rangle \qquad \mathcal{C}_{\mathsf{API}}\langle \mathcal{C}_{\mathsf{e}} \rangle \langle e_0 \rangle = \langle s_0, i_0 \rangle \ \cdots \ \mathcal{C}_{\mathsf{API}}\langle \mathcal{C}_{\mathsf{e}} \rangle \langle e_n \rangle = \langle s_n, i_n \rangle$$

$$\hat{e} = \mathsf{Replace}[[e, \$\hat{v}_{i_0}, \ldots, \$\hat{v}_{i_n}]] \qquad \mathcal{C}_{\mathsf{e}}\langle \hat{e} \rangle = \langle \hat{s}, i \rangle$$

$$
s_{\mathsf{api}} =
\begin{cases}
s_0 \ \ldots \ s_n \\
\$ \mathit{if}_{\mathsf{sig}} = \$apiRegister(\$\hat{v}_{i_0}, \ldots, \$\hat{v}_{i_n}); \\
\mathsf{if}(\$\mathit{if}_{\mathsf{sig}})\{ \\
\quad \$\mathit{if}_{\mathsf{sig}}.check(\$\hat{v}_{i_0}, \ldots, \$\hat{v}_{i_n}, \$\hat{l}_{i_0}, \ldots, \$\hat{l}_{i_n}); \\
\quad \$\hat{v}_i = \hat{e}; \\
\quad \$\hat{l}_i = \$\mathit{if}_{\mathsf{sig}}.label(\$\hat{v}_i, \$\hat{v}_{i_0}, \ldots, \$\hat{v}_{i_n}, \$\hat{l}_{i_0}, \ldots, \$\hat{l}_{i_n}); \\
\} \ \mathsf{else} \ \{\hat{s}\}
\end{cases}
\qquad
s' = \begin{cases} s_{\mathsf{api}} & \text{if } \hat{e} \in \mathsf{Intercept} \\ \hat{s} & \text{otherwise} \end{cases}
$$

$$\mathcal{C}_{\mathsf{API}}\langle \mathcal{C}_{\mathsf{e}} \rangle \langle e \rangle = \langle s', i \rangle$$

Fig. 2. Extended compiler $\mathcal{C}_{\mathsf{API}}$.

4.1 IFlow Signatures

We propose *IFlow signatures* to simulate monitored executions of API relations. IFlow signatures are composed of three methods – *domain*, *check*, and *label*. Method *domain* checks whether or not to apply the API, *check* checks if the constraints associated with the API are verified, and *label* updates the instrumented labeling and outputs the reading effect associated with a call to the API. Functions *check* and *label* must be specified separately because *check* has to be executed before calling the API (in order to prevent its execution when it can potentially trigger a security violation), whereas *label* must be executed after calling the API (so that it can label the memory resulting from its execution). Formally, we define an *IFlow Signature* as a triple $\langle \#check, \#label, \#domain \rangle$, where: $\#check$ is the reference of the *check* function object, $\#label$ is the reference of the *label* function object, and $\#domain$ is the reference of the *domain* function object.

Runtime API Register. We assume the existence of a runtime function called the *runtime API register*, that simulates the API Register, which we denote by $\$apiRegister$. The function $\$apiRegister$ makes use of the *domain* method of each API in its range to decide whether there is an API relation associated with its inputs, in which case it outputs an object containing the corresponding IFlow Signature, otherwise it returns *null*.

Meta-compiler. Figure 2 presents a new meta-compiler, $\mathcal{C}_{\mathsf{API}}$, that receives as input an inlining compiler for JavaScript expressions, $\mathcal{C}_{\mathsf{e}}$, and outputs a new inlining compiler that can handle the invocation of the APIs whose signatures are in the range of the API register simulated by $\$apiRegister$. Since statement redexes are not intercepted, the compilation function $\mathcal{C}_{\mathsf{s}}$ is left unchanged except that it uses the new compilation function for expressions for compiling the subexpressions of the given statement. The specification of the meta-compiler makes use of a syntactic function $\mathsf{Replace}$ that receives as input an expression and a sequence of variables and outputs the result of substituting each one of its subexpressions by the corresponding sequence variable. $\mathsf{Intercept}$ is the set of all statements that contain an expression redex whose execution is to be intercepted by the monitored semantics. Each expression that can be an interception point

$$\mathcal{R}_{\mathsf{API}}^{\mathsf{DOM}}(\mu, \langle r, m, \ldots \rangle) = \begin{cases} \Downarrow_{\mathsf{cre}} & \text{if } m = \text{``createElement''} \wedge r = \#doc \\ \Downarrow_{\mathsf{app}} & \text{if } m = \text{``appendChild''} \wedge @tag \in \mathsf{dom}(\mu(r)) \\ \Downarrow_{\mathsf{rem}} & \text{if } m = \text{``removeChild''} \wedge @tag \in \mathsf{dom}(\mu(r)) \\ \Downarrow_{\mathsf{len}} & \text{if } m = \text{``length''} \wedge @tag \in \mathsf{dom}(\mu(r)) \\ \Downarrow_{\mathsf{par}} & \text{if } m = \text{``parentNode''} \wedge @tag \in \mathsf{dom}(\mu(r)) \\ \Downarrow_{\mathsf{ind}} & \text{if } m \in \mathsf{Number} \wedge @\mathsf{tag} \in \mathsf{dom}(\mu(\mathsf{r})) \\ \Downarrow_{\mathsf{sib}} & \text{if } m = \text{``nextSibling''} \wedge @tag \in \mathsf{dom}(\mu(r)) \end{cases}$$

Fig. 3. API register $\mathcal{R}_{\mathsf{API}}^{\mathsf{DOM}}$ for the DOM API.

of the semantics is compiled by the compiler generated by the meta-compiler to a statement, which: (1) executes the statements corresponding to the compilation of its subexpressions, (2) tests if the sequence of values corresponding to the subexpressions of the expression to compile is associated with an IFlow signature, (3) if the test is true, it executes the *check* method of the corresponding IFlow signature, an expression equivalent to the original expression, and the *label* method of the corresponding IFlow signature. If the test is false, it executes the compilation of an expression equivalent to the original one by the original inlining compiler. For simplicity, we do not take into account expressions that manipulate control flow, meaning that the evaluation of a given expression implies the evaluation of all its subexpressions. Therefore, we do not consider the JavaScript conditional expression. This limitation can be surpassed by re-writing all conditional expressions as IF statements before applying the compiler.

Note that the meta-compiler proposed in this section allows the developer of the inlining compiler to extend it in a modular way, developing and proving each API IFlow signature at a time.

5   Implementation and DOM API Extension

An implementation of a meta-compiler based on the JavaScript inlining compiler of [10] can be found in [20] together with an online testing tool and a set of IFlow signatures that includes all those studied in the paper. As a case study, we give a high-level description of our the DOM API extension.

Interaction between client-side JavaScript programs and the HTML document is done *via* the DOM API [17]. In order to access the functionalities of this API, JavaScript programs manipulate a special kind of objects, here named *DOM objects*. In contrast to the ECMA Standard [1] that specifies in full detail the internals of objects created at runtime, the DOM API only specifies the behavior that DOM interfaces are supposed to exhibit when a program interacts with them. Hence, browser vendors are free to implement the DOM API as they see fit. In fact, in all major browsers, the DOM is not managed by the JavaScript engine. Instead, there is a separate engine, often called the *render engine*, whose role is to do so. Therefore, interactions between a JavaScript program and the DOM may potentially stop the execution of the JavaScript engine and trigger a call to the render engine. Thus, a monitored JavaScript engine has no access to the implementation of the DOM API.

We model DOM objects as standard JavaScript objects and we assume that every memory contains a *document* object denoted *doc*, which is accessed through the property "doc" and stored in fixed reference #*doc*. Each DOM object defines a property @*tag* that specifies its tag (for instance, $\langle div \rangle$, $\langle html \rangle$, $\langle a \rangle$) and, possibly, an arbitrary number of indexes $0, ..., n$ each pointing to one of its $n+1$ children. DOM Element objects form a *forest*, such that the displayed HTML document corresponds to the tree hanging from the object pointed to by #*doc*. Due to lack of space, we only present the labeled API relation for removing a DOM Element object from its parent object in the DOM forest. This API method gives rise to implicit information flows [2,18,23] that its labeled version needs to take into account.

Example 6 (Leak via removeChild - Order Leak). Suppose that in the original memory there are three orphan DIV nodes bound to variables div1, div2, and div3.

```
1  div1.appendChild(div2); div1.appendChild(div3);
2  if(h) { div1.removeChild(div2); }
3  l = div1[0];
```

After the execution of this program, depending on the value of the high variable h, the value of the low variable l can be either that of div2 or div3, meaning that the final level associated with variable l must be H in both executions. This example shows that, when removing a node, the new indexes of its right siblings are affected. To tackle this problem, the labelled DOM API methods enforce that the level of the property through which a DOM object is accessed is always lower than or equal to the levels of the properties corresponding to its right siblings.

Below we give the specification of the labeled API relation $\Downarrow_{\sf rem}$ for removing a DOM object from its parent in the DOM forest. This rule receives a sequence of arguments $\langle r_0, m_1, r_2 \rangle$ as input and removes the object pointed to by r_2 from the children of the object pointed to by r_1. To this end, it first checks that $\mu(r_0)$ is in fact the parent of $\mu(r_2)$. Then, the object $\mu(r_0)$ is updated by shifting by -1 all the indexes equal to or higher than i (the index of the object being removed) and by removing its index n. The levels of the indexes of the right siblings of the node to remove are accordingly shifted by -1. The constraint of the rule prevents a program from removing in a high context a node that was inserted in a low context. Function $\mathcal{R}_{\sf \#Children}$ receives a memory μ as input and outputs a binary relation such that if $\langle r, n \rangle \in \mathcal{R}_{\sf \#Children}(\mu)$, then the DOM node pointed to by r has n children (with indexes $0, \ldots, n-1$).

$domain = $ function$(o_0, m)\{$return $o_0[@tag]$ && $(m == $ "removeChild"$);\}$

$check = $ function$(o_0, m_1, o_2, \sigma_0, \sigma_1, \sigma_2)\{$
    var $i = \$index(o_0, o_2);$
    return $\boxed{\$check(\sigma_0 \sqcup \sigma_1 \sqcup \sigma_2 \leq o_0[\$shadow(i)]);}^{\dagger}$
$\}$

$label = $ function$(ret, o_0, m_1, o_2, \sigma_0, \sigma_1, \sigma_2)\{$
    var $j = \$index(o_0, o_2);$
    while$(j < o_0.length - 1)\{$
        $\boxed{o_0[\$shadow(j)] = o_0[\$shadow(j+1)];}^{\dagger\dagger}$
    $\}$
    return $\boxed{\sigma_0 \sqcup \sigma_1 \sqcup \sigma_2}^{\dagger\dagger\dagger};$
$\}$

Fig. 4. IFlow signature of $\Downarrow_{\mathsf{rem}}$

REMOVECHILD

$$\frac{\begin{array}{c} \mu(r_0)(i) = r_2 \quad \langle r_0, n+1 \rangle \in \mathcal{R}_{\#\mathsf{Children}}(\mu) \quad \mathsf{dom}(o_0) = \mathsf{dom}(\gamma_0) = \mathsf{dom}(\mu(r_0))\backslash\{n\} \\ \forall_{0 \leq j < i} \cdot o_0(j) = \mu(r_0)(j) \quad \forall_{i \leq j < n} \cdot o_0(j) = \mu(r_0)(j+1) \quad o_0(@tag) = \mu(r_0)(@tag) \\ \forall_{0 \leq j < i} \cdot \gamma_0(j) = \Gamma(r_0)(j) \; \forall_{i \leq j < n} \cdot \boxed{\gamma_0(j) = \Gamma(r_0)(j+1)}^{\dagger\dagger} \quad \gamma_0(@tag) = \Gamma(r_0)(@tag) \\ \mu' = \mu[r_0 \mapsto o_0] \quad \Gamma' = \Gamma[r_0 \mapsto \gamma_0] \quad \boxed{\sigma_0 \sqcup \sigma_1 \sqcup \sigma_2 \leq \Gamma(r_0)(i)}^{\dagger} \end{array}}{\langle \mu, \Gamma, \Sigma, \langle r_0, m_1, r_2 \rangle, \langle o_0, \sigma_1, \sigma_2 \rangle \rangle \Downarrow_{\mathsf{rem}} \langle \mu', \Gamma', \Sigma, r_2, \boxed{\sigma_0 \sqcup \sigma_1 \sqcup \sigma_2}^{\dagger\dagger\dagger} \rangle}$$

In order for DOM API relations to be added to the semantics, one has to add them to the API register. Hence, we assume that the $\mathcal{R}_{\mathsf{API}}$ extends the API register given in Fig. 3. The following lemma validates the hypotheses of the security theorem (Theorem 1) for $\mathcal{R}_{\mathsf{API}}^{\mathsf{DOM}}$, allowing us to conclude that the extension of a noninterferent JavaScript monitor with the DOM API relations here defined is noninterferent.

Lemma 1 (Conf. and NI for the DOM API). $\mathbf{Conf}(\mathcal{R}_{\mathsf{API}}^{\mathsf{DOM}}) \wedge \mathbf{NI}(\mathcal{R}_{\mathsf{API}}^{\mathsf{DOM}})$

Figure 4 presents a possible IFlow signature for the API relation $\Downarrow_{\mathsf{rem}}$, which makes use of the following runtime functions: (1) $\$check$ diverges if its argument is different from *true* and returns *true* otherwise; (2) $\$shadow$ receives as input a property name and outputs the name of the corresponding shadow property; and (3) $\$index$ outputs the index of its second argument in the list of children of its first argument. The labeled boxes in the API relation rule and in the code of the IFlow signature are intended to emphasize the correspondence between the two.

6   Conclusion

In summary, we have proposed a methodology for extending arbitrary monitored JavaScript semantics with secure APIs, which allows to prove the security of the extended monitor in a modular way. As a case study, we extend the inlining compiler of [10] with a fragment of the DOM Core Level 1 API. Further related technical developments, as well as an implementation that includes the IFlow signatures of the APIs studied in the paper, can be found in [20].

Acknowledgments. Fragoso Santos acknowledges funding from the EPSRC grant reference EP/K032089/1. No new data was collected in the course of this research.

References

1. The 5.1th edition of ECMA 262, ECMAScript Language Specification. Technical report, ECMA 2011, June 2011
2. Almeida-Matos, A., Fragoso Santos, J., Rezk, T.: An information flow monitor for a core of DOM. In: Maffei, M., Tuosto, E. (eds.) TGC 2014. LNCS, vol. 8902, pp. 1–16. Springer, Heidelberg (2014)
3. Austin, T.H., Flanagan, C.: Efficient purely-dynamic information flow analysis. In: PLAS (2009)
4. Austin, T.H., Flanagan, C.: Permissive dynamic information flow analysis. In: PLAS (2010)
5. Austin, T.H., Flanagan, C.: Multiple facets for dynamic information flow. In: POPL (2012)
6. Banerjee, A., Naumann, D.A.: Secure information flow and pointer confinement in a java-like language. In: CSFW (2002)
7. Bielova, N.: Survey on javascript security policies and their enforcement mechanisms in a web browser. Special Issue on Automated Specification and Verification of Web Systems of JLAP (2013)
8. Chudnov, A., Naumann, D.A.: Information flow monitor inlining. In: CSF (2010)
9. Denning, D.E.: A lattice model of secure information flow. Commun. ACM **19**(5), 236–243 (1976)
10. Santos, J.F., Rezk, T.: An information flow monitor-inlining compiler for securing a core of javascript. In: Cuppens-Boulahia, N., Cuppens, F., Jajodia, S., Abou El Kalam, A., Sans, T. (eds.) SEC 2014. IFIP AICT, vol. 428, pp. 278–292. Springer, Heidelberg (2014)
11. Gardner, P., Smith, G., Wheelhouse, M.J., Zarfaty, U.: Dom: Towards a formal specification. In: PLAN-X (2008)
12. Le Guernic, G.: Confidentiality Enforcement Using Dynamic Information Flow Analyses. Ph.D. thesis, Kansas State University (2007)
13. Guha, A., Lerner, B., Gibbs Politz, J., Krishnamurthi, S.: Web API verification: Results and challenges. In: Analysis of Security APIs (2012)
14. Hedin, D., Birgisson, A., Bello, L., Sabelfeld, A.: JSFlow: Tracking information flow in JavaScript and its APIs. In: SAC (2014)
15. Hedin, D., Sabelfeld, A.: Information-flow security for a core of javascript. In: CSF (2012)

16. Magazinius, J., Russo, A., Sabelfeld, A.: On-the-fly inlining of dynamic security monitors. Comput. Secur. **31**, 827–843 (2012)
17. W3C Recommendation. DOM: Document Object Model (DOM). Technical report, W3C (2005)
18. Russo, A., Sabelfeld, A., Chudnov, A.: Tracking information flow in dynamic tree structures. In: Backes, M., Ning, P. (eds.) ESORICS 2009. LNCS, vol. 5789, pp. 86–103. Springer, Heidelberg (2009)
19. Sabelfeld, A., Myers, A.C.: Language-based information-flow security. J. Sel. Areas Commun. **21**, 5–19 (2003)
20. Santos, J.F., Rezk, T.: Information flow monitor-inlining compiler. http://www-sop.inria.fr/indes/ifJS/
21. Taly, A., Erlingsson, U., Mitchell, J.C., Miller, M.S., Nagra, J.: Automated analysis of security-critical javascript apis. In: SP (2011)
22. Venkatakrishnan, V.N., Xu, W., DuVarney, D.C., Sekar, R.: Provably correct run-time enforcement of non-interference properties. In: Ning, P., Qing, S., Li, N. (eds.) ICICS 2006. LNCS, vol. 4307, pp. 332–351. Springer, Heidelberg (2006)
23. Garg, D., Rajani, V., Bichhawat, A., Hammer, C.: Information Flow control for Event Handling and the DOM in Web Browsers. In: CSF (2015). to appear

Hybrid Typing of Secure Information Flow in a JavaScript-Like Language

José Fragoso Santos[1]([⊠]), Thomas Jensen[2], Tamara Rezk[2],
and Alan Schmitt[2]

[1] Imperial College London, London, UK
jose.fragoso.santos@imperial.ac.uk
[2] Inria, Sophia Antipolis, France
{thomas.jensen,tamara.rezk,alan.schmitt}@inria.fr

Abstract. As JavaScript is highly dynamic by nature, static information flow analyses are often too coarse to deal with the dynamic constructs of the language. To cope with this challenge, we present and prove the soundness of a new hybrid typing analysis for securing information flow in a JavaScript-like language. Our analysis combines static and dynamic typing in order to avoid rejecting programs due to imprecise typing information. Program regions that cannot be precisely typed at static time are wrapped inside an internal *boundary* statement used by the semantics to interleave the execution of statically verified code with the execution of code that must be dynamically checked.

1 Introduction

The dynamic aspects of JavaScript make the analysis of JavaScript programs very challenging. On one hand, one may use a purely static analysis, but either restrict the language to exclude these dynamic aspects or over-approximate them; this is too coarse to be applicable in practice. On the other hand, one may use purely dynamic mechanisms, such as monitoring or secure multi-executions [1,6,8,16]; but the gained precision comes at the cost of a much lower performance compared to the original code [7].

We propose a general hybrid analysis to statically verify secure information flow in a core of JavaScript. Following the hybrid typing motto "static analysis where possible with dynamic checks where necessary"[5], we are able to reduce the runtime overhead introduced by purely dynamic analyses without excluding dynamic field operations. In fact, our analysis can handle some of the most challenging JavaScript features, such as prototype-based inheritance, extensible objects, and constructs for checking the existence of object properties. Its key ingredient is an internal boundary statement inspired by recent work in inter-language interoperability [10]. The static component of our analysis wraps program regions that cannot be precisely verified inside an internal *boundary* statement instead of rejecting the whole program. This boundary statement identifies the regions of the program that must be verified at runtime—which may be as small as a single statement—and enables the initial set up required

© Springer International Publishing Switzerland 2016
P. Ganty and M. Loreti (Eds.): TGC 2015, LNCS 9533, pp. 63–78, 2016.
DOI: 10.1007/978-3-319-28766-9_5

by the dynamic analysis. In summary, the proposed boundary statement allows the semantics to effortlessly interleave the execution of statically verified code with the execution of code that must be verified at runtime.

Although our work is generally motivated by the verification of dynamic features of JavaScript, we choose to focus on the particular case of constructs that rely on dynamic computation of object field names, which we call *dynamic field operations*. In JavaScript, one can access a field f of an object o either by writing o.f or o[e], where e is an expression that dynamically evaluates to the string f. Dynamic computation of field names is one of the major sources of imprecision of static analyses for JavaScript [9].

Example 1 (Running example: the challenge of typing dynamic field operations). Below we present a program that creates an object o with a secret field secret1 and two public fields public1 and public2.

```
o = {}; o.secret1 = secret_input();
o.public1 = public_input(); o.public2 = public_input(); public = o[g()]
```

The secret field secret1 gets a secret input via function secret_input, while the two public fields public1 and public2 each get a public input via function public_input. The program then assigns the value of one of the three fields to the public variable public, as determined by the return value of function g. Concretely, when g returns the string "secret1", the program assigns a secret value to public and the execution is insecure. On the other hand, when g returns either "public1" or "public2", the program assigns a public value to public and the execution is secure. However, in order to make sure that g never returns "secret1", a static analysis needs to predict the dynamic behaviour of g, which is, in general, undecidable.

The loss of precision introduced by the dynamic computation of field names is not exclusive to field projections. It also occurs in method calls, field deletions, and membership checks. We account for the use of these operations by verifying them at runtime. When verifying a statement containing a dynamic field operation, the static component of the analysis wraps it inside a boundary statement. In the case of the running example, all statements except the last one are statically typed. In contrast, the last assignment is re-written as @monitor(@type_env, @pc, @ret, public = o[g()]), where the first three arguments of the monitor statement are used for the setup of the runtime analysis. Hence, when the program is executed the only overhead introduced by the dynamic component of our hybrid analysis regards the security checks for validating or rejecting the statement public = o[g()].

Contributions. The main contribution of the paper is the design of a new hybrid analysis for verifying secure information flow in a JavaScript-like language. To achieve this, we introduce: **(1)** a type language specifically designed to control information flow in a subset of JavaScript, **(2)** a static type system for verifying statements not containing dynamic field operations, **(3)** a dynamic typing analysis for verifying statements containing dynamic field operations, and **(4)** a novel boundary operator for interleaving the execution of statically verified

Table 1. Core JS syntax - expressions and statements

$$
\begin{aligned}
v \in \mathcal{V}al \quad &::= \quad lit \mid \underline{lit} \mid l \mid \lambda x : \dot{\tau}.s \\
e \in \mathcal{E}xpr \quad &::= \quad v \mid \text{this} \mid x \mid x = e \mid \{\,\} \,[\dot{\tau}] \mid e.f \mid e_1[e_2] \mid e_1.f = e_2 \\
&\quad\;\; \mid e_1[e_2] = e_3 \mid f \,\text{in}\, e \mid [e_1] \,\text{in}\, e_2 \mid \text{delete}\, e.f \mid \text{delete}\, e_1[e_2] \\
&\quad\;\; \mid \text{function}\, (x)[\dot{\tau}]\{s\} \mid e_1(e_2) \mid e_1.x(e) \mid e_1[e_2](e_3) \\
s \in \mathcal{S}tmt \quad &::= \quad e \mid \text{var}\, x \,[\dot{\tau}] \mid s_1;\, s_2 \mid \text{if}(e)\,\{s_1\}\,\text{else}\,\{s_2\} \mid \text{return}\, e
\end{aligned}
$$

regions with dynamically verified ones. Finally, we have implemented a prototype as well as a case study, available online at [15].

2 Core JS

Syntax. The syntax of Core JS is given in Table 1. Expressions include values, the keyword this, variables, variable assignments, object literals, static and dynamic field projections, static and dynamic field assignments, static and dynamic membership checks, static and dynamic field deletions, function literals, function calls, and static and dynamic method calls. Statements include expression statements, variable declarations, sequences, conditional statements, and return statements. We distinguish two types of *values*: literal values and runtime values. Literal values include numbers, booleans, strings, and undefined. Runtime values, ranged over by $\underline{v}$, include parsed literal values, locations, and parsed function literals. Object literals, function literals, and variable declarations are annotated with their respective *security types* (which are explained in Sect. 3). In the following, we use $\mathcal{E}xpr_{\sharp}$ for the set of Core JS dynamic field operations.

Memory Model. A heap $H \in \mathcal{H}eap : \mathcal{L}oc \times \mathcal{X} \rightharpoonup \mathcal{V}al$ is a partial mapping from locations in $\mathcal{L}oc$ and field names in $\mathcal{X}$ to values in $\mathcal{V}al$. We denote a heap cell by $(l, f) \mapsto v$, the union of two disjoint heaps by $H_1 \uplus H_2$, a read operation by $H(l, f)$, and a heap update operation by $H[l.f \mapsto v]$. An object can be seen as a set of heaps cells addressed by the same location but with different field names. We use $l \mapsto \{f_1 : v_1, \ldots, f_n : v_n\}$ as an abbreviation for the object $(l, f_1) \mapsto v_1 \uplus \ldots \uplus (l, f_n) \mapsto v_n$.

Every object has a prototype, whose location is stored in a special field _proto_. In order to determine the value of a field f of an object o, the semantics first checks whether f is one of the fields of o. If that is the case, the field look-up yields that value. Otherwise, the semantics checks whether f belongs to the fields of the prototype of o and so forth. The sequence of objects that can be accessed from a given object through the inspection of the respective prototypes is called a prototype chain. The prototype chain inspection procedure is modelled by the semantic function π given in appendix. Informally, the expression $\pi(H, l, f)$ denotes the location of the first object that defines f in the prototype chain of the object pointed to by l (if no such object exists, π returns null). Given that most

Table 2. Evaluation contexts

$$
\begin{aligned}
\hat{E} ::=\ &\square \mid x = \hat{E} \mid \hat{E}.f \mid \hat{E}[e] \mid l[\hat{E}] \mid \hat{E}.f = e \mid \hat{E}[e_1] = e_2 \\
&\mid l[\hat{E}] = e \mid l[f] = \hat{E} \mid [\hat{E}] \,\text{in}\, e \mid [f] \,\text{in}\, \hat{E} \mid \text{delete}\ \hat{E}.f \mid \text{delete}\ \hat{E}[e] \\
&\mid \text{delete}\ l[\hat{E}] \mid \hat{E}(e) \mid l(\hat{E}) \mid \hat{E}.f(e) \mid \hat{E}[e](e) \mid l[\hat{E}](e) \mid l[f](\hat{E}) \\
E ::=\ &\hat{E} \mid E;\, s \mid \text{if}(\hat{E})\,\{s_1\}\,\text{else}\,\{s_2\} \mid \text{return}\ \hat{E}
\end{aligned}
$$

implementations of JavaScript allow for explicit prototype mutation, we include this feature in Core JS. For instance, $x.\_proto\_$ evaluates to the prototype of the object bound to x and $x.\_proto\_ = y$ sets the prototype of the object bound to x to the object bound to y.

Scope is modelled using *environment records*. An environment record is simply an internal object that maps variable names to their respective values. An environment record is created for every function or method call. We use $\mathsf{act}(l, x, v, s, l')$ to denote the environment record that: **(1)** is identified by location l where it is stored, **(2)** maps x to v, **(3)** maps all the variables declared in s to undefined, and **(4)** maps the field @*this* to the location l'. (Note that environment records map a single variable because functions have a single argument. Moreover, in the execution of a method call, the field @*this* is used to store the location of the object on which the method was invoked.) Variables are resolved with respect to a list of environment record locations, called *scope chain*. The variable inspection procedure is modelled by the semantic function σ given in appendix. We let $\sigma(H, L, x)$ denote the location of the first environment record that defines x in the scope chain L. The global object, assumed to be pointed to by a fixed location l_g, is the environment record that binds global variables.

Since functions are first-class citizens, the evaluation of a function literal triggers the creation of a special type of object, called *function object*. Every function object has two fields: @*body* and @*scope*, which respectively store the corresponding parsed function literal and the scope chain that was active when the function literal was evaluated. Functions execute in the scope in which the they were evaluated.

Semantics. Figure 1 presents a fragment of the semantics of Core JS in the style of Wright and Felleisen [19] (the full semantics is given in appendix). A configuration Ψ has the form $\langle H, L, s \rangle$ where H is the current heap, L the current scope chain, and s the statement to execute. Transitions are labelled with an internal event α for the use of the dynamic analysis. The evaluation order is specified with the help of evaluation contexts, whose syntax is given in Table 2. In the following, we use $l :: L$ for the list obtained by prepending l to L and $\mathsf{head}(L)$ for the first element of L.

Rule VARIABLE uses σ to determine the location l' of the environment record that defines x and reads its value from the heap. Rule DYN FIELD PROJECTION uses π to determine the location l'' of the object that defines f in the prototype chain of the object pointed to by l' and then reads its value from the heap. Rule

---

VARIABLE
$l = \mathsf{head}(L) \qquad l' = \sigma(H, L, x)$
$\underline{v} = H(l', x)$

$$\langle H, L, x \rangle \xrightarrow{\mathsf{var}_l(x)} \langle H, L, \underline{v} \rangle$$

DYN. FIELD PROJECTION
$l = \mathsf{head}(L) \qquad l'' = \pi(H, l', f)$
$\underline{v} = H(l'', f)$

$$\langle H, L, l'[f] \rangle \xrightarrow{\mathsf{f\text{-}proj}_l(f)} \langle H, L, \underline{v} \rangle$$

DYN. FIELD ASSIGNMENT
$l' = \mathsf{head}(L) \qquad H' = H[l.f \mapsto \underline{v}]$

$$\langle H, L, l[f] = \underline{v} \rangle \xrightarrow{\mathsf{f\text{-}ass}_{l'}(f)} \langle H', L, \underline{v} \rangle$$

MEMBERSHIP CHECK - TRUE
$l' = \mathsf{head}(L) \qquad \pi(H, l, f) \neq \mathsf{null}$

$$\langle H, L, [f] \, \mathsf{in} \, l \rangle \xrightarrow{\mathsf{in}_{l'}(f)} \langle H, L, \mathsf{true} \rangle$$

FUNCTION LITERAL
$l = \mathsf{head}(L) \qquad l' = \mathsf{fresh}(H, \dot\tau) \qquad H' = H \uplus l' \mapsto \{@scope : L, @body : \lambda x : \dot\tau.s\}$

$$\langle H, L, \mathsf{function} \, (x)[\dot\tau]\{s\} \rangle \xrightarrow{\mathsf{push}_l(\dot\tau)} \langle H', L, l' \rangle$$

FUNCTION CALL
$l' = \mathsf{head}(L) \quad l'' \notin \mathsf{dom}(H) \quad \lambda x : \dot\tau.s = H(l, @body)$
$L' = H(l, @scope) \quad H' = H \uplus \mathsf{act}(l'', x, \underline{v}, s, l_g)$

$$\langle H, L, l(\underline{v}) \rangle \xrightarrow{\mathsf{f\text{-}call}_{l'}} \langle H', l'' :: L', @\mathsf{FunExe}(L, s) \rangle$$

IF END
$l = \mathsf{head}(L)$

$$\langle H, L, @\mathsf{EI}(\underline{v}) \rangle \xrightarrow{\curvearrowright_l} \langle H, L, \underline{v} \rangle$$

IF - TRUE
$l = \mathsf{head}(L) \quad \neg\mathsf{false}(\underline{v}) \quad s' = @\mathsf{EI}(s_1)$

$$\langle H, L, \mathsf{if}(\underline{v}) \, \{s_1\} \, \mathsf{else} \, \{s_2\} \rangle \xrightarrow{\mathsf{if}_l} \langle H, L, s' \rangle$$

CONTEXTUAL PROPAGATION
$\langle H, L, s \rangle \xrightarrow{\alpha} \langle H', L', s' \rangle$

$$\langle H, L, E[s] \rangle \xrightarrow{\alpha} \langle H', L', E[s'] \rangle$$

Fig. 1. Fragment of the small-step semantics of core JS

DYN FIELD ASSIGNMENT updates the current heap with a mapping from l and f to $\underline{v}$. Rule MEMBERSHIP CHECK - TRUE checks if f is defined in the prototype chain of the object pointed to by l and evaluates to true. Rule FUNCTION LIT-ERAL adds a new function object to the heap. Rule FUNCTION CALL extends the heap with a new environment record for the evaluation of the function pointed to by l. The current scope chain L is replaced with the scope chain L' that was active when the corresponding function literal was evaluated extended with the location l'' of the newly created environment record. The semantics makes use of an internal statement $@\mathsf{FunExe}(L, s)$ for keeping track of the caller's scope chain during the execution of the function's body. Rule IF - TRUE checks if the guard of the conditional does not belong to the set of *falsy* values –{false, 0, undefined, null}– and replaces the whole conditional with its then-branch followed by an internal statement $@\mathsf{EI}$ for notifying the dynamic analysis of the end of that branch. CONTEXTUAL PROPAGATION is standard.

3 Static Typing Secure Information Flow in Core JS

In this section, we present both a new type language for controlling information flow in JavaScript and the static component of our analysis. Here, the specification of security policies relies on two key elements: a lattice of security levels and a typing environment that maps resources to security types, which can be viewed as safety types annotated with security levels. In the examples, we use $\mathcal{L} = \{H, L\}$ with $L \sqsubset H$, meaning that L-labelled resources (*low* resources) are less confidential than those labelled with H (*high*). We use $\sqcup$, $\bot$, and $\top$ for the least upper bound (*lub*), the *bottom* level, and the *top* level, respectively.

Security Types. A security type $\dot{\tau} = \tau^{\sigma}$ is obtained by pairing up a *raw type* τ with a security level σ, called its *external level*. The external level of a security type establishes an upper bound on the levels of the resources on which the values of that type may depend. For instance, a primitive value of type PRIM^L may only depend on *low* resources. The syntax of raw types is given and explained below:

$$\tau ::= \mathrm{PRIM} \mid \langle \dot{\tau}.\dot{\tau} \xrightarrow{\sigma} \dot{\tau} \rangle \mid \langle \kappa.\dot{\tau} \xrightarrow{\sigma} \dot{\tau} \rangle$$
$$\mid \mu\kappa.\langle f^{\sigma} : \dot{\tau}, \cdots, f^{\sigma} : \dot{\tau}, *^{\sigma} : \dot{\tau} \rangle \mid \mu\kappa.\langle f^{\sigma} : \dot{\tau}, \cdots, f^{\sigma} : \dot{\tau} \rangle$$

- The type PRIM is the type of expressions which evaluate to primitive values.
- The type $\langle \dot{\tau}_0.\dot{\tau}_1 \xrightarrow{\sigma} \dot{\tau}_2 \rangle$ is the type of expressions which evaluate to functions that map values of type $\dot{\tau}_1$ to values of type $\dot{\tau}_2$ and during the execution of which, the keyword this is bound to an object of type $\dot{\tau}_0$. Level σ is the *writing effect* [14] of functions of this type, that is, a lower bound on the levels of the resources updated or created during their execution. When specifying a function type inside an object type, one can use the type variable bound by that object type as the type of the keyword this (in the syntax of types, κ ranges over the set of type variables).
- The type $\mu\kappa.\langle f_0^{\sigma_0} : \dot{\tau}_0, \cdots, f_n^{\sigma_n} : \dot{\tau}_n, *^{\sigma_*} : \dot{\tau}_* \rangle$ is the type of expressions which evaluate to objects that *may* define the fields f_0 to f_n mapping each field f_i to a value of security type $\dot{\tau}_i$. The security type assigned to $*$ is the *default security type*, which is the security type of all fields not in $\{f_0, \cdots, f_n\}$. Every field f_i is further associated with an *existence level* σ_i that establishes an upper bound on the levels of the contexts in which the field can be created or deleted. The level σ_* is the *default existence level*. When no default security type is declared, the objects of the type may only define explicitly declared fields.

The reason why we do not precisely track the presence of fields in object types is that we do not want the type of an object to change at runtime even though its structure may change. Notice that the absence of a field in a type does not mean it cannot be accessed in objects of that type: this field may still be defined in the prototype chain. We could have flattened security types for objects by requiring every object type to explicitly declare all the fields accessible through the prototype chains of the objects of that type, but this would have two disadvantages. First, object types would be less precise, and second, they would be much larger as the types of prototype fields would be duplicated. The cost of this design choice is a more complex STATIC FIELD PROJECTION typing rule that has to take the prototype chain into account.

Given a security type $\dot{\tau}$, the expression $\mathrm{lev}(\dot{\tau})$ denotes its external level and $\lfloor \dot{\tau} \rfloor$ its raw type (for instance, $\mathrm{lev}(\mathrm{PRIM}^L) = L$ and $\lfloor \mathrm{PRIM}^L \rfloor = \mathrm{PRIM}$). We define $\dot{\tau}^{\sigma}$

Table 3. Typing environment for the Examples 1 to 6

$$\Gamma(\texttt{public}) = \text{PRIM}^L$$
$$\Gamma(\texttt{secret}) = \text{PRIM}^H$$
$$\Gamma(\texttt{secret\_input}) = \langle \dot\tau_{g.\_} \xrightarrow{H} \text{PRIM}^H \rangle^L$$
$$\Gamma(\texttt{public\_input}) = \langle \dot\tau_{g.\_} \xrightarrow{H} \text{PRIM}^L \rangle^L$$
$$\Gamma(\texttt{g}) = \langle \dot\tau_{g.\_} \xrightarrow{H} \text{PRIM}^L \rangle^L \quad \Gamma(\texttt{o0}) = \mu\kappa.\langle\_\texttt{proto}\_^H : \dot\tau_o \rangle^L$$

$$\dot\tau_o = \mu\kappa \cdot \left\langle \begin{array}{l} \texttt{public1}^L : \text{PRIM}^L, \\ \texttt{public2}^L : \text{PRIM}^L, \\ \texttt{secret1}^H : \text{PRIM}^H \\ \texttt{secret2}^H : \text{PRIM}^H \end{array} \right\rangle^L$$

$$\Gamma(\texttt{o}) = \Gamma(\texttt{o1}) = \Gamma(\texttt{o2}) = \dot\tau_o$$

as $\lfloor \dot\tau \rfloor^{\text{lev}(\dot\tau) \sqcup \sigma}$ (for example, $(\text{PRIM}^L)^H = \text{PRIM}^H$). Given a function security type $\dot\tau = \langle \dot\tau_0.\dot\tau_1 \xrightarrow{\sigma} \dot\tau_2 \rangle^{\sigma'}$, we use $\dot\tau$.this, $\dot\tau$.arg, $\dot\tau$.ret, and $\dot\tau$.wef to denote $\dot\tau_0$, $\dot\tau_1$, $\dot\tau_2$, and σ, respectively. Given an object security type $\dot\tau$, we use $\text{dom}(\dot\tau)$ for the set containing all field names explicitly declared in $\dot\tau$ (including $*$, if present). Given a field name f and an object security type $\dot\tau$, $\dot\tau.f$ ($\dot\tau.\overline{f}$, resp.) denotes either the security type (existence level resp.) with which $\dot\tau$ associates f or its default security type (existence level, resp.) when $f \notin \text{dom}(\dot\tau)$ and $* \in \text{dom}(\dot\tau)$. The ordering $\sqsubseteq$ on security levels induces a simple ordering $\preceq$ on security types: $\dot\tau_0 \preceq \dot\tau_1$ *iff* $\text{lev}(\dot\tau_0) \sqsubseteq \text{lev}(\dot\tau_1)$ and $\lfloor \dot\tau_0 \rfloor = \lfloor \dot\tau_1 \rfloor$. We use $\dot\tau_g$ for the type of the global object. Finally, a typing environment Γ is simply a mapping from variables to security types.

Example 2. Table 3 presents the typing environment used to type the programs given in Examples 1 to 6. Since secret_input, public_input, and g are to be used as functions, their respective types use the type of the global object as the type of the keyword this. Since none of these three functions expects an argument or updates the heap, their respective types omit the type of the argument and declare a *high* writing effect. Our design choice of not flattening object types can also be seen in this example: the type of o0 is much shorter as it does not need to mention at top level the fields declared in $\dot\tau_o$.

Static Type System. The key insight of the static type system is that it wraps program regions which cannot be precisely analysed at static time within a boundary statement @$monitor(\Gamma, pc, \dot\tau_r, s)$ responsible for turning on the typing analysis at runtime. The parameters Γ, pc, and $\dot\tau_r$ are the typing environment, the context level [14], and the type of the function whose body is being typed, respectively. Given a typing environment Γ, a level pc, and an expression e, the typing judgment $\Gamma, pc \vdash_e e \hookrightarrow e' : \dot\tau$ means that e is rewritten as a semantically equivalent expression e', which may include boundary statements, has raw type $\lfloor \dot\tau \rfloor$, and reads variables or fields of level at most $\text{lev}(\dot\tau)$. Typing judgements for statements, with the form $\Gamma, pc, \dot\tau_r \vdash_s s \hookrightarrow s'$, differ from typing judgements for expressions in that they do not assign a type to the statement. When e (s resp.) coincides with e' (s' resp.), we omit $\hookrightarrow e'$ ($\hookrightarrow s'$ resp.) from the typing rules. The most relevant typing rules are given in Fig. 2 and described below. (We omit

LITERAL
$\Gamma, pc \vdash_e lit : \mathsf{PRIM}^\perp$

VARIABLE
$\Gamma, pc \vdash_e x : \Gamma(x)$

ASSIGNMENT
$$\frac{\Gamma, pc \vdash_e e : \dot{\tau} \qquad \dot{\tau}^{pc} \preceq \Gamma(x)}{\Gamma, pc \vdash_e x = e : \dot{\tau}}$$

STATIC FIELD PROJECTION
$$\frac{\Gamma, pc \vdash_e e : \dot{\tau} \qquad \dot{\tau}_f = \pi(\dot{\tau}, f)}{\Gamma, pc \vdash_e e.f : \dot{\tau}_f^{\mathsf{lev}(\dot{\tau})}}$$

STATIC MEMBER CHECK
$$\frac{\Gamma, pc \vdash_e e : \dot{\tau} \qquad \sigma = \mathsf{lev}(\dot{\tau}) \sqcup \bar{\pi}(\dot{\tau}, f)}{\Gamma, pc \vdash_e f \text{ in } e : \mathsf{PRIM}^\sigma}$$

STATIC FIELD ASSIGNMENT
$$\frac{\forall_{i=1,2} \; \Gamma, pc \vdash_e e_i : \dot{\tau}_i \\ \dot{\tau}_2 \preceq \dot{\tau}_1.f \qquad pc \sqcup \mathsf{lev}(\dot{\tau}_1) \sqsubseteq \dot{\tau}_1.\bar{f}}{\Gamma, pc \vdash_e e_1.f = e_2 : \dot{\tau}_2}$$

STATIC FIELD DELETION
$$\frac{\Gamma, pc \vdash_e \mathsf{delete} \, e : \dot{\tau} \\ pc \sqcup \mathsf{lev}(\dot{\tau}) \sqsubseteq \dot{\tau}.\bar{f} = \sigma_f}{\Gamma, pc \vdash_e \mathsf{delete} \, e.f : \mathsf{PRIM}^{\sigma_f}}$$

FUNCTION LITERAL
$$\frac{\Gamma' = \mathsf{hoist}(\Gamma[x \mapsto \dot{\tau}.\mathsf{arg}, this \mapsto \dot{\tau}.\mathsf{this}], s) \\ pc' = \dot{\tau}.\mathsf{wef} \quad \mathsf{lev}(\dot{\tau}) \sqcup pc \sqsubseteq pc' \quad \Gamma', pc', \dot{\tau} \vdash_s s \hookrightarrow s'}{\Gamma, pc \vdash_e \mathsf{function} \, (x)[\dot{\tau}]\{s\} \hookrightarrow \mathsf{function} \, (x)[\dot{\tau}]\{s'\} : \dot{\tau}}$$

STATIC METHOD CALL
$$\frac{\forall_{i=1,2} \; \Gamma, pc \vdash_e e_i : \dot{\tau}_i \qquad \dot{\tau}_f = \pi(\dot{\tau}_1, f) \qquad \sigma = pc \sqcup \mathsf{lev}(\dot{\tau}_1) \sqcup \mathsf{lev}(\dot{\tau}_f) \\ \sigma \sqsubseteq \dot{\tau}_f.\mathsf{wef} \qquad \dot{\tau}_1^\sigma \preceq \dot{\tau}_f.\mathsf{this} \qquad \dot{\tau}_2^\sigma \preceq \dot{\tau}_f.\mathsf{arg}}{\Gamma, pc \vdash_e e_1.f(e_2) : (\dot{\tau}_f.\mathsf{ret})^\sigma}$$

VERIFIED EXPR STMT
$$\frac{\Gamma, pc \vdash_e e \hookrightarrow e' : \dot{\tau}}{\Gamma, pc, \dot{\tau}_{ret} \vdash_s e \hookrightarrow e'}$$

DYN. EXPRESSION STMT
$$\frac{e \in \mathcal{E}xpr_\sharp \qquad s = @monitor(\Gamma, pc, \dot{\tau}_r, e)}{\Gamma, pc, \dot{\tau}_r \vdash_s e \hookrightarrow s}$$

(PARTIALLY) VERIFIED CONDITIONAL
$$\frac{\Gamma, pc \vdash_e e \hookrightarrow e' : \dot{\tau} \qquad \forall_{i=0,1} \; \Gamma, pc \sqcup \mathsf{lev}(\dot{\tau}), \dot{\tau}_r \vdash_s s_i \hookrightarrow s'_i}{\Gamma, pc, \dot{\tau}_{ret} \vdash_s \mathsf{if}(e) \, \{s_1\} \, \mathsf{else} \, \{s_2\} \hookrightarrow \mathsf{if}(e') \, \{s'_1\} \, \mathsf{else} \, \{s'_2\}}$$

MONITORED CONDITIONAL
$$\frac{e \in \mathcal{E}xpr_\sharp \qquad s = @monitor(\Gamma, pc, \dot{\tau}_{ret}, \mathsf{if}(e) \, \{s_1\} \, \mathsf{else} \, \{s_2\})}{\Gamma, pc, \dot{\tau}_{ret} \vdash_s \mathsf{if}(e) \, \{s_1\} \, \mathsf{else} \, \{s_2\} \hookrightarrow s}$$

Fig. 2. Static typing core JS expressions

the explanations of Rules LITERAL, VARIABLE, and ASSIGNMENT as they are standard).

STATIC FIELD PROJECTION. As a given field may be defined anywhere in the prototype chain of the inspected object, this rule needs to take into account the whole prototype chain of that object. To this end, we overload function π to model a static prototype chain inspection procedure. Informally, $\pi(\dot{\tau}, f)$ computes the *lub* between the security types of f in the prototype chain of objects of type $\dot{\tau}$ and upgrades the external level of this type with the *lub* between the existence levels of the field *_proto_* in that prototype chain.

Example 3 (Leaks via Prototype Mutations). The program below creates three
empty objects bound to: o0, o1, and o2. Then, it creates a field named public1 in
both o1 and o2, which is set to 0 in o1 and to 1 in o2. Depending on the value of
a *high* variable secret, the prototype of o0 is either set to o1 or to o2. Finally, the
low variable public1 is set to the value of the field public1 of the prototype of o0
(because o0 does not define that field), thereby creating an implicit information
flow between secret and public.

```
o0 = {}; o1 = {}; o2 = {}; o1.public1 = 0; o2.public1 = 1;
if(secret){o0._proto_ = o1} else {o0._proto_ = o2}; public = o0.public1
```

Letting Γ be the typing environment of Table 3, it follows that
$\pi(\Gamma(\text{o0}), \text{public1}) = \text{PRIM}^H$ because $\Gamma(\text{o0}).\overline{\text{\_proto\_}} = H$. Hence, the assignment
public = o0.public1 is not typable as the type of o0.public1, PRIM^H, is not lower
than or equal to PRIM^L.

STATIC MEMBER CHECK. Since the domain of an object can change at execution
time and since programs can check if a given field is defined using the keyword
in, the mere existence of a field may disclose secret information. The existence
security levels declared in object security types serve to control this type of
information flows. However, analogously to field projections, this rule needs to
take into account the whole prototype chain of the inspected object, because the
field whose existence is being checked may be defined anywhere in that prototype
chain. To this end, we make use of the static function $\bar{\pi}(\dot{\tau}, f)$ that computes the
lub between the existence levels of f and *_proto_* in the prototype chain of objects
of type $\dot{\tau}$.

Example 4 (Leaks via Membership Checks). The program below creates an
object with two fields secret1 and secret2. Then, depending on the value of
a *high* variable secret, it deletes either secret1 or secret2 from the domain of
o. Finally, the *low* variable public is assigned to true if secret1 is defined in the
prototype chain of o or to false if it is not, thereby creating an implicit flow
between secret and public.

```
o = {}; o.secret1 = 0; o.secret2 = 0;
if (secret) { delete o.secret1 } else { delete o.secret2 }; public = secret1 in o
```

Letting Γ be the typing environment of Table 3, it follows that $\bar{\pi}(\Gamma(\text{o}), \text{secret1}) =$
PRIM^H because $\Gamma(\text{o}).\overline{\text{secret1}} = H$. Hence, the last assignment is not typable as the
type of the expression secret1 in o, PRIM^H, is not lower than or equal to PRIM^L.

STATIC FIELD ASSIGNMENT. The first constraint of the rule checks if the type of
the assigned expression is a subtype of the assigned field type, thus preventing
the assignment of a secret value to a public field. The second constraint checks if
the context level is lower than or equal to the existence level of the assigned field,
thereby preventing the creation of a visible field depending on secret information.

FIELD DELETION. The rule checks if the context level is lower than or equal to
the field's existence level, thereby preventing visible fields from being deleted in
invisible contexts.

FUNCTIONAL LITERAL. This rule checks if the context level is lower than or equal to the writing effect of the type of the function literal, thereby preventing the evaluation of function literals that update or create *public* resources inside secret contexts. Then, the type system types the body of the function literal using the typing environment obtained by extending the current one with the type of the the formal argument, the type of the keyword this, and the types of the variables declared in the body of the function literal. To this end, we make use of a syntactic function hoist that extends the typing environment given as its first argument with the mappings from the variables declared in the statement given as its second argument to their respective security types. Note that this rule may re-write the the body of the function literal in order to enable the dynamic analysis.

METHOD CALL. This rule first verifies if the context level is lower than or equal to the writing effect of the method to call, thereby preventing the calling of a method that creates or updates *public* resources depending on *secret* values. Then, the rule checks if the type of the object on which the method is called and the type of the function argument match the type of the keyword this and the type of the formal parameter. The method call is finally typed with the return type of the method type upgraded with the context level.

DYN. EXPRESSION STATEMENT. This rule wraps every expression that contains a dynamic field operation inside a boundary statement. Recall that $\mathcal{E}xpr_{\sharp}$ denotes the set of Core JS dynamic field operations.

CONDITIONAL. If the conditional guard contains a dynamic field operation, the whole conditional is wrapped inside a boundary statement. In the opposite case, the type system types both branches, upgrading the context level with the external level of the security type of the conditional guard.

Example 5 (Hybrid versus Static Typing of the Running Example). Consider the program from Example 1 and the typing environment of Table 3. When typing the assignment public = o[g()], which contains a dynamic field operation, the type system applies the DYN. EXPRESSION STATEMENT rule and wraps the whole assignment inside a boundary statement. All the other statements, which do not contain dynamic field operations, are fully statically verified and, therefore, left unchanged. Hence, the resulting program is given by:

```
o = {}; o.secret1 = secret_input(); o.public1 = public_input();
o.public2 = public_input(); @monitor(@type_env, @pc, @ret, public = o[g()])
```

If, instead, the type system tried to statically type this assignment, it would need to check that the type of o[g()] was less than or equal to the type of public, PRIM^{L}. Since we do not know the value to which the call to g evaluates, the type system would need to use the *lub* between the types of all the fields declared in the type of o. Consequently, as one of those fields has type PRIM^{H}, the assignment would not be typable.

MONITOR SYNC

$$\frac{\Psi \overset{\alpha_l}{\to} \Psi' \quad \omega \overset{\alpha_l}{\to} \omega'}{(\!|\Psi, \Omega \cup \{\omega\}|\!) \to (\!|\Psi', \Omega \cup \{\omega'\}|\!)}$$

UNMONITORED STEP

$$\frac{\Psi \overset{\alpha_l}{\to} \Psi' \quad \forall_{\omega \in \Omega} \, \mathsf{er}(\omega) \neq l}{(\!|\Psi, \Omega|\!) \to (\!|\Psi', \Omega|\!)}$$

MONITOR CONFIGURATION +

$$\frac{l = \mathsf{head}(L) \quad \forall_{\omega \in \Omega} \, \mathsf{er}(\omega) \neq l \quad \omega' = \langle \Gamma, \dot{\tau}_r, l, pc :: [\,], [\,]\rangle}{(\!|\langle H, L, E[@monitor(\Gamma, \dot{\tau}_r, pc, s)]\rangle, \Omega|\!) \to (\!|\langle H, L, E[@monitor(s)]\rangle, \Omega \cup \{\omega'\}|\!)}$$

MONITOR CONFIGURATION - 1
$\Psi = \langle H, L, E[@monitor(v)]\rangle$
$\mathsf{head}(L) = \mathsf{er}(\omega) \quad \Psi' = \langle H, L, E[v]\rangle$

$$\frac{}{(\!|\Psi, \Omega \cup \{\omega\}|\!) \to (\!|\Psi', \Omega|\!)}$$

MONITOR CONFIGURATION - 2
$\Psi = \langle H, L, E[@monitor(\mathsf{return}\, v)]\rangle$
$\mathsf{head}(L) = \mathsf{er}(\omega) \quad \Psi' = \langle H, L, E[\mathsf{return}\, v]\rangle$

$$\frac{}{(\!|\Psi, \Omega \cup \{\omega\}|\!) \to (\!|\Psi', \Omega|\!)}$$

Fig. 3. Monitored semantics rules

4   Dynamic Typing Secure Information Flow in Core JS

The goal of a boundary statement is to enable and disable the information flow analysis at runtime. In this section, we define the semantics of the boundary operator by extending the semantics of Core JS with optional tracking of security types and verification of security constraints.

Monitored Semantics. A configuration of the monitored semantics has the form $(\!|\Psi, \Omega|\!)$ where Ψ is a Core JS configuration and Ω is a possibly empty set of monitor configurations. A monitor configuration ω is associated to a specific function call and has the form $\omega = \langle \Gamma, \dot{\tau}_r, l, o, \rho\rangle$ where: **(1)** Γ is a typing environment, **(2)** $\dot{\tau}_r$ is the type of the function that is executing, **(3)** l is the identifier of the environment record associated to the function call that is being monitored, **(4)** o is a *control context*, which is a list containing the levels of the expressions on which the monitored statement branched in order to reach the current context, and **(5)** ρ is an *expression context*, which is a list consisting of the security types of the values of the current evaluation context. The rules of the monitored semantics are given in Fig. 3 and described below. We use $\mathsf{er}(\omega)$ to denote the location of the environment record associated with ω.

Rule MONITOR SYNC corresponds to a monitored step. The transition of the monitor is synchronised with the transition of Core JS semantics through an *internal event* α_l, where l identifies the running function that performed a computation step.

Rule UNMONITORED STEP models the case where there is no matching monitor configuration for the current computation step. In this case, Core JS semantics performs an unconstrained computation step (that takes place outside a boundary statement).

Rule MONITOR CONFIGURATION + generates a new monitor configuration for verifying the statement inside a boundary statement. In order to account for computation steps inside boundary statements, we extend the syntax of evaluation contexts with a special boundary context: $E = @monitor(E')$.

LITERAL
$$\frac{\rho' = \mathsf{PRIM}^\perp :: \rho}{\Gamma, \dot\tau_r, l \vdash \langle o, \rho \rangle \xrightarrow{\mathsf{lit}_l} \langle o, \rho' \rangle}$$

THIS
$$\frac{\rho' = \Gamma(this) :: \rho}{\Gamma, \dot\tau_r, l \vdash \langle o, \rho \rangle \xrightarrow{\mathsf{this}_l} \langle o, \rho' \rangle}$$

VARIABLE
$$\frac{\rho' = \Gamma(x) :: \rho}{\Gamma, \dot\tau_r \vdash \langle o, \rho \rangle \xrightarrow{\mathsf{var}_l(x)} \langle o, \rho' \rangle}$$

VARIABLE ASSIGNMENT
$$\frac{pc = \mathsf{head}(o) \quad \dot\tau = \mathsf{head}(\rho) \quad \dot\tau^{pc} \preceq \Gamma(x)}{\Gamma, \dot\tau_r, l \vdash \langle o, \rho \rangle \xrightarrow{\mathsf{v\text{-}ass}_l(x)} \langle o, \rho \rangle}$$

FIELD PROJECTION
$$\frac{pc = \mathsf{head}(o) \quad \rho = \dot\tau_2 :: \dot\tau_1 :: \rho' \quad \dot\tau = \pi(\dot\tau_1, f) \quad \sigma = pc \sqcup \mathsf{lev}(\dot\tau_1) \sqcup \mathsf{lev}(\dot\tau_2)}{\Gamma, \dot\tau_r, l \vdash \langle o, \rho \rangle \xrightarrow{\mathsf{f\text{-}proj}_l(f)} \langle pc :: o, \rho, \dot\tau^\sigma :: \rho' \rangle}$$

MEMBERSHIP CHECK
$$\frac{pc = \mathsf{head}(o) \quad \rho = \dot\tau_2 :: \dot\tau_1 :: \rho' \quad \sigma = \bar\pi(\dot\tau_1, f) \sqcup \mathsf{lev}(\dot\tau_1) \sqcup \mathsf{lev}(\dot\tau_2) \sqcup pc}{\Gamma, \dot\tau_r, l \vdash \langle o, \rho \rangle \xrightarrow{\mathsf{in}_l(f)} \langle o, \mathsf{PRIM}^\sigma :: \rho \rangle}$$

FIELD ASSIGNMENT
$$\frac{\rho = \dot\tau_3 :: \dot\tau_2 :: \dot\tau_1 :: \rho' \quad pc = \mathsf{head}(o) \quad \sigma = \mathsf{lev}(\dot\tau_1) \sqcup \mathsf{lev}(\dot\tau_2) \sqcup pc \quad \dot\tau_3^\sigma \preceq \dot\tau_1.f \quad \sigma \sqsubseteq \dot\tau_1.\bar f}{\Gamma, \dot\tau_r, l \vdash \langle o, \rho \rangle \xrightarrow{\mathsf{f\text{-}ass}_l(f)} \langle o, \dot\tau_3 :: \rho' \rangle}$$

FIELD DELETION
$$\frac{\rho = \dot\tau_2 :: \dot\tau_1 :: \rho' \quad \sigma = \dot\tau_1.\bar f \quad \mathsf{lev}(\dot\tau_1) \sqcup \mathsf{lev}(\dot\tau_2) \sqcup \mathsf{head}(o) \sqsubseteq \sigma}{\Gamma, \dot\tau_r, l \vdash \langle o, \rho \rangle \xrightarrow{\mathsf{del}_l(f)} \langle o, \mathsf{PRIM}^\sigma :: \rho' \rangle}$$

METHOD CALL
$$\frac{\rho = \dot\tau_3 :: \dot\tau_2 :: \dot\tau_1 :: \rho' \quad pc = \mathsf{head}(o) \quad \dot\tau_f = \pi(\dot\tau_1, f) \quad \sigma = \mathsf{lev}(\dot\tau_1) \sqcup \mathsf{lev}(\dot\tau_2) \sqcup pc \quad \sigma \sqsubseteq \dot\tau_f.\mathsf{wef} \quad \dot\tau_1^\sigma \preceq \dot\tau_f.\mathsf{this} \quad \dot\tau_3^\sigma \preceq \dot\tau_f.\mathsf{arg}}{\Gamma, \dot\tau_r, l \vdash \langle o, \rho \rangle \xrightarrow{\mathsf{m\text{-}call}_l(f)} \langle o, (\dot\tau_f.\mathsf{ret})^\sigma :: \rho \rangle}$$

IF - BRANCH
$$\frac{o' = \mathsf{lev}(\dot\tau) :: o}{\Gamma, \dot\tau_r, l \vdash \langle o, \dot\tau :: \rho \rangle \xrightarrow{\mathsf{if}_l} \langle o', \rho \rangle}$$

IF - END
$$\Gamma, \dot\tau_r, l \vdash \langle \sigma :: o, \rho \rangle \xrightarrow{\succ \mathsf{if}_l} \langle o, \rho \rangle$$

Fig. 4. Dynamic typing core JS expressions and statements

Rules MONITOR CONFIGURATION - 1 and MONITOR CONFIGURATION - 2 remove a monitor configuration from the current set of monitor configurations when its corresponding statement finishes executing.

Monitoring Rules. Monitor transitions are defined in Fig. 4. We use $\Gamma, \dot\tau_r, l \vdash \langle o, \rho \rangle \xrightarrow{\alpha_l} \langle o', \rho' \rangle$ as shorthand for $\langle \Gamma, \dot\tau_r, l, o, \rho \rangle \xrightarrow{\alpha_l} \langle \Gamma, \dot\tau_r, l, o', \rho' \rangle$. The constraints enforced by the monitor are the same as the constraints enforced by the type system of Sect. 3. However, in contrast to the type system, the monitor can precisely type dynamic expressions, since it has access to field names computed at runtime.

Example 6 (Monitoring a Dynamic Field Look-up). In the following, we present the sequence of monitor configurations generated when executing the statement: @monitor(@type_env, @pc, @ret, public = o[g()]) (check the running example).

$$\langle \perp, [] \rangle \xrightarrow{\mathsf{var}_l(o)} \langle L, \dot\tau_o \rangle \xrightarrow{\mathsf{var}_l(g)} \langle L, \langle \dot\tau_g .\_ \xrightarrow{H} \mathsf{PRIM}^L \rangle :: \dot\tau_o \rangle \xrightarrow{\mathsf{f\text{-}call}_l} \langle L, \mathsf{PRIM}^L :: \dot\tau_o \rangle$$

If g() returns public1: $\xrightarrow{\mathsf{f\text{-}proj}_l(\mathsf{public1})} \langle L, \mathsf{PRIM}^L \rangle \xrightarrow{\mathsf{v\text{-}ass}_l(\mathsf{public})} \langle L, \mathsf{PRIM}^L \rangle$

If g() returns private1: $\xrightarrow{\mathsf{f\text{-}proj}_l(\mathsf{private1})} \langle L, \mathsf{PRIM}^H \rangle \xrightarrow{\mathsf{v\text{-}ass}_l(\mathsf{public})} \not\rightarrow$

We consider two different cases: the case in which g() evaluates to public1 and the case in which it evaluates to secret1. While in the first case, the execution is allowed to go through, in the second one it gets stuck, because the program tries to assign a secret value to a public variable.

Let us now briefly explain the rules that better illustrate our choices when designing the monitor. Since, by default, all literal values are public, when a *literal* value is evaluated, the monitor simply pushes $\mathsf{PRIM}^\perp$ onto the expression stack. In contrast, when a *variable* is evaluated, the monitor has to read its type from the typing environment and push it onto the expression stack. When a *field projection* is evaluated, the first two types on the expression stack are the types of the expressions that evaluate to the field name and to the inspected object, respectively. Furthermore, the name of the inspected field is available in the internal event that labels the transition. Hence, the monitor simply has to replace the first two types of the expression stack with the type of the inspected field upgraded with the external levels of the types of the current subexpressions. When an *if statement* is evaluated, the type of the conditional guard is on top of the expression stack. Hence, the monitor simply pops that type out of the expression stack and pushes its external level (upgraded with the current *pc*) onto the control stack. Complementarily, when the execution leaves the branch of a conditional, the monitor just pops out the top of the control stack.

Implementation. Instead of wrapping statements containing dynamic field operations within boundary statements, which are not part of the JavaScript language, the prototype of the hybrid type system [15] in-lines the monitoring logic in the statement itself [16]. This approach has the advantage of being immediately deployable. The prototype implementation was used to secure simple Web application accessible online [15].

5   Security Guarantees

This section describes the security guarantees offered by the proposed analysis. To formally define the absence of information leaks, we rely on an intuitive notion of *low-projection* [14] that establishes the part of a heap that an attacker at a given security level can see. Informally, given a heap H, an attacker at level σ can observe:

1. the existence of a field f in the domain of an object whose type has external level $\leq \sigma$ and associates f with an existence level $\leq \sigma$ and
2. the value of a field f in the domain of an object whose type has external level $\leq \sigma$ and associates f with a security type with external level $\leq \sigma$.

Figure 5 presents a labelled object together with its low-projection at level L. The object in the figure has three fields: f_1, f_2, and f_3. An attacker at level L can observe both the existence and the value of f_1 since it has *low* existence level and is associated with a visible value and the existence but not the value of f_2, since it has *low* existence level but is associated with an invisible value. The attacker

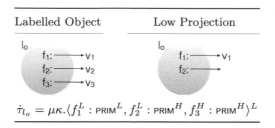

Labelled Object	Low Projection

$$\dot{\tau}_{l_o} = \mu\kappa.\langle f_1^L : \text{PRIM}^L, f_2^L : \text{PRIM}^H, f_3^H : \text{PRIM}^H\rangle^L$$

Fig. 5. A labelled object and its low projection

can neither observe the value nor the existence of f_3 because it has *high* existence level and is associated with an invisible value. Two heaps H_0 and H_1 are said to be *low-equal* at level σ, written $H_0 \sim_\sigma H_1$, if they coincide in their respective low-projections. Theorem 1 states that the monitored successfully-terminating execution of a program generated by the static type system on two low-equal heaps always yields two low-equal heaps. A sketch of the proof of Theorem 1 is given in the long-version of the paper available online at [15].

Theorem 1 (Noninterference). *For any typing environment* Γ, *levels* σ *and* pc, *security type* $\dot{\tau}$, *statement,* s, *and two heaps* H_0 *and* H_1, *such that* $\Gamma, pc, \dot{\tau} \vdash_s s \hookrightarrow s'$, $H_0 \sim_\sigma H_1$, *and* $(\langle H_i, [\,], s'\rangle, \{\}) \to^* (\langle H_i', [\,], v_i\rangle, \{\})$ *for* $i = 0, 1$, *it holds that* $H_0' \sim_\sigma H_1'$.

6   Related Work

There is a wide variety of mechanisms for enforcing and verifying secure information flow, ranging from purely static type systems [14,18] to different flavours of dynamic analysis [2,13]. The main mechanisms for securing information flow in JavaScript [1,6,8] are mostly-dynamic due to the dynamicity of the language.

There is a long line of research on safety types for JavaScript which dates back to the seminal work of Thieman [17]. Since then, the TypeScript programming language [11] was proposed as a flexible language that adds optional types to JavaScript with the goal of harnessing the flexibility of real JavaScript, while at the same time providing some of the advantages otherwise reserved for statically typed languages, such as informative compiling errors. Recently, Rastogi et al. [12] designed and implemented a new gradual type system for safely compiling TypeScript to JavaScript. The soundness of the proposed approach is guaranteed by combining strict static checks with residual runtime checks. We believe that our work can serve as a basis for extending TypeScript types with security labels in order to verify secure information flow in TypeScript web applications.

Gradual type systems for secure information flow have been proposed for a pure lambda calculus [3] and for a core ML-like language with references [4]. The goal of these two works is significantly different from ours, as their main intent is to cater for the use of *polymorphic* security labels. For instance, the type language proposed in [4] includes a special annotation "?" representing an unknown security level at static time. Expressions that use variables whose types contain the unknown level annotation, "?", cannot be precisely typed at static time. The programmer can introduce runtime casts in points where values of a pre-determined security type are expected. Then the dynamic analysis checks whether or not a cast can be *securely* performed during execution. However, in order to verify such casts at runtime, these analyses must track security labels during the execution of both dynamically verified and statically verified program regions. In contrast, our analysis only needs to dynamically verify the execution of program regions which were not statically verified.

7   Conclusions

We propose a sound hybrid typing analysis for enforcing secure information flow in a core of JavaScript that includes dynamic field operations. Furthermore, our analysis can be easily extended to handle other dynamic constructs of the language such as eval or unknown code, which only need to be wrapped inside the proposed boundary statement. Finally, we have implemented our analysis and used it to verify a web application available online [15].

This work follows a well-established trend on combining static and dynamic analysis to devise more permissive and efficient hybrid mechanisms [13]. Our approach can be applied to other scenarios, such as the verification of isolation properties [9], where it could be used to derive mostly-static lightweight enforcement mechanisms from prior purely static specifications.

Acknowledgments. We acknowledge funding from the EPSRC grant reference EP/K032089/1 (Fragoso Santos) and the ANR project AJACS ANR-14-CE28-0008 (Jensen, Rezk, and Schmitt). No new data was collected in the course of this research.

References

1. Bichhawat, A., Rajani, V., Garg, D., Hammer, C.: Information flow control in webkit's javascript bytecode. In: Abadi, M., Kremer, S. (eds.) POST 2014 (ETAPS 2014). LNCS, vol. 8414, pp. 159–178. Springer, Heidelberg (2014)
2. Devriese, D., Piessens, F.: Noninterference through secure multi-execution. In: SP (2010)
3. Disney, T., Flanagan, C.: Gradual information flow typing. In: STOP (2011)
4. Fennell, L., Thiemann, P.: Gradual security typing with references. In: CSF (2013)
5. Flanagan, C.: Hybrid type checking. In: POPL (2006)
6. De Groef, W., Devriese, D., Nikiforakis, N., Piessens, F.: Flowfox: a web browser with flexible and precise information flow control. In: CCS (2012)
7. Hedin, D., Birgisson, A., Bello, L., Sabelfeld, A.: JSFlow: tracking information flow in JavaScript and its APIs. In: SAC (2014)
8. Hedin, D., Sabelfeld, A.: Information-flow security for a core of JavaScript. In: CSF (2012)

9. Maffeis, S., Taly, A.: Language-based isolation of untrusted JavaScript. In: CSF (2009)
10. Matthews, J., Findler, R.B.: Operational semantics for multi-language programs. In: ACM TOPLAS (2009)
11. Microsoft. TypeScript language specification. Technical report, Microsoft (2014)
12. Rastogi, A., Swamy, N., Fournet, C., Bierman, G., Vekris, P.: Safe & efficient gradual typing for TypeScript. In: POPL (2015)
13. Russo, A., Sabelfeld, A.: Dynamic vs. static flow-sensitive security analysis. In: CSF (2010)
14. Sabelfeld, A., Myers, A.C.: Language-based information-flow security. IEEE J. Sel. Areas Commun. **21**(1), 5–19 (2003)
15. Santos, J.F.: Online materials - hybrid type system 2015. http://www.doc.ic.ac.uk/~jfaustin
16. Santos, J.F., Rezk, T.: An information flow monitor-inlining compiler for securing a core of javascript. In: Cuppens-Boulahia, N., Cuppens, F., Jajodia, S., Abou El Kalam, A., Sans, T. (eds.) SEC 2014. IFIP AICT, vol. 428, pp. 278–292. Springer, Heidelberg (2014)
17. Thiemann, P.: Towards a type system for analyzing javascript programs. In: Sagiv, M. (ed.) ESOP 2005. LNCS, vol. 3444, pp. 408–422. Springer, Heidelberg (2005)
18. Volpano, D.M., Irvine, C.E., Smith, G.: A sound type system for secure flow analysis. J. Comput. Secur. **4**(2), 167–187 (1996)
19. Wright, A., Felleisen, M.: A syntactic approach to type soundness. Inf. Comput. **115**(1), 38–94 (1994)

Fault Ascription in Concurrent Systems

Gregor Gössler$^{(\boxtimes)}$ and Jean-Bernard Stefani

INRIA Grenoble – Rhône-Alpes, Université Grenoble – Alpes, Grenoble, France
gregor.goessler@inria.fr

Abstract. Fault diagnosis is becoming increasingly important and difficult with the growing pervasiveness and complexity of computer systems. We propose in this paper a general semantic framework for fault ascription, a precise form of fault diagnosis that relies on counterfactual analysis for identifying necessary and sufficient causes of faults in component-based systems. Our framework relies on configuration structures to handle concurrent systems, partial and distributed observations in a uniform way. It defines basic conditions for a counterfactual analysis of necessary and sufficient causes, and it presents a refined analysis that conforms to our basic conditions while avoiding various infelicities.

1 Introduction

The increasing reliance of our modern societies on computer systems makes the diagnosis of faults in such systems a crucial necessity. In complex computer systems, for instance in large distributed systems, fault diagnosis is a difficult proposition. Several approaches to fault diagnosis have been put forward in the literature, e.g. using techniques from artificial intelligence [16,17], from automatic control [12], or from concurrency theory [3,9].

In this paper, we contribute to the latter line of work by developing a general framework for *fault ascription* in concurrent systems. Fault ascription, also called *blaming* [6], is a form of fault diagnosis that goes beyond the identification of *explanations*, typically understood as executions that are congruent with observed behavior, to identify *necessary* and *sufficient* causes for some observed behavior, and that can pinpoint the origin of a fault in the failure of given components to meet their specification.

Intuitively, a *necessary cause* is a set of events that must take place in order for a fault to occur in the context of given observations; a *sufficient cause* is a set of events that is enough to trigger an observed fault. These notions are reminiscent of similar notions in philosophy and legal reasoning [4,14]. They are required in order to determine, in a complex system, which components are responsible for the occurrence of a fault, and to ascribe legal responsibility for a fault occurring in multi-vendor systems [15]. In contrast to classical fault diagnosis and fault isolation, fault ascription requires some form of *counterfactual reasoning* of the form "would f also have occurred if c had not occurred?" in order to assess the modality of causes.

© Springer International Publishing Switzerland 2016
P. Ganty and M. Loreti (Eds.): TGC 2015, LNCS 9533, pp. 79–94, 2016.
DOI: 10.1007/978-3-319-28766-9_6

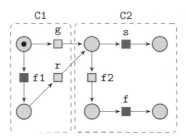

Fig. 1. Running example (color figure online)

Example 1. As a very simple example, consider the system depicted by the small Petri net in Fig. 1, where observable transitions are colored dark blue, while unobservable ones are colored light grey. The system comprises two components, C1 and C2. C1 can either perform action g (its normal behavior), or perform action f1 (a fault), followed by action r. C2 can either perform action s (its normal behavior), or perform action f2 (a fault), followed by action f. The composition of the two components enforces the serialization of executions of C1 and C2. The overall behavior of the composition is given by the unfolding of the Petri net in Fig. 1, which consists of the following event configurations: $\{\emptyset, \{g\}, \{g,s\}, \{g,f2\}, \{g,f2,f\}, \{f1\}, \{f1,r\}, \{f1,r,s\}, \{f1,r,f2\}, \{f1,r,f2,f\}\}$.

Consider now an observation on the execution of this system that consists of the recording of the following observable event configurations $\{\emptyset, \{f1\}, \{f1,f\}\}$, and assume we are interested in knowing which faulty component behavior is to blame for the occurrence of the fault f. Intuitively, it seems clear that C1 is *not* to blame: indeed, even if C1 performs the faulty transition f1, the system can recover from this fault via transition r, and let C2 behave normally. It would thus appear that C2 is to blame, and that the fault that is necessary for f to occur is just f2, for *had* C2 *not misbehaved via action* f2, then the whole system *would not have experienced fault* f. In contrast, the fact that C1 had a fault f1 during the observed execution has no bearing on the final fault since *even without the fault* f1, *the fault* f2 *alone would have been sufficient to entail* f.

In this paper, we develop a general concurrency theoretic framework which formalizes the counterfactual analysis required to analyse fault ascription scenarios as in the above example. It is based on configuration structures [19], and encompasses truly concurrent executions, as well as partial and distributed observations.

The paper is organized as follows. Section 2 details the notations and operations on configuration structures we use in the paper, defines our formalization of component-based systems, of faults and of observation logs. Section 3 motivates constructions needed for fault ascription by means of a simple example, and presents our abstract framework for fault ascription. Section 4 presents an instance of our framework, with definite constructions for ascertaining necessary and sufficient causes of faults, which generalizes previous works based on traces

[6, 7, 20]. Section 5 discusses several examples that illustrate various features of our framework. Section 6 discusses related work. Section 7 concludes the paper.

2 Preliminaries

Notations. We use $[n]$ to denote the finite set of naturals $\{1, \ldots, n\}$. We use boldface to denote tuples of elements taken from a given set, as in $\mathbf{s} = \langle s_1, \ldots, s_n \rangle$. We use $\bigcup S$ to denote $\bigcup_{s \in S} s$. A predicate $\mathcal{P}$ that applies to elements of a set $\mathbb{S}$ is identified with a subset of $\mathbb{S}$. In the paper, we use both set operations, e.g. $s \in \mathcal{P}$, or predicate notation, e.g. $\mathcal{P}(s)$, where appropriate.

2.1 Operations on Configuration Structures

Definition 1 (Configuration Structure). *A* configuration structure *is a tuple* $(\mathbb{E}, \mathcal{C})$, *where* $\mathbb{E}$ *is a set (of events), and* $\mathcal{C} \subseteq 2^{\mathbb{E}}$ *is a set of subsets of* $\mathbb{E}$, *called* configurations.
  A rooted configuration structure $(\mathbb{E}, \mathcal{C})$ *is such that* $\emptyset \in \mathcal{C}$.

We now define some operations on configuration structures.

- $(\mathbb{E}_1, \mathcal{C}_1) \parallel (\mathbb{E}_2, \mathcal{C}_2) = (\mathbb{E}, \mathcal{C})$ where $\mathbb{E} = \mathbb{E}_1 \cup \mathbb{E}_2$ and $\mathcal{C} = \{c \in 2^{\mathbb{E}} \mid c \cap \mathbb{E}_i \in \mathcal{C}_i, i = 1, 2\}$
- $(\mathbb{E}_1, \mathcal{C}_1) \sqcap (\mathbb{E}_2, \mathcal{C}_2) = (\mathbb{E}_1 \cap \mathbb{E}_2, \mathcal{C}_1 \cap \mathcal{C}_2)$
- $(\mathbb{E}_1, \mathcal{C}_1) \subseteq (\mathbb{E}_2, \mathcal{C}_2)$ iff $\mathbb{E}_1 \subseteq \mathbb{E}_2 \wedge \mathcal{C}_1 \subseteq \mathcal{C}_2$
- $\max \mathcal{C} = \{c \in \mathcal{C} \mid \forall c' \in \mathcal{C} : c \subseteq c' \Rightarrow c = c'\}$
- $(\mathbb{E}, \mathcal{C})_{\downarrow \mathbb{F}} = (\mathbb{E} \cap \mathbb{F}, \mathcal{C}_{\downarrow \mathbb{F}})$ where $\mathcal{C}_{\downarrow \mathbb{F}} = \{c_{\downarrow \mathbb{F}} \mid c \in \mathcal{C}\}$, and $c_{\downarrow \mathbb{F}} = c \cap \mathbb{F}$.
- Let $(\mathbb{E}, \mathcal{C})$ be a configuration structure, and let $\mathbb{F}$ be a set such that $\mathbb{E} \subseteq \mathbb{F}$. We define $c^{\uparrow \mathbb{F}} = \{c' \subseteq \mathbb{F} \mid c' \cap \mathbb{E} = c\}$, $\mathcal{C}^{\uparrow \mathbb{F}} = \bigcup_{c \in \mathcal{C}} c^{\uparrow \mathbb{F}}$, and $(\mathbb{E}, \mathcal{C})^{\uparrow \mathbb{F}} = (\mathbb{F}, \mathcal{C}^{\uparrow \mathbb{F}})$.

Remark 1. When $\mathbb{E} \subseteq \mathbb{F}$, we have by definition: $\forall d \in c^{\uparrow \mathbb{F}}, d_{\downarrow \mathbb{E}} = c$.

Definition 2 (Hasse Diagram). *For a set of configurations* $\mathcal{C}$ *we define the graph* $H_{\mathcal{C}} = (V, E)$ *with vertices* $V = \mathcal{C}$ *and edges*

$$E = \{(c, c') \mid c, c' \in \mathcal{C} \wedge c \subseteq c' \wedge \forall c'' \in \mathcal{C} : c \subseteq c'' \subseteq c' \implies c = c'' \vee c'' = c'\}$$

Definition 3 (Conflict). *Let* $C = (\mathbb{E}, \mathcal{C})$ *be a configuration structure. We say that a pair of events* (e, e') *is* conflictual *in* C *if there exists no* $c \in \mathcal{C}$ *such that* $\{e, e'\} \subseteq c$. C *is* conflict-free *if no pair of events of* $\mathbb{E}$ *is conflictual.*

2.2 Systems and Components

A *component specification* is a rooted configuration structure. A component specification is the expected behavior of an actual component. Similarly, a *system specification* is the abstraction of a system composed of a set of interacting components:

Definition 4 (System Specification). *A system specification is a pair* $(\mathbf{S}, B)$, *where:*

- $\mathbf{S} = (S_i)_{i \in I}$ *is a finite tuple of component specifications* $S_i = (\mathbb{E}_i, \mathcal{C}_i)$, *where the sets* $\mathbb{E}_i$ *are assumed to be mutually disjoint, i.e.* $\forall i, j \in I, i \neq j \implies \mathbb{E}_i \cap \mathbb{E}_j = \emptyset$.
- $B = (\mathbb{B}, \mathcal{B})$ *is a rooted configuration structure, where* $\mathbb{B} \subseteq \mathbb{E} = \bigcup_{i \in I} \mathbb{E}_i$.

We use the word "component" in a broad sense to denote part of a system behavior. The configuration structure B plays the role of a behavioral model: it is used to express assumptions and constraints on the possible (correct and incorrect) behaviors. In particular, B may be used to model synchronization and coordination between components. The component specifications define the *correct* behavior of components, in the sense of *normality* of [10]; the actual component behavior may violate those specifications. Note that B may contain behaviors not in $S = \|_{i \in I} S_i$, for instance events in $(\bigcup_{i \in I} \mathbb{E}_i) \setminus (\bigcup_{i \in I} \bigcup \mathcal{C}_i)$. Conversely, part of the behaviors of S may not be feasible according to B.

Remark 2. An alternate definition for a system specification that explicitly accounts for events $\mathbb{E}^*$ not appearing in component specifications could be defined as follows:
System specification – alternate definition. A system specification is a pair $(\mathbf{S}, B)$, where:

- $\mathbf{S} = (S_i)_{i \in I}$ is a finite tuple of component specifications $S_i = (\mathbb{E}_i, \mathcal{C}_i)$
- $B = (\mathbb{B}, \mathcal{B})$ is a rooted configuration structure where $\mathbb{B} \subseteq \mathbb{E} \cup \mathbb{E}^*$, where $\mathbb{E} = \bigcup_{i \in I} \mathbb{E}_i$ and $\mathbb{E}^* \cap \mathbb{E} = \emptyset$.

However, one can always transform a system specification $(\mathbf{S}, B)$ according to the above definition into a system specification $\mathsf{A}(\mathbf{S}, B)$ complying with Definition 4: it suffices to define $\mathsf{A}(\mathbf{S}, B) = (\mathbf{S}', B)$, where $\mathbf{S}' = \mathbf{S}, \top_{E^*}$ and $\top_{E^*} = (\mathbb{E}^*, 2^{\mathbb{E}^*})$.

2.3   Faults and Logs

Given a system specification $(\mathbf{S}, B)$ with events in $\mathbb{E}$, a *fault* is an incorrect behavior. To define a fault, we require a predicate $\mathcal{P} \subseteq 2^{\mathbb{E}}$, which characterizes the correct configurations. In this paper, we focus on safety properties, using the standard transition system associated with a configuration structure under the asynchronous interpretation [19]. A fault occurs whenever $\mathcal{P}$ is violated. We require that system specifications be *consistent with respect to the given property*, which amounts to say that when all the components behave according to their specification, the system is not at fault. Formally:

Definition 5 (Consistent System Specification). *A consistently specified system is a tuple* $(\sigma, \mathcal{P})$ *where* $\sigma = (\mathbf{S}, B)$ *is a system specification with* $\mathbf{S} = ((\mathbb{E}_i, \mathcal{C}_i))_{i \in [n]}$, *and* $\mathcal{P}$ *is a predicate such that* $\|_{i \in [n]} \mathcal{C}_i \cap B \subseteq \mathcal{P}$.

Under a consistent specification, property $\mathcal{P}$ may be violated only if at least one of the components violates its specification. In contrast, the violation of a component specification does not necessarily entail a violation of $\mathcal{P}$. This is useful e.g. to model systems that tolerate certain component failures. Throughout this paper we consider only consistent system specifications.

Remark 3. In addition to being consistent, a meaningful specification of a system should satisfy $\|_{i \in [n]} S_i \cap B \neq \emptyset$ — i.e. B should allow for some correct behavior of its components —, although this is not required for the analysis described below.

Observations of the execution of a system specified by $(\mathbf{S}, B)$, with events $\mathbb{E}$, take the form of *logs*.

Definition 6 (Logs, Observables and Detected Faults). *A log of a system with specification $(\mathbf{S}, B)$ is a rooted conflict-free configuration structure $(\mathbb{O}, \mathcal{L})$ such that $(\mathbb{O}, \mathcal{L}) \subseteq B_{\downarrow \mathbb{O}}$, with $\mathbb{O} \subseteq \mathbb{E}$. We call $\mathbb{O}$ the set of observable events or observables. Given a consistently specified system $((\mathbf{S}, B), \mathcal{P})$ and a set of observables $\mathbb{O}$, we say a fault is* detected *by a log $(\mathbb{O}, \mathcal{L})$ whenever $\mathcal{L} \not\subseteq \mathcal{P}_{\downarrow \mathbb{O}}$.*

Definition 7 (Filtering $\odot$). *Let $L = (\mathbb{O}, \mathcal{L})$ and $B = (\mathbb{B}, \mathcal{B})$ be two configuration structures such that $\mathbb{O} \subseteq \mathbb{B}$. We define the filter of B by L, noted $L \odot B$, as follows:*

$$L \odot B = \{ c \in \mathcal{L}^{\uparrow \mathbb{B}} \cap \mathcal{B} \mid \exists c' \in \mathcal{B} : c \cup \bigcup \mathcal{L} \subset c' \}$$

The filtering operation extracts configurations from B that are compatible with observations provided by L, avoiding introducing configurations that would be inconsistent with observations (because of conflicts between unobservable events and observed events).

Example 2. For $B = (\mathbb{B}, \mathcal{B})$ with $\mathbb{B} = \{\tau, a, b\}$, $\mathcal{B} = \{\emptyset, \{\tau\}, \{a\}, \{a, b\}\}$, $\mathbb{O} = \{a\}$, and a log $L = (\mathbb{O}, \mathcal{L})$ with $\mathcal{L} = \{\emptyset, \{a\}\}$ we have $L \odot B = \{\emptyset, \{a\}, \{a, b\}\}$. The configuration $\{\tau\}$ is consistent with the observed configuration $\emptyset \in \mathcal{L}$ but inconsistent with the observation $\{a\}$, hence we do not have $\{\tau\}$ in $L \odot B$.

We use filtering $L \odot B$, as in the example above, to retrieve explanations for the observed behavior recorded in a log. One might want to refine the definition of $L \odot B$ so as to be more precise concerning inferred non-observable behavior, that is, eliminate configurations that are not consistent with observed configurations in the log. This is standard practice in fault diagnosis [5]. However, for the sake of simplicity, we will stick in this paper to the definition of filtering given in Sect. 2, and the simple consistency check it provides.

Example 3. Figure 1 illustrates an example system specification. The system B is specified by the unfolding of the Petri net in the figure (following e.g. [19]). The specification of component C1 is given by the configurations $\{\emptyset, \{g\}\}$ built on events $\mathbb{E}_1 = \{g, f1, r\}$. The specification of component C2 is given by the configurations $\{\emptyset, \{s\}\}$ over $\mathbb{E}_2 = \{s, f2, f\}$. The behavior B adds the faulty transitions f1, f2, f to the behavior of components, as well as the synchronization constraint forcing the occurrence of transitions s or f2 after the occurrence of transitions g or r. The set of events of B is $\mathbb{B} = \{g, f1, r, s, f2, f\}$. The configurations of B are $\mathcal{B} = \{\emptyset, \{g\}, \{g, s\}, \{g, f2\}, \{g, f2, f\}, \{f1\}, \{f1, r\}, \{f1, r, s\}, \{f1, r, f2\}, \{f1, r, f2, f\}\}$. Observables $\mathbb{O}$ are events $\{f1, s, f\}$, marked in dark blue in Fig. 1. The configurations of the log L in this example are $\{\emptyset, \{f1\}, \{f1, f\}\}$.

Remark 4. To simplify notations in the following sections, given a system specification and its behavioral model $(\mathbb{B}, \mathcal{B})$, we often write $\mathcal{P}$ and in general sets of configurations $\mathcal{X} \subseteq \mathcal{B}$ using logical formulas with events as propositional variables indicating the occurrence of these events. For instance, $\mathcal{X} = f_1$ stands for $\mathcal{X} = \{c \in \mathcal{B} \mid f_1 \in c\}$.

3   A General Framework for Fault Ascription

In this section we define causality of component behaviors for the violation of a system-level property. We assume the following inputs to be given:

- a system specification $\sigma = (\mathbf{S}, B)$ with component specifications $S = ((\mathbb{E}_i, \mathcal{C}_i))_{i \in I}$ and $B = (\mathbb{B}, \mathcal{B})$, with $\mathbb{B} \subseteq \bigcup_{i \in I} \mathbb{E}_i$;
- a set $\mathbb{O} \subseteq \mathbb{B}$ of observable events;
- a property $\mathcal{P}$ such that $(\sigma, \mathcal{P})$ is consistently specified;
- a log $L = (\mathbb{O}, \mathcal{L})$;
- a set $\mathcal{X} \subseteq \mathcal{B} \setminus \|_i \mathcal{C}_i$ of faulty configurations to be checked for causality.

Notice that the set of faulty configurations $(L \odot B) \setminus \|_i \mathcal{C}_i$ is, in general, incomparable with $(L \odot B) \setminus \mathcal{P}$: a violation of $\mathcal{P}$ does not need to occur simultaneously with the violation of component specifications.

In order to verify whether the violations $\mathcal{X}$ are a cause for the violation of $\mathcal{P}$ in L, we construct the (hypothetical) system behavior where the failures in $\mathcal{X}$ and their effects on the observed execution do not occur, under the contingency that the parts of the log that are not impacted by $\mathcal{X}$ remain consistent with the actual observations. We then verify whether all obtained behaviors satisfy $\mathcal{P}$. Let $\mathsf{CF}_\mathcal{X}$ ("counterfactuals with respect to $\mathcal{X}$") be an operation on configuration structures with the following property, for $L = (\mathbb{O}, \mathcal{L})$:

$$\begin{cases} \mathsf{CF}_\mathcal{X}(\mathcal{L}) \subseteq \mathcal{B} \setminus \mathcal{X} \ \wedge \\ \quad \forall i \in [n] : \big((L \odot B)_{\downarrow \mathbb{E}_i} \subseteq \mathcal{C}_i \Rightarrow \mathsf{CF}_\mathcal{X}(\mathcal{L})_{\downarrow \mathbb{E}_i} \subseteq \mathcal{C}_i\big) & \text{if } (L \odot B) \cap \mathcal{X} \neq \emptyset \quad (1) \\ \mathsf{CF}_\mathcal{X}(\mathcal{L}) = L \odot B & \text{if } (L \odot B) \cap \mathcal{X} = \emptyset \end{cases}$$

Intuitively, the set of configurations $\mathsf{CF}_\mathcal{X}(\mathcal{L})$ models the system behavior "if $\mathcal{X}$ had not happened", while avoiding the introduction of new component failures.

For a given $\mathsf{CF}_\mathcal{X}$ we can now define the notions of necessary and sufficient causality.

Definition 8 (Necessary Causality). *Consider a consistently specified system* $((\mathbf{S}, B), \mathcal{P})$ *with component specifications* $\mathbf{S} = \langle S_1, ..., S_n \rangle$ *and* $S_i = (\mathbb{E}_i, \mathcal{C}_i)$, *a log* $L = (\mathbb{O}, \mathcal{L})$ *with* $L \odot B \nsubseteq \mathcal{P}$, *and a predicate* $\mathcal{X}$ *of faulty configurations.* $\mathcal{X}$ *is a* necessary cause *of the violation of* $\mathcal{P}$ *in* L *(with respect to counterfactual operator* CF*) if* $\mathsf{CF}_{\mathcal{X}}(\mathcal{L}) \subseteq \mathcal{P}$. *The faults of a subset* $\mathcal{I}$ *of components are a* necessary cause *if* $\mathcal{X} \triangleq \{c \in \mathcal{B} \mid \exists i \in \mathcal{I} : c_{\downarrow \mathbb{E}_i} \notin \mathcal{C}_i\}$ *is a necessary cause.*

That is, the incorrect configurations in $\mathcal{X}$ are a necessary cause for the violation of $\mathcal{P}$ in L if, in the counterfactual scenarios where configurations in $\mathcal{X}$ do not occur, $\mathcal{P}$ would have been satisfied.

The definition of necessary causality above is parameterized by a counterfactual operator CF. We can check that, regardless of the counterfactual operator used, this definition agrees with a naive notion of necessary causality as necessary condition, defined as follows:

Definition 9 (Naive Necessary Causality). *Let* $B = (\mathbb{B}, \mathcal{B})$ *be a system specification, and let* $\mathcal{P} \subseteq 2^{\mathbb{B}}$ *be a property. Let* $x \subseteq \mathbb{B}$ *and* $\mathcal{Y} \subseteq 2^{\mathbb{B}}$. *We say that* x *is a* naive necessary cause *for the violation of* $\mathcal{P}$ *in* $\mathcal{Y}$, *if* x *appears as a subset of all faulty configurations in* $\mathcal{Y}$, *formally:* $\forall c \in \mathcal{Y} \setminus \mathcal{P}, x \subseteq c$.

Example 4. Naive necessary causality is not satisfactory for analyzing causality *relative* to the behavior recorded in the log. To see this, consider two components with specifications $(\mathbb{E}_i, \mathcal{C}_i)$ with $\mathbb{E}_i = \{a_i, f_i\}$, $\mathcal{C}_i = \{\emptyset, \{a_i\}\}$, $i = 1, 2$, the behavioral model $\mathcal{B} = 2^{\mathbb{E}}$ with $\mathbb{E} = \mathbb{E}_1 \cup \mathbb{E}_2$, and the property $\mathcal{P} = \neg(f_1 \vee f_2)$: a failure f_i of any of the components violates $\mathcal{P}$. For the log $L = (\mathbb{E}, \mathcal{L})$ with $\mathcal{L} = \{\emptyset, \{a_1\}, \{a_1, f_2\}\}$, f_2 is not a naive necessary cause with respect to $\mathcal{B}$, but it is a necessary cause in L (that is, under the contingency that f_1 has not occurred) since $\mathsf{CF}_{\mathcal{X}}(\mathcal{L}) \subseteq \mathcal{P}$.

Proposition 1 (Soundness with Respect to Naive Necessary Causality). *Let* $((\mathbf{S}, (\mathbb{B}, \mathcal{B})), \mathcal{P})$ *be a consistently specified system and* $L = (\mathbb{O}, \mathcal{L})$ *be a log as specified in Definition 8. Assume that there exists* $e \in \mathbb{B}$ *such that* $\{e\}$ *is a naive necessary cause for the violation of* $\mathcal{P}$ *in* $\mathcal{B}$. *Then* $\mathcal{X} = e$ *is a necessary cause of the violation of* $\mathcal{P}$ *in* L.

Proof. By definition of naive necessary causality, e belongs to all faulty configurations. Hence, we have $\mathcal{B} \setminus \mathcal{P} = \mathcal{X}$. Since $L \odot B \nsubseteq \mathcal{P}$ (by Definition 8), we have $(L \odot B) \cap \mathcal{X} \neq \emptyset$ and thus $\mathsf{CF}_{\mathcal{X}}(\mathcal{L}) \subseteq \mathcal{P}$, as required.

Example 5. Returning to our simple example in Fig. 1, it is easy to check that $\mathcal{X} = \mathtt{f2}$ is identified as a naive necessary cause for the violation of $\mathcal{P} = \neg f$ in $\mathcal{B}$, and as a necessary cause for the violation of $\mathcal{P}$ in L using any counterfactual operation meeting Condition 1. Note that in a system consisting of two copies of the Petri Net in Fig. 1 running in parallel, with the second copy having primed events $\mathtt{x}'$ where the first has event $\mathtt{x}$, $\mathcal{X} = \mathtt{f2}$ is still identified as a necessary cause for the violation of $\mathcal{P}' = \mathtt{f} \vee \mathtt{f}'$ in L using any counterfactual operation meeting Condition 1, but is *not* a naive necessary cause for the violation of $\mathcal{P}'$ in $\mathcal{B} \parallel \mathcal{B}'$.

Definition 10 (Inevitable). *Given sets C, C' of configurations with $\emptyset \in C$, we call C' inevitable in C if for any $c \in \max C$, any path from $\emptyset$ to c in the Hasse diagram H_C transits by some configuration in C', and only a finite subset of C is reachable from $\emptyset$ in H_C without transiting by some configuration in C'.*

C is inevitably faulty with respect to a predicate P if $C \setminus P$ — that is, a violation of P — is inevitable in C.

Intuitively, a set of configurations is inevitably faulty with respect to P if all its maximal elements can only be reached through some intermediate configuration violating P.

The definition of *sufficient causality* is dual to necessary causality, where in the alternative worlds we remove the failures *not in* $\mathcal{X}$ and verify whether P is *still violated*. In order for the definition to correctly cope with configurations simultaneously encompassing component failures within and outside of $\mathcal{X}$, we only define sufficient causality on the level of components, rather than faulty configurations.

Definition 11 (Sufficient Cause). *Given*

- *a consistently specified system $((\mathbf{S}, B), P)$ with $\mathbf{S} = \langle S_1, ..., S_n \rangle$ and $S_i = (\mathbb{E}_i, C_i)$,*
- *a log $L = (\mathbb{O}, \mathcal{L})$ such that $L \odot B$ is inevitably faulty with respect to P; and*
- *a subset $\mathcal{I} \subseteq [n]$ of components,*

the failures of components in $\mathcal{I}$ are a sufficient cause for the violation of P in L if with $\mathcal{X} \triangleq \{c \in B \mid \exists i \in [n] \setminus \mathcal{I} : c_{\downarrow \mathbb{E}_i} \notin C_i\}$, $CF_{\mathcal{X}}(\mathcal{L})$ is inevitably faulty with respect to P.

That is, the failures of components in $\mathcal{I}$ are a sufficient cause for the violation of P if for the counterfactual scenarios where failures of components other than $\mathcal{I}$ do not occur, a violation of P is still inevitable.

Remark 5. One may wonder whether we have for sufficient causes an equivalent of Proposition 1. Unfortunately, we don't. We can certainly mirror what we did with necessary causality, and define a notion of sufficient cause as *sufficient condition* for a failure, i.e. say that some configuration c is a sufficient cause for a failure f if the occurrence of the events in c inevitably leads to the occurrence of failure f. The two definitions of sufficient and of naive sufficient causality in general lead to different identification of sufficient causes, though. This is because the configuration structures on which inevitable faultiness is verified, are incomparable.

Proposition 2 (Soundness). *If $\mathcal{X}$ is a necessary cause for the violation of P in the log $L = (\mathbb{O}, \mathcal{L})$ then $(L \odot B) \cap \mathcal{X} \neq \emptyset$.*

If the failures of components $\mathcal{I}$ are a sufficient cause for the violation of P in the log $L = (\mathbb{O}, \mathcal{L})$ then $(L \odot B)_{\downarrow \mathbb{E}_i} \not\subseteq C_i$ for some $i \in \mathcal{I}$.

Intuitively, any cause contains some configuration of the log where at least one component has violated its specification.

Proof. Necessary causality: Let $\mathcal{X}$ be such that $(L \odot B) \cap \mathcal{X} = \emptyset$. We show that $\mathcal{X}$ is not a cause. Let $\mathcal{C} = \mathsf{CF}_{\mathcal{X}}(\mathcal{L})$. By hypothesis on $\mathsf{CF}_{\mathcal{X}}$ we have $\mathcal{C} = L \odot B$, thus $\neg(\mathcal{C} \subseteq \mathcal{P})$, and $\mathcal{X}$ is not a cause for the violation of $\mathcal{P}$ in L.

Sufficient causality: Let $\mathcal{I}$ be such that $\forall i \in \mathcal{I}, (L \odot B)_{\downarrow \mathbb{E}_i} \subseteq \mathcal{C}_i$. We have $\mathcal{X} = \{c \in \mathcal{B} \mid \exists i \in [n] \setminus \mathcal{I} : c_{\downarrow \mathbb{E}_i} \notin \mathcal{C}_i\}$. Let $\mathcal{C} = \mathsf{CF}_{\mathcal{X}}(\mathcal{L})$. By hypothesis on $\mathsf{CF}_{\mathcal{X}}$ we have $\mathcal{C} \subseteq \mathcal{B} \setminus \mathcal{X} \ \wedge \ \forall i \in [n] : ((L \odot B)_{\downarrow \mathbb{E}_i} \subseteq \mathcal{C}_i \Rightarrow \mathsf{CF}_{\mathcal{X}}(\mathcal{L})_{\downarrow \mathbb{E}_i} \subseteq \mathcal{C}_i)$, hence $\mathcal{C} \subseteq \mathcal{B} \cap \|_i \mathcal{C}_i$. By consistency of the specification it follows that $\mathsf{CF}_{\mathcal{X}}(\mathcal{L})$ is not inevitably faulty with respect to $\mathcal{P}$, hence the failures of components in $\mathcal{I}$ are not a sufficient cause.

Proposition 3 (Completeness). *Each violation (resp. inevitable violation) of $\mathcal{P}$ in $L \odot B$ has a necessary (resp. sufficient) cause.*

Proof. Necessary causality: Let $\mathcal{X} = \mathcal{B} \setminus \|_i \mathcal{C}_i$ and $\mathcal{C} = \mathsf{CF}_{\mathcal{X}}(\mathcal{L})$. By hypothesis on $\mathsf{CF}_{\mathcal{X}}$ we have $\mathcal{C} \subseteq \mathcal{B} \setminus \mathcal{X}$. Thus, $\mathcal{C}$ contains only observations consistent with executions where all components behave correctly. By consistency of the specification we have $\mathsf{CF}_{\mathcal{X}}(\mathcal{L}) \subseteq \mathcal{P}$, thus $\mathcal{X}$ is a necessary cause for the violation of $\mathcal{P}$ in L.

Sufficient causality: Suppose that $L \odot B$ is inevitably faulty with respect to $\mathcal{P}$, and let $\mathcal{I} = \{i \in [n] \mid (L \odot B)_{\downarrow \mathbb{E}_i} \not\subseteq \mathcal{C}_i\}$. We have $\mathcal{X} = \emptyset$. Let $\mathcal{C} = \mathsf{CF}_{\mathcal{X}}(\mathcal{L})$. By hypothesis on $\mathsf{CF}_{\mathcal{X}}$ we have $\mathcal{C} = L \odot B$. Since $L \odot B$ is inevitably faulty with respect to $\mathcal{P}$, so is $\mathcal{C}$, hence $\mathcal{X}$ is a sufficient cause for the violation of $\mathcal{P}$ in L.

Proposition 4. *If the failures of a subset $\mathcal{I}$ of components are a necessary (resp. sufficient) cause then the failures of components $[n] \setminus \mathcal{I}$ are not a sufficient (resp. necessary) cause.*

Proof. If $\mathcal{X} = \{c \in \mathcal{B} \mid \exists i \in \mathcal{I} : c_{\downarrow \mathbb{E}_i} \notin \mathcal{C}_i\}$ is a necessary cause then $\mathsf{CF}_{\mathcal{X}}(\mathcal{L}) \subseteq \mathcal{P}$, thus $\mathsf{CF}_{\mathcal{X}}(\mathcal{L})$ is not inevitably faulty, thus $[n] \setminus \mathcal{I}$ is not a sufficient cause.

Conversely, if $\mathcal{I}$ is a sufficient cause then $\mathsf{CF}_{\mathcal{X}}(\mathcal{L})$, with $\mathcal{X} = \{c \in \mathcal{B} \mid \exists i \in [n] \setminus \mathcal{I} : c_{\downarrow \mathbb{E}_i} \notin \mathcal{C}_i\}$, is inevitably faulty with respect to $\mathcal{P}$, hence $\neg(\mathsf{CF}_{\mathcal{X}}(\mathcal{L}) \subseteq \mathcal{P})$, and $[n] \setminus \mathcal{I}$ is not a necessary cause.

4   An Instantiation

Following Stalnaker's and Lewis' *closest world assumption* [14, 18], $\mathcal{X}$ is a cause for the violation of $\mathcal{P}$ if among the worlds (that is, alternative behaviors) where $\mathcal{X}$ is true, some world where $\mathcal{P}$ is violated is *closer* to the actual world L than any world where $\mathcal{P}$ holds. In this section we first illustrate with Example 6 why "closeness" of the counterfactuals is important also in our framework, and then propose a concrete definition for $\mathsf{CF}_{\mathcal{X}}$. The goal of this instantiation is to construct from L — in the spirit of the closest world assumption — a counterfactual configuration structure where exactly the faults $\mathcal{X}$ to be checked for causality and their effects are eliminated and replaced with correct behaviors.

The following example illustrates that, with the extreme choices of $\mathsf{CF}_{\mathcal{X}}$ satisfying Condition (1), Definitions 8 and 11 do not pinpoint the expected cause.

Example 6 (Extreme choices of $\mathsf{CF}_{\mathcal{X}}$). Let us illustrate why the extreme choices of $\mathsf{CF}_{\mathcal{X}}$ satisfying Condition (1) are not useful in practice.

First, take $\mathsf{CF}^1_{\mathcal{X}}(\mathcal{L}) = \{\emptyset\}$ and consider the component alphabets $\mathbb{E}_i = \{f_i\}$ and component specifications $\mathcal{C}_i = \{\emptyset\}$, $i = 1, 2$, the behavioral model $\mathcal{B} = \{\emptyset, \{f_1\}, \{f_2\}, \{f_2, f_3\}\}$, the property $\mathcal{P} = \neg(f_1 \vee f_2)$, the log $L = (\mathbb{E}, \mathcal{L})$ with $\mathbb{E} = \mathbb{E}_1 \cup \mathbb{E}_2$ and $\mathcal{L} = \{\emptyset, \{f_1\}, \{f_1, f_2\}\}$, and $\mathcal{X} = f_1$. Intuitively, both components produce a fault event f_i, each of which is sufficient to violate $\mathcal{P}$. The counterfactual configuration structure where $\mathcal{X}$ does not happen is $\mathsf{CF}^1_{\mathcal{X}}(\mathcal{L}) = \{\emptyset\} \subseteq \mathcal{P}$, thus $\mathcal{X}$ is (wrongly) considered as a necessary cause. This is because $\mathsf{CF}^1_{\mathcal{X}}$ discards all configurations of $\mathcal{L}$, resulting in complete loss of information about the observed behavior of the second component. In other words, $\mathsf{CF}^1_{\mathcal{X}}$ is not a closest world to L where $\mathcal{X}$ does not happen. Similarly, f_2 is not recognized as a sufficient cause since $\mathsf{CF}^1_{\mathcal{X}}$ is not inevitably faulty with respect to $\mathcal{P}$.

Now take $\mathsf{CF}^2_{\mathcal{X}}(\mathcal{L}) = \{c \in \mathcal{B} \setminus \mathcal{X} \mid \forall i \in [n] : (L \odot B)_{\downarrow \mathbb{E}_i} \subseteq \mathcal{C}_i \Rightarrow c_{\downarrow \mathbb{E}_i} \in \mathcal{C}_i\}$ and consider the component specifications $(\mathbb{E}_i, \mathcal{C}_i)$, $i = 1, 2$, with $\mathbb{E}_1 = \{f_1\}$, $\mathbb{E}_2 = \{f_2, f_3\}$, and $\mathcal{C}_i = \{\emptyset\}$, $i = 1, 2$, the behavioral model $\mathcal{B} = 2^{\mathbb{E}}$ with $\mathbb{E} = \mathbb{E}_1 \cup \mathbb{E}_2$, the property $\mathcal{P} = \neg(f_1 \vee f_3)$, the log $(\mathbb{E}, \mathcal{L}')$ with $\mathcal{L}' = \{\emptyset, \{f_1\}, \{f_2\}\}$, and $\mathcal{X} = f_1$. Intuitively, the first component is faulty and violates $\mathcal{P}$, whereas the second component is faulty but does not contribute to the violation of $\mathcal{P}$. The counterfactual configuration structure where $\mathcal{X}$ does not happen is $\mathsf{CF}^2_{\mathcal{X}}(\mathcal{L}') = \{\emptyset, \{f_2\}, \{f_3\}, \{f_2, f_3\}\}$. The occurrence of f_3 violates $\mathcal{P}$, thus $\mathcal{X}$ is (wrongly) not considered as a necessary cause. This is because $\mathsf{CF}^2_{\mathcal{X}}$ encompasses all configurations not satisfying $\mathcal{X}$, including those where the second component fails with f_3, in contrast to its observed behavior.

We now develop a concrete definition of $\mathsf{CF}_{\mathcal{X}}$ where the set of counterfactuals is represented by a configuration structure computed by the composition of a *pruning* and a *grafting* operations. Pruning restricts the faulty configurations in $(L \odot B) \cap \mathcal{X}$ to the maximal non-faulty sub-configurations, while remembering the original configuration.

Definition 12 (Pruning). *The* pruning *of a log $L = (\mathbb{O}, \mathcal{L})$ with respect to a predicate $\mathcal{X}$ is*

$$L / \mathcal{X} = \{(c', c \setminus c') \mid c \in L \odot B \wedge c' \text{ is a maximal subset of } c \text{ s.t. }$$
$$\neg \mathcal{X}(c') \wedge \forall i \in [n] : c'_{\downarrow \mathbb{E}_i} \in \mathcal{B}_{\downarrow \mathbb{E}_i}\}$$

Example 7. For $L = (\mathbb{O}, \mathcal{L})$ with $\mathcal{L} = \{\emptyset, \{f_1, f_2\}\}$, $\mathcal{B} = \{\emptyset, \{f_1\}, \{f_2\}, \{f_1, f_2\}\}$, and $\mathcal{X} = \{\{f_1, f_2\}\}$ we have $L / \mathcal{X} = \{(\emptyset, \emptyset), (\{f_1\}, \{f_2\}), (\{f_2\}, \{f_1\})\}$.

Before instantiating the counterfactual operator CF, we introduce an auxiliary function that will be used to remove the effects of a set $\mathcal{X}$ of faulty configurations in the counterfactual model $\mathsf{CF}_{\mathcal{X}}(\mathcal{L})$.

Definition 13 (Predecessor Closure, wf). *Given sets of configurations $\mathcal{C}$ and $\mathcal{C}'$, a configuration $c \in \mathcal{C}$ is* predecessor-closed *in $\mathcal{C}$ with respect to $\mathcal{C}'$ if $c = \emptyset$*

or $\max\{c' \in \mathcal{C}' \mid c' \subsetneq c\} \cap \mathcal{C} \neq \emptyset$. *We say that $\mathcal{C}$ is predecessor-closed with respect to $\mathcal{C}'$ if all its elements are predecessor-closed with respect to $\mathcal{C}'$. Let $wf_{\mathcal{C}'}(\mathcal{C})$ be the greatest transitively predecessor-closed subset of $\mathcal{C}$ with respect to $\mathcal{C}'$.*

Intuitively, a configuration $c \in \mathcal{C}$ is *predecessor-closed* in $\mathcal{C}$ with respect to $\mathcal{C}'$ if some immediate predecessor of c in $\mathcal{C}'$ is in $\mathcal{C}$.

Example 8. For $\mathcal{C} = \{\emptyset, \{a, b\}, \{d\}, \{c, d\}\}$ and $\mathcal{C}' = \{\emptyset, \{a\}, \{a, b\}, \{c\}, \{c, d\}\}$ we have $wf_{\mathcal{C}'}(\mathcal{C}) = \{\emptyset, \{d\}, \{c, d\}\}$.

The goal of grafting is to construct from $L/\mathcal{X}$ a configuration structure modeling the alternative behaviors where the configurations in $\mathcal{X}$ do not occur.

Definition 14 (Grafting). *Let $\mathbf{S}$ be a vector of component specifications $S_i = (\mathbb{E}_i, \mathcal{C}_i)$. The grafting of a set of tuples S — obtained by pruning $\mathcal{L}$ with respect to a set $\mathcal{X}$ — with a set of configurations $\mathcal{C}$ is $S \triangleright_{\mathcal{L},\mathcal{X},\mathbf{S}} \mathcal{C} = wf_{\mathcal{B}}(Y)$ where*

$$Y = \{c \mid (c, \emptyset) \in S\} \cup \{c \in \mathcal{C} \setminus \mathcal{X} \mid \exists (c', c'') \in S : c'' \neq \emptyset \wedge c' \subseteq c \wedge \quad (2)$$

$$\forall i : \big(c''_{\downarrow \mathbb{E}_i} = \emptyset \Rightarrow c_{\downarrow \mathbb{E}_i} = c'_{\downarrow \mathbb{E}_i}\big) \wedge \quad (3)$$

$$\big((c' \cup c'')_{\downarrow \mathbb{E}_i} \in \mathcal{C}_i \Rightarrow c_{\downarrow \mathbb{E}_i} \in \mathcal{C}_i\big) \wedge \quad (4)$$

$$\big(c_{\downarrow \mathbb{E}_i} \notin \mathcal{C}_i \Rightarrow c_{\downarrow \mathbb{E}_i} = (c' \cup c'')_{\downarrow \mathbb{E}_i}\big)\} \quad (5)$$

That is, the set Y is the union of the unpruned original configurations where $\mathcal{X}$ does not hold, and the configurations of $\mathcal{C}$ that are supersets of some pruned configuration (line (2)). For the latter set, Condition (3) ensures that, for each component, only pruned configurations are grafted. Component configurations of the log that have not been pruned could be observed the same way in the counterfactual model, and are not grafted to stay as close as possible to the observed log. Condition (4) ensures the extensions to preserve invariance of the component specifications, that is, no new component failures are introduced. Condition (5) makes sure that configurations of a component that violate its specification are not grafted since in the absence of a fault model — representing all possible incorrect behaviors — we have no knowledge about how to extend faulty behaviors.

A path in $H_{\mathcal{B}}$ from $\emptyset$ to a configuration $c \in L \odot B$ can be seen as an *explanation* of how c may have been reached in L. Intuitively, configurations that cannot be explained in Y represent effects of $\mathcal{X}$ that would not have occurred without $\mathcal{X}$. The role of $wf_{\mathcal{B}}$ in grafting is to remove those configurations.

Proposition 5. *If $L = (\mathbb{O}, \mathcal{L})$ is such that $L \odot B$ is predecessor-closed with respect to $\mathcal{B}$ then with $\mathsf{CF}_{\mathcal{X}}(L) = (L/\mathcal{X}) \triangleright_{\mathcal{L},\mathcal{X},\mathbf{S}} \mathcal{B}$, Condition (1) is satisfied.*

Proof. If $(L \odot B) \cap \mathcal{X} \neq \emptyset$, the fact that $\mathsf{CF}_{\mathcal{X}}(L) \subseteq \mathcal{B} \setminus \mathcal{X} \wedge \forall i \in [n] : \big((L \odot B)_{\downarrow \mathbb{E}_i} \subseteq \mathcal{C}_i \Rightarrow \mathsf{CF}_{\mathcal{X}}(L)_{\downarrow \mathbb{E}_i} \subseteq \mathcal{C}_i\big)$ follows immediately from the observation that both sets whose union defines Y in Definition 14, exclude any configuration satisfying $\mathcal{X}$, or introducing failures of components that behave correctly in L. On the other hand, if $(L \odot B) \cap \mathcal{X} = \emptyset$ we have $L/\mathcal{X} = \{(c, \emptyset) \mid c \in L \odot B\}$ and $\mathsf{CF}_{\mathcal{X}}(L) = (L/\mathcal{X}) \triangleright_{\mathcal{L},\mathcal{X},\mathbf{S}} \mathcal{B} = wf_{\mathcal{B}}(L \odot B) = L \odot B$.

$L \odot B$ is predecessor-closed with respect to $\mathcal{B}$ for any log that is obtained as the projection $\mathcal{M}_{\downarrow \mathbb{O}}$ of some rooted path $\mathcal{M}$ in $H_{\mathcal{B}}$.

5 Examples

Example 9 (Use of grafting). Consider two components with specifications $(\mathbb{E}_i, \mathcal{C}_i)$ where $\mathbb{E}_i = \{e_i, f_i\}$ and $\mathcal{C}_i = \{\emptyset, \{e_i\}\}$, $i = 1, 2$, the behavioral model $\mathcal{B} = 2^{\mathbb{E}}$ with $\mathbb{E} = \mathbb{E}_1 \cup \mathbb{E}_2$, the property $\mathcal{P} = \neg((f_1 \wedge f_2) \vee (f_1 \wedge e_2) \vee (e_1 \wedge f_2))$ — that is, a failure event f_i becomes fatal once the other component produces some event —, and the log $L = (\mathbb{E}, \mathcal{L})$ with $\mathcal{L} = \{\emptyset, \{f_1\}, \{f_1, f_2\}\}$. In order to check whether $\mathcal{X}_1 = f_1$ is a necessary cause for the violation of $\mathcal{P}$ we compute $L \odot B = \mathcal{L}$, $L/\mathcal{X}_1 = \{(\emptyset, \emptyset), (\emptyset, \{f_1\}), (\{f_2\}, \{f_1\})\}$, and $\mathsf{CF}_{\mathcal{X}_1}(\mathcal{L}) = (L/\mathcal{X}_1) \rhd_{\mathcal{L}, \mathcal{X}_1, \mathbf{S}} \mathcal{B} = wf_{\mathcal{B}}(\{\emptyset, \{e_1\}, \{f_2\}, \{e_1, f_2\}\}) = \{\emptyset, \{e_1\}, \{f_2\}, \{e_1, f_2\}\}$. The obtained configuration structure still violates $\mathcal{P}$, hence $\mathcal{X}_1$ is not a necessary cause for the violation of $\mathcal{P}$. Intuitively, *even if the first component had behaved correctly,* $\mathcal{P}$ would have been violated. Simply taking the projection of $L/\mathcal{X}_1$ on the first configuration of the tuples we would have given the set of configurations $\{\emptyset, \{f_2\}\} \subseteq \mathcal{P}$.

Example 10 (Causal over-determination). Consider a system of two components with the same specifications and behavioral model as in Example 9, the property $\mathcal{P} = \neg(f_1 \vee f_2)$, and the log $L = (\mathbb{E}, \mathcal{L})$ with $\mathcal{L} = \{\emptyset, \{f_1\}, \{f_1, f_2\}\}$. In order to check whether $\mathcal{X}_1 = f_1$ is a necessary cause for the violation of $\mathcal{P}$ we compute $L/\mathcal{X}_1 = \{(\emptyset, \emptyset), (\emptyset, \{f_1\}), (\{f_2\}, \{f_1\})\}$ and $\mathsf{CF}_{\mathcal{X}_1}(\mathcal{L}) = (L/\mathcal{X}_1) \rhd_{\mathcal{L}, \mathcal{X}_1, \mathbf{S}} \mathcal{B} = wf_{\mathcal{B}}(\{\emptyset, \{e_1\}, \{f_2\}, \{e_1, f_2\}\}) = \{\emptyset, \{e_1\}, \{f_2\}, \{e_1, f_2\}\}$. This configuration structure still violates $\mathcal{P}$, hence $\mathcal{X}_1$ is not a necessary cause for the violation of $\mathcal{P}$. Symmetrically, $\mathcal{X}_2 = f_2$ is not a necessary cause either. On the other hand, as $\mathsf{CF}_{\mathcal{X}_1}(\mathcal{L})$ (resp. $\mathsf{CF}_{\mathcal{X}_2}(\mathcal{L})$) is inevitably faulty with respect to $\mathcal{P}$, the failures of the second (resp. first) component are found to be a sufficient cause for the violation of $\mathcal{P}$.

Example 11 (Joint causation). Consider the same component specifications, behavioral model, and log as in Example 10, and the property $\mathcal{P} = \neg(f_1 \wedge f_2)$. In order to check whether $\mathcal{X}_1 = f_1$ is a necessary cause for the violation of $\mathcal{P}$ we compute, as above, $\mathsf{CF}_{\mathcal{X}_1}(\mathcal{L})$ that satisfies our new property, hence $\mathcal{X}_1$ is a necessary cause for the violation of $\mathcal{P}$. As $\mathsf{CF}_{\mathcal{X}_1}(\mathcal{L})$ (resp. $\mathsf{CF}_{\mathcal{X}_2}(\mathcal{L})$) is not inevitably faulty with respect to $\mathcal{P}$, the failure of the second (resp. first) component alone is not a sufficient cause for the violation of $\mathcal{P}$.

Example 12 (Use of wf in grafting). Consider two components with specifications $(\mathbb{E}_i, \mathcal{C}_i)$ where $\mathbb{E}_1 = \{f_1, a\}$, $\mathbb{E}_2 = \{f_2\}$, and $\mathcal{C}_1 = \mathcal{C}_2 = \{\emptyset\}$, with observable events $\mathbb{O} = \{f_1, a, f_2\}$, the behavioral model $\mathcal{B} = \{\emptyset, \{f_1\}, \{f_1, a\}, \{f_2\}, \{f_1, f_2\}, \{f_1, a, f_2\}\}$, the property $\mathcal{P} = \neg(f_1 \wedge a)$, the log $L = (\mathbb{E}_1 \cup \mathbb{E}_2, \mathcal{L})$ with $\mathcal{L} = \{\emptyset, \{f_1\}, \{f_1, f_2\}, \{f_1, a, f_2\}\}$, and $\mathcal{X} = f_1 \wedge \neg a$: both components produce a fault event f_i; the conjunction of f_1 and a violates $\mathcal{P}$. We have $L/\mathcal{X} = \{(\emptyset, \emptyset), (\emptyset, \{f_1\}), (\{f_2\}, \{f_1\}), (\{f_1, a, f_2\}, \emptyset)\}$ and $(L/\mathcal{X}) \rhd_{\mathcal{L}, \mathcal{X}, \mathbf{S}} \mathcal{B} = wf_{\mathcal{B}}(\mathcal{C}) = \{\emptyset, \{f_2\}\} \subseteq \mathcal{P}$, where $\mathcal{C} = \{\emptyset, \{f_2\}, \{f_1, a, f_2\}\}$. Hence $\mathcal{X}$ is a necessary cause. The configuration $\{f_1, a, f_2\}$ is not reachable in $H_{\mathcal{B}}$ by any path passing only through the configurations in $\mathcal{C}$, therefore it is removed by $wf_{\mathcal{B}}$. Without applying $wf_{\mathcal{B}}$ we would have obtained the set of configurations $\mathcal{C}$ that still violates $\mathcal{P}$, thus $\mathcal{X}$ would not be found to be a necessary cause.

Example 13 (Comparison with [7]). Consider three components S (scheduler), C_1 and C_2 (clients) with the following event sets and specifications: $\mathbb{E}_S = \{go_1, go_2\}$, $\mathcal{C}_S = \{\emptyset, \{go_1\}, \{go_2\}\}$, $\mathbb{E}_{C_1} = \{p_1, w_1\}$, $\mathcal{C}_{C_1} = \{\emptyset, \{p_1\}, \{w_1\}\}$ $\mathbb{E}_{C_2} = \{p_2, w_2, f_2\}$, $\mathcal{C}_{C_2} = \{\emptyset, \{p_2\}, \{w_2\}\}$, the behavioral model $\mathcal{B} = (p_1 \Rightarrow go_1) \wedge (p_2 \Rightarrow go_2)$, and the property $\mathcal{P} = \neg(p_1 \wedge p_2) \wedge \neg(w_1 \wedge f_2)$. Intuitively, the scheduler grants one of the components access to some critical section. Client C_i may enter with p_i if it has been granted access, or do w_i. The second component may fail with event f_2. The property requires mutual exclusion, and absence of f_2 in conjunction with w_1. We want to analyze causality of $\mathcal{X} = go_1 \wedge go_2$ on the log $L = (\mathbb{E}_S \cup \mathbb{E}_{C_1} \cup \mathbb{E}_{C_2}, \mathcal{L})$ with $\mathcal{L} = \{\emptyset, \{f_2\}, \{f_2, go_1\}, \{f_2, go_1, p_1\}, \{f_2, go_2\}, \{f_2, go_2, p_2\}, \{f_2, go_1, go_2, p_1\}, \{f_2, go_1, go_2, p_2\}, \{f_2, go_1, go_2, p_1, p_2\}\}$. We have $(L/\mathcal{X}) \triangleright_{\mathcal{L}, \mathcal{X}, \mathbf{s}} \mathcal{B} = \{\emptyset, \{f_2\}, \{f_2, go_1\}, \{f_2, go_1, p_1\}, \{f_2, go_2\}, \{f_2, go_2, p_2\}\}$. Thus, $\mathcal{X}$ is a necessary cause for the violation of $\mathcal{P}$, and the failure f_2 of C_2 is not a sufficient cause.

The trace-based formalism of [7] cannot express the fact that the log does not distinguish any order among go_1 and go_2; if we fix this by introducing a new fault event go_{12}, then the *unaffected prefixes* — that is, the longest prefixes that could have been observed if go_{12} had not occurred — of the vector of component logs $(go_{12}; p_1; f_2.p_2)$ are $(\epsilon; \epsilon; f_2)$, and the set of counterfactual traces includes the vector of component traces $(go_1; w_1; f_2)$ that still violates $\mathcal{P}$. Hence, the fault of the scheduler is (incorrectly) not recognized as a necessary cause due to the fact that the information that the first client actually performed p_1, is lost.

In contrast, in the approach we present here, the use of configuration structures enables us to represent disjunctive counterfactual scenarios as in the example above that share different (sub-)configurations with the log that are incompatible among each other (here, $\{f_2, go_1, p_1\}$ and $\{f_2, go_2, p_2\}$).

Example 14 (Unobservable failure events). Consider the component specifications $(\mathbb{E}_i, \mathcal{C}_i)$ with $\mathbb{E}_1 = \{f_1, e_1\}$, $\mathbb{E}_2 = \{f_2\}$, $\mathbb{E}_3 = \{f_3, e_3\}$, and $\mathcal{C}_i = \{\emptyset\}$, $i = 1, ..., 3$, with observable events $\mathbb{O} = \{e_1, f_2, e_3\}$, the behavioral model $\mathcal{B} = (e_1 \Rightarrow f_1) \wedge (e_3 \Rightarrow f_3)$, the property $\mathcal{P} = \neg(e_1 \vee f_2)$, the log $L = (\mathbb{O}, \mathcal{L})$ with $\mathcal{L} = \{\emptyset, \{e_1\}, \{e_1, e_3\}\}$, and $\mathcal{X} = f_1$. Intuitively, the first and third component produce an unobservable violation of their specification; event e_1 following f_1 violates $\mathcal{P}$, whereas the second component behaves correctly. We have $(L/\mathcal{X}) \triangleright_{\mathcal{L}, \mathcal{X}, \mathbf{s}} \mathcal{B} = \{\emptyset, \{f_3\}, \{f_3, e_3\}\} \subseteq \mathcal{P}$, thus $\mathcal{X}$ is correctly recognized as a necessary cause.

Example 15 (Running example). For Example 3, $L = (\mathbb{O}, \mathcal{L})$ with $\mathcal{L} = \{\emptyset, \{\mathtt{f1}\}, \{\mathtt{f1}, \mathtt{f}\}\}$, $\mathcal{X}_1 = \mathtt{f1}$, and the property $\mathcal{P} = \neg\mathtt{f}$ we obtain $L/\mathcal{X}_1 = \{(\emptyset, \emptyset), (\emptyset, \{f_1\}), (\emptyset, \{f_1, r\}), (\{f_2\}, \{f_1, r\}), (\{f_2, f\}, \{f_1, r\})\}$ and $\mathsf{CF}_{\mathcal{X}_1}(\mathcal{L}) = (L/\mathcal{X}_1) \triangleright_{\mathcal{L}, \mathcal{X}_1, \mathbf{s}} \mathcal{B} = \{\emptyset, \{\mathtt{g}\}, \{\mathtt{g}, \mathtt{f2}\}, \{\mathtt{g}, \mathtt{f2}, \mathtt{f}\}\}$ which still violates $\mathcal{P}$, hence $\mathcal{X}_1$ is not a necessary cause for the violation of $\mathcal{P}$. On the other hand, for $\mathcal{X}_2 = \mathtt{f2}$ we have $\mathsf{CF}_{\mathcal{X}_2}(\mathcal{L}) =$

$(L/\mathcal{X}_2) \rhd_{\mathcal{L},\mathcal{X}_1,\mathbf{s}} \mathcal{B} = \{\emptyset, \{\mathtt{f1}\}, \{\mathtt{f1,r}\}, \{\mathtt{f1,r,s}\}\} \subseteq \mathcal{P}$, hence $\mathcal{X}_2$ is a necessary cause. Conversely, as $\mathsf{CF}_{\mathcal{X}_1}(\mathcal{L})$ is inevitably faulty whereas $\mathsf{CF}_{\mathcal{X}_2}(\mathcal{L})$ is not, the failure of the second component is a sufficient cause but not the failure of the first component.

6 Related Work

As we remarked in the introduction, fault diagnosis is an active research field, with diverse questions and techniques drawn from different areas, including concurrency theory, discrete event systems, artificial intelligence, and control theory. We consider in this section only what we believe to be the most relevant works in these areas.

With respect to the techniques we use, our work is clearly related to works on diagnosis in discrete event systems [5,21] and specifically diagnosis via unfolding [9]. The diagnosis questions in these works are actually very different from ours. They include *diagnosability* questions, which amount to determining the possible occurrence of (types of) hidden faults from the observation of executions, and *explanation* questions, which amount to determining which (prefix of) executions are compatible with observations recorded in a given log. Finding explanations is the key objective in the work by Haar et al. [3,9]. In the terms of our framework, their goal is to find efficient algorithms (using Petri net unfolding techniques) for computing prefixes of $L \odot B$, where L records observed configurations, and B is the system specification. They also extended their techniques to finding explanations in systems with evolving topology [1], which we do not consider in this paper. To the best of our knowledge, these works do not consider fault ascription as we do here.

Closest to our approach on fault ascription are [7,20], which also target fault ascription, and share a similar setting of black-box components equipped with specifications, and a log in the form of a vector of component traces. In contrast to the work presented here these works do not consider unobservable events, they are limited to linear component traces and, as pointed out in Example 13, they use a construction of the (sub-)configurations shared between the log and the counterfactuals that may result in either loss of information or inconsistencies in the counterfactual scenarios.

With their definition of *actual causality* based on a model of *structural equations* over a set of propositional variables [11], Halpern and Pearl have proposed the most influential definition of causality in computer science to date. Intuitively, the observed values of a set X of variables is an actual cause for an observed property φ if with different values of X, φ would not hold, and there exists a contingency in which the observed values of X entail φ. At first glance, it would seem that the notion of actual causality does not coincide with our notions of necessary and sufficient causality, but pinpointing the exact reasons for the difference, and characterizing the situations leading to different results, appears non-trivial, and we leave this as a question for further study.

Several approaches use [11] to encode and analyze execution traces. [2] determines potential causes for the first violation of an LTL formula by a trace.

As [11] only considers a propositional setting without any temporal connectors, the trace is modeled as a matrix of propositional variables. The structure of the formula is used as a model to determine which events may have caused the violation of the property. The reported causes are, in general, neither necessary nor sufficient. [13] extends the definition of actual causality to totally ordered sequences of events, and uses this definition to construct from a set of traces a probabilistic fault tree. The accuracy of the diagnostic depends on the number of traces used to construct the model.

The use of a distance metric is explored in [8] to localize, from a counter-example from model-checking, a possible fault as the difference between the error trace and a closest correct trace. This work features a "white box" approach that relies on access to source code, with no component specification.

7   Conclusion

We have presented in this paper a general framework for fault ascription, based on configuration structures. The framework supports the definition of analyses providing notions of necessary and sufficient causes for failures in component-based systems. Analyses in our framework relies on operators $\mathsf{CF}_\mathcal{X}$ for constructing counterfactual configurations, which we characterize abstractly via a simple constraint. The key contribution of this framework lies in the definition of notions of necessary and sufficient causality relative to an observed execution, recorded in a log, which we prove to be sound (each necessary or sufficient cause indeed explains an observed failure by some component failures) and complete (each failure has a necessary cause and a sufficient cause). We have also presented an instantiation of the framework that presents pruning and grafting constructions used to define a non-trivial counterfactual operator. Our framework generalizes previous works on fault ascription based on traces [7,20], and we have shown by means of an example that our pruning and grafting constructions help solve the problem of inaccurate counterfactuals — leading to inconsistencies or loss of information — inherent in the trace-based approach.

Much work remains to be done however. For a start, we intend to formalize a symbolic algorithm implementing our definitions of fault ascription directly on Petri nets and synchronized products of transition systems, similar to the symbolic approach to fault ascription in real-time systems of [6] based on timed automata. For increased precision, we intend to leverage in our analysis techniques developed for fault diagnosis, especially those relying on unfolding [9]. Finally, following up the work of Baldan et al. on fault diagnosis in systems with evolving topology [1], we intend to extend our framework and causal analysis for fault ascription to dynamically configurable systems.

References

1. Baldan, P., Chatain, T., Haar, S., König, B.: Unfolding-based diagnosis of systems with an evolving topology. In: van Breugel, F., Chechik, M. (eds.) CONCUR 2008. LNCS, vol. 5201, pp. 203–217. Springer, Heidelberg (2008)

2. Beer, I., Ben-David, S., Chockler, H., Orni, A., Trefler, R.J.: Explaining counterexamples using causality. Formal Methods Syst. Des. **40**(1), 20–40 (2012)
3. Benveniste, A., Haar, S., Fabre, E., Jard, C.: Distributed monitoring of concurrent and asynchronous systems. In: Amadio, R.M., Lugiez, D. (eds.) CONCUR 2003. LNCS, vol. 2761, pp. 1–26. Springer, Heidelberg (2003)
4. Brennan, A.: Necessary and sufficient conditions. In: Zalta, E.N., (ed.) The Stanford Encyclopedia of Philosophy. Winter 2012 (edn.) (2012)
5. Cassandras, C.G., Lafortune, S.: Introduction to Discrete Event Systems, 2nd edn. Springer, New York (2008)
6. Gössler, G., Astefanoaei, L.: Blaming in component-based real-time systems. In: 2014 International Conference on Embedded Software, EMSOFT. IEEE (2014)
7. Gössler, G., Le Métayer, D.: A general framework for blaming in component-based systems. Sci. Comput. Program. **113**, 223–235 (2015). (in Press)
8. Groce, A., Chaki, S., Kroening, D., Strichman, O.: Error explanation with distance metrics. STTT **8**(3), 229–247 (2006)
9. Haar, S., Fabre, E.: Diagnosis with petri net unfoldings. In: Seatzu, C., Silva Suárez, M., van Schuppen, J.H. (eds.) Control of Discrete-event Systems. LNCIS, vol. 433, pp. 301–318. Springer, Heidelberg (2013)
10. Halpern, T.Y., Hitchcock, C.: Graded causation and defaults. CoRR (2013). abs/1309.1226
11. Halpern, J.Y., Pearl, J.: Causes and explanations: a structural approach. part i: causes. Br. J. Philos. Sci. **56**(4), 843–887 (2005)
12. Hwang, I., Kim, S., Kim, Y., Seah, C.E.: A survey of fault detection, isolation and reconfiguration methods. IEEE Trans. Control Syst. Technol. **18**(3), 636–653 (2010)
13. Kuntz, M., Leitner-Fischer, F., Leue, S.: From probabilistic counterexamples via causality to fault trees. In: Flammini, F., Bologna, S., Vittorini, V. (eds.) SAFECOMP 2011. LNCS, vol. 6894, pp. 71–84. Springer, Heidelberg (2011)
14. Lewis, D.: Counterfactuals, 2nd edn. Blackwell, Oxford (2000)
15. Le Métayer, D., Maarek, M., et al.: Liability issues in software engineering: the use of formal methods to reduce legal uncertainties. Commun. ACM **54**(4), 99–106 (2011)
16. Pearl, J.: Causality: Models, Reasoning and Inference, 2nd edn. Cambridge University Press, Cambridge (2009)
17. Reiter, R.: A theory of diagnosis from first principles. Artif. Intell. **32**(1), 57–95 (1987)
18. Stalnaker, R.: A Theory of Conditionals. Studies in Logical Theory. Blackwell, Oxford (1968)
19. van Glabbeek, R.J., Plotkin, G.D.: Configuration structures, event structures and petri nets. Theor. Comput. Sci. **410**(41), 4111–4159 (2009)
20. Wang, S., Ayoub, A., Ivanov, R., Sokolsky, O., Lee, I.: Contract-based blame assignment by trace analysis. In: 2nd ACM Interational Conference HiCoNS. ACM (2013)
21. Zaytoon, J., Lafortune, S.: Overview of fault diagnosis methods for discrete event systems. Ann. Rev. Control **37**(2), 308–320 (2013)

Disjunctive Information Flow
for Communicating Processes

Ximeng Li[1]([✉]), Flemming Nielson[1], Hanne Riis Nielson[1], and Xinyu Feng[2]

[1] DTU Compute, Technical University of Denmark, Kongens Lyngby, Denmark
{ximl,fnie,hrni}@dtu.dk
[2] University of Science and Technology of China, Hefei, China
xyfeng@ustc.edu.cn

Abstract. The security validation of practical computer systems calls for the ability to specify and verify information flow policies that are dependent on data content. Such policies play an important role in concurrent, communicating systems: consider a scenario where messages are sent to different processes according to their tagging. We devise a security type system that enforces content-dependent information flow policies in the presence of communication and concurrency. The type system soundly guarantees a compositional noninterference property. All theoretical results have been formally proved in the Coq proof assistant [9].

1 Introduction

Language-based information flow control [27] aims to provide end-to-end guarantees against inadvertent information leakage in the execution of programs. The security enforcement is usually achieved by static type systems [32], dynamic monitoring [13], or a mixture of both [4]. The security guarantee is usually provided by noninterference properties (e.g., [10,26]) requiring that the public parts of a system should stay invariant against variations in the confidential parts [8]. The area has gained practical impact in securing voting systems [7], cryptographic implementations such as RSA encryption (e.g., [27]), and in the end-to-end confidentiality enforcement in real-world programming languages like PHP [18] and JavaScript [3,15].

In recent years, an emerging concern in information flow control is the enforcement of content-dependent flow policies ([1,6,20]). In this setting, different security classes are assigned to a variable under different memory contents. Content-dependent policies are useful in concurrent systems — consider processes exchanging messages whose destinations depend on their tagging. However, despite all the aforementioned existing work (all in a sequential setting), the interaction between content-dependent policies on the one hand, and concurrency and communication on the other, is largely unexplored so far.

In this paper, we enforce content-dependent information flow policies in a concurrent language, where processes make use of local variables and communicate with each other to share information. The selection of relevant policies

© Springer International Publishing Switzerland 2016
P. Ganty and M. Loreti (Eds.): TGC 2015, LNCS 9533, pp. 95–111, 2016.
DOI: 10.1007/978-3-319-28766-9_7

at each program point is achieved with the help of a Hoare logic [2] component in our information flow type system. We consider synchronous communication much in the manner of a process calculus like CCS [23]. The types of communication channels act as bridges between the modular typing of the individual processes. The *presence* and *content* of communication behaviors are treated separately (e.g., [21,24]), which leads to a more flexible confidentiality enforcement, and a more intuitive formulation of noninterference property (termed "communication-aware security") that is bisimulation-based, progress-sensitive [16], and *compositional*.

This paper is structured as follows. A motivating example where a multiplexer and a demultiplexer communicate with each other, is introduced in Sect. 2. We then introduce the simple concurrent language used throughout our development in Sect. 3. Our security policies, termed *disjunctive policies*, are introduced in Sect. 4. This is followed by the presentation of our information flow type system in Sect. 5, and noninterference property in Sect. 6. The security of the motivating example is guaranteed by its well-typedness. We conclude and discuss certain elements of our development and related work in Sect. 7.

All theoretical results in this paper have been formally proved[1] in the Coq proof assistant [9].

2   Motivating Example

The MILS security architecture [25] aims to achieve controlled information flow between different system partitions that share certain resources. A typical kind of shared component is a multiplexer (e.g., [12]) that directs confidential input from partition I to confidential output to partition II, and public input from partition III to public output to partition IV. Separation between confidential traffic and public traffic is to be enforced.

Consider a (simple-minded) concretization of this scenario with the processes in Fig. 1. A multiplexer process (S_M) wraps up the source data in x_1 or x_2, along with tags 1 and 2 respectively, and forwards it over the dyadic channel c to a demultiplexer process (S_D). The demultiplexer will then unwrap the data and forward it to the sinks z_1 or z_2, depending on the tag value.

Multiplexer (S_M) : while true do   Demultiplexer (S_D) : while true do
           $c!(1, x_1)$; $c?(y, z)$;
           $c!(2, x_2)$ if $y = 1$
                                        then $z_1 := z$
                                        else $z_2 := z$

Fig. 1. The code for the multiplexer and the demultiplexer

---

[1] The proof script is accessible at http://lbtweb.pbworks.com/w/file/fetch/97133580/dif_com_coq.zip.

Suppose the variable x_1 is confidential, whereas x_2 is public. The information flow analysis should then reveal that z_1 needs to be confidential, while z_2 can be public.

For modularity reasons, a *type-based analysis* needs to assign a confidentiality level to the channel c, to be able to type S_M and S_D separately. In the demultiplexer process S_D, both z_1 and z_2 obtain data from c, depending on whether the tag is 1 or not. It would then be desirable for the type system to have the knowledge that *either* c is confidential and communicating $(1, \_)$, *or* c is public and communicating $(2, \_)$. This is precisely what our disjunctive policies aim to capture, in the setting of concurrent systems.

Moreover, when it is said that "c is confidential", what is actually meant is that it communicates confidential *content*. The observation of the mere *presence* of any communication action over c, without observing the content communicated, does not jeopardize the confidentiality of x_1. We thus distinguish between the presence and content of channel communication (e.g., [19,21]), for a more fine-grained, permissive enforcement of our disjunctive policies.

3   The Language

We introduce the concurrent imperative language to be used, and specify its structural operational semantics.

Syntax. A system Σ consists of a fixed number of concurrent processes. All variables are local to their own processes, and information sharing is achieved by means of communication.

All processes are assumed to have distinct identifiers in $\{1, 2, \dots\}$. For a system Σ with the set $Pid(\Sigma)$ of process identifiers, its set of variables can thus be denoted by $\mathbf{Var}_\Sigma = \biguplus_{i \in Pid(\Sigma)} \mathbf{Var}_{\Sigma,i}$, where the process with identifier i can only use variables from $\mathbf{Var}_{\Sigma,i}$. For communication, the set of polyadic channels is $\mathbf{PCh}$ and the set of atomic channels is $\mathbf{Ch} = \{c.1, \cdots, c.m \mid c \in \mathbf{PCh}$, and c has arity $m\}$.

We write x, y, z for variables, X for sets of variables, c for either a polyadic channel name or an atomic channel name (it will always be clear from the context which is the case), n for unspecified constants, op for unspecified arithmetic operators, rel for unspecified relational operators, and $\mathbf{tt}$ for the boolean constant denoting truth. The set of variables contained in an arithmetic expression a (resp. boolean expression b) is $fv(a)$ (resp. $fv(b)$).

The syntax of our language is given by:

$$a ::= n \mid x \mid a_1 \; op \; a_2$$
$$b ::= \mathbf{tt} \mid a_1 \; rel \; a_2 \mid b_1 \wedge b_2 \mid \neg b$$
$$S ::= \mathsf{nil} \mid \mathsf{skip} \mid x := a \mid S_1; S_2 \mid \mathsf{if}\ b\ \mathsf{then}\ S_1\ \mathsf{else}\ S_2 \mid \mathsf{while}\ b\ \mathsf{do}\ S \mid c?x \mid c!a$$
$$\Sigma ::= i : S_i \mid \Sigma_1 || \Sigma_2 \mid \Sigma \setminus \Omega$$

Sequential processes S can contain communication binders: $c!\boldsymbol{a}$ for output of the vector $\boldsymbol{a}$ of arithmetic expressions over the polyadic channel c and $c?\boldsymbol{x}$ for input from the polyadic channel c into the vector $\boldsymbol{x}$ of variables. The process nil is an inert process that cannot perform any computation.

Systems are composed of concurrent, communicating processes. The construct $i : S_i$ represents a process running the statement S_i, with process identifier i. The construct $\Sigma_1 || \Sigma_2$ represents two systems running concurrently. We require $Pid(\Sigma_1) \cap Pid(\Sigma_2) = \emptyset$ for the well-formedness of $\Sigma_1 || \Sigma_2$. Finally the construct $\Sigma \setminus \Omega$ is the system that can perform all the input/output actions of Σ provided that those actions are not over the polyadic channels in Ω. This last construct is similar to the CCS restriction operator [23], whose introduction allows to specify whether each channel used by a process is shared with another process or with the environment.

Table 1. Small-step semantics of processes and systems.

$$\vdash_i \langle \text{skip}; \sigma \rangle \xrightarrow{\tau} \langle \text{nil}; \sigma \rangle \qquad\qquad \vdash_i \langle x := a; \sigma \rangle \xrightarrow{\tau} \langle \text{nil}; \sigma[x \mapsto \mathcal{A}[\![a]\!]\sigma] \rangle$$

$$\vdash_i \langle c!\boldsymbol{a}; \sigma \rangle \xrightarrow{c!\boldsymbol{v}} \langle \text{nil}; \sigma \rangle \ \text{ if } \boldsymbol{v} = \mathcal{A}[\![\boldsymbol{a}]\!]\sigma \qquad \vdash_i \langle c?\boldsymbol{x}; \sigma \rangle \xrightarrow{c?\boldsymbol{v}} \langle \text{nil}; \sigma[\boldsymbol{x} \mapsto \boldsymbol{v}] \rangle$$

$$\frac{\vdash_i \langle S_1; \sigma \rangle \xrightarrow{\alpha} \langle S_1'; \sigma' \rangle}{\vdash_i \langle S_1; S_2; \sigma \rangle \xrightarrow{\alpha} \langle S_1'; S_2; \sigma' \rangle} \ \text{if } S_1' \neq \text{nil} \qquad \frac{\vdash_i \langle S_1; \sigma \rangle \xrightarrow{\alpha} \langle \text{nil}; \sigma' \rangle}{\vdash_i \langle S_1; S_2; \sigma \rangle \xrightarrow{\alpha} \langle S_2; \sigma' \rangle}$$

$$\vdash_i \langle \text{if } b \text{ then } S_1 \text{ else } S_2; \sigma \rangle \xrightarrow{\tau} \langle S_1; \sigma \rangle \ \text{ if } \mathcal{B}[\![b]\!]\sigma = \mathbf{tt}$$

$$\vdash_i \langle \text{if } b \text{ then } S_1 \text{ else } S_2; \sigma \rangle \xrightarrow{\tau} \langle S_2; \sigma \rangle \ \text{ if } \mathcal{B}[\![b]\!]\sigma = \mathbf{ff}$$

$$\vdash_i \langle \text{while } b \text{ do } S; \sigma \rangle \xrightarrow{\tau} \langle (S; \text{while } b \text{ do } S); \sigma \rangle \ \text{ if } \mathcal{B}[\![b]\!]\sigma = \mathbf{tt}$$

$$\vdash_i \langle \text{while } b \text{ do } S; \sigma \rangle \xrightarrow{\tau} \langle \text{nil}; \sigma \rangle \ \text{ if } \mathcal{B}[\![b]\!]\sigma = \mathbf{ff}$$

$$\frac{\vdash_i \langle S_i; \sigma \rangle \xrightarrow{\alpha} \langle S_i'; \sigma' \rangle}{\langle i : S_i; \sigma \rangle \xrightarrow{\alpha}_i \langle i : S_i'; \sigma' \rangle} \qquad \frac{\langle \Sigma; \sigma \rangle \xrightarrow{\alpha}_\eta \langle \Sigma'; \sigma' \rangle}{\langle \Sigma \setminus \Omega; \sigma \rangle \xrightarrow{\alpha}_\eta \langle \Sigma' \setminus \Omega; \sigma' \rangle} \ \text{if } ch(\alpha) \notin \Omega$$

$$\frac{\langle \Sigma_1; \sigma_1 \rangle \xrightarrow{c\rho\boldsymbol{v}}_i \langle \Sigma_1'; \sigma_1' \rangle \ \langle \Sigma_2; \sigma_2 \rangle \xrightarrow{c\bar{\rho}\boldsymbol{v}}_j \langle \Sigma_2'; \sigma_2' \rangle}{\langle \Sigma_1 || \Sigma_2; \sigma_1 \uplus \sigma_2 \rangle \xrightarrow{\tau}_{i,j} \langle \Sigma_1' || \Sigma_2'; \sigma_1' \uplus \sigma_2' \rangle} \ \text{where } \rho \in \{!, ?\}$$

$$\frac{\langle \Sigma_1; \sigma_1 \rangle \xrightarrow{\alpha}_\eta \langle \Sigma_1'; \sigma_1' \rangle}{\langle \Sigma_1 || \Sigma_2; \sigma_1 \uplus \sigma_2 \rangle \xrightarrow{\alpha}_\eta \langle \Sigma_1' || \Sigma_2; \sigma_1' \uplus \sigma_2 \rangle} \qquad \frac{\langle \Sigma_2; \sigma_2 \rangle \xrightarrow{\alpha}_\eta \langle \Sigma_2'; \sigma_2' \rangle}{\langle \Sigma_1 || \Sigma_2; \sigma_1 \uplus \sigma_2 \rangle \xrightarrow{\alpha}_\eta \langle \Sigma_1 || \Sigma_2'; \sigma_1 \uplus \sigma_2' \rangle}$$

Semantics. The structural operational semantics of our language is presented in Table 1. In order to handle communication, the transitions are annotated with the *action* taking place; an action α takes one of three forms: $c!\boldsymbol{v}$ (for output over c), $c?\boldsymbol{v}$ (for input over c) or τ (for the remaining cases) where $\boldsymbol{v} \in \mathbf{Val}^\star$ denotes the sequence of values being communicated over the channel. We tacitly assume that arities match without having explicitly to require this in the semantics.

The evaluation of arithmetic and boolean expressions is specified using the functions $\mathcal{A}$ and $\mathcal{B}$, respectively.

The general form of the transitions for processes is $\vdash_i \langle S; \sigma \rangle \xrightarrow{\alpha} \langle S'; \sigma' \rangle$, where i is the identifier of the process being executed, and $\sigma, \sigma' \in \mathbf{Var}_{\Sigma,i} \to \mathbf{Val}$. The transition rules are fairly standard.

Lifting the semantics to systems, the configurations take the form $\langle \Sigma; \sigma \rangle$, where we tacitly assume that $\sigma \in \mathbf{St}_\Sigma$, and $\mathbf{St}_\Sigma$ is $\mathbf{Var}_\Sigma \to \mathbf{Val}$. The transitions are of the form $\langle \Sigma; \sigma \rangle \xrightarrow{\alpha}_\eta \langle \Sigma'; \sigma' \rangle$ where η is the list of identifiers for the processes executed. For a polarity ! or ?, we have $\tilde{!} =?$ and $\tilde{?} =!$. For a mapping A, we write $\mathbf{D}_A$ for its domain. For two mappings A and B such that $\mathbf{D}_A \cap \mathbf{D}_B = \emptyset$, we denote by $A \uplus B$ the mapping with domain $\mathbf{D}_A \uplus \mathbf{D}_B$, such that $(A \uplus B)(i) = \begin{cases} A(i) & (\text{if } i \in \mathbf{D}_A) \\ B(i) & (\text{if } i \in \mathbf{D}_B) \end{cases}$. Then the transition rules for systems are mostly self-explanatory. In particular, the second rule says that $\langle \Sigma \setminus \Omega; \sigma \rangle$ can perform an action α of $\langle \Sigma; \sigma \rangle$ if the channel used by α is not in Ω.

Example 1. The combination of the multiplexer and demultiplexer considered in Sect. 2 can be represented by the system $\Sigma_{\mathrm{MD}} = (1 : S_{\mathrm{M}} \,\|\, 2 : S_{\mathrm{D}}) \setminus \{c\}$.   □

4   Security Policies

Each confidentiality level is taken from the two-point confidentiality lattice $\mathbf{Lab_S} = (\{L, H\}, \sqsubseteq)$ where $L \sqsubseteq H$, throughout our development. The level H (resp. L) represents high (resp. low) confidentiality. A generalization to arbitrary security lattices is straightforward but induces notational sophistication; hence we stay with $\mathbf{Lab_S}$. We will also allow to write $\mathbf{Lab_S}$ for the underlying set $\{L, H\}$.

$$\begin{aligned}
\mathcal{P} &= [1 \mapsto \mathcal{P}(1)] \uplus \ldots \uplus [n \mapsto \mathcal{P}(n)] \\
\mathcal{P}(i) &= \{P \mid P = (P_S, P_V), \text{ where } P_S \in \mathbf{Var}_{\Sigma,i} \to \mathbf{Lab_S}, \ P_V \in \mathbf{Lab_F}\} \\[6pt]
\mathcal{P}^{\mathrm{ch}} &= \{P^\circ, P_1^\bullet, P_2^\bullet, ..., P_m^\bullet\} \\
P^\circ &\in \mathbf{PCh} \to \mathbf{Lab_S} \\
P_j^\bullet &= (P_{jS}^\bullet, P_{jV}^\bullet), \text{ where } P_{jS}^\bullet = \mathbf{Ch} \to \mathbf{Lab_S}, \text{ and } P_{jV}^\bullet = \mathbf{Ch} \to \mathbf{Lab_V}
\end{aligned}$$

Fig. 2. The structure of policy environments and policies

The structure of our policies is illustrated by Fig. 2. For systems Σ, we introduce policy environments $\mathcal{P}$ such that for each $i \in Pid(\Sigma)$, $\mathcal{P}(i)$ is a set of policies for the variables in $\mathbf{Var}_{\Sigma,i}$. Each variable policy $P \in \mathcal{P}(i)$ consists of two components, $P_S : \mathbf{Var}_{\Sigma,i} \to \mathbf{Lab_S}$ and $P_V : \mathbf{Lab_F}$, where P_S contains the confidentiality level of each variable in $\mathbf{Var}_{\Sigma,i}$ and P_V is a logical formula describing the possible values of these variables. Given a set $X \subseteq$ $\mathbf{Var}_{\Sigma,i}$, we define $P_{\mathsf{S}}[X]$ as $\bigsqcup_{x \in X} P_{\mathsf{S}}(x)$. We denote by $P \in \mathcal{P}$ the fact that $P \in \{(\biguplus_{i \in \mathbf{D}_{\mathcal{P}}} P_{i\mathsf{S}}, \bigwedge_{i \in \mathbf{D}_{\mathcal{P}}} P_{i\mathsf{V}}) \mid \forall i \in \mathbf{D}_{\mathcal{P}} : P_i \in \mathcal{P}(i)\}$.

We also allow to specify a (global) set $\mathcal{P}^{\mathrm{ch}}$ of channel policies. The set $\mathcal{P}^{\mathrm{ch}}$ has a distinguished member $P^{\circ} : \mathbf{PCh} \to \mathbf{Lab}_{\mathsf{S}}$ that gives the confidentiality level of the "presence" of communications over each polyadic channel. Apart from P°, there is at least one content policy $P^{\bullet} \in \mathcal{P}^{\mathrm{ch}}$. Each $P^{\bullet}$ has two components $P_{\mathsf{S}}^{\bullet} : \mathbf{Ch} \to \mathbf{Lab}_{\mathsf{S}}$ and $P_{\mathsf{V}}^{\bullet} : \mathbf{Ch} \to \mathbf{Lab}_{\mathsf{V}}$, where for each atomic channel c, $P_{\mathsf{S}}^{\bullet}(c)$ is the confidentiality level of the communication contents over c, and $P_{\mathsf{V}}^{\bullet}(c)$ is the set of values potentially communicated over c.

For a variable policy P, P_{V} can capture "relational constraints" between different variables. For instance, given an output $c!(x - y)$, it is valid to have $P_{\mathsf{V}} = (p(x) = p(y))$ where $p(-)$ is the *parity* function. Correspondingly, a channel policy $P^{\bullet}$ may come with *the set of even numbers* for $P_{\mathsf{V}}^{\bullet}(c.1)$.

Each $\mathcal{P}(i)$ ($i \in Pid(\Sigma)$) resembles a disjunctive formula of variable policies (where each policy is a conjunction over the confidentiality and content information provided by it). The same analogy is enjoyed by the set $\mathcal{P}_{\bullet}^{\mathrm{ch}} = \{P^{\bullet} \mid P^{\bullet} \in \mathcal{P}^{\mathrm{ch}}\}$ of content policies for channels. Hence we term our policies *disjunctive policies*. Hereafter, the parameterization on $\mathcal{P}^{\mathrm{ch}}$ in our formulations will often be elided since $\mathcal{P}^{\mathrm{ch}}$ is treated as a global constant. The distinguished presence policy $P^{\circ} \in \mathcal{P}^{\mathrm{ch}}$ will be left implicit for the same reason.

Example 2. We will use the following policies for the multiplexer example presented in Sect. 2, where $\mathbb{Z}$ is the set of all integers.

$$\mathcal{P}_{\mathrm{MD}}(1) = \{P_{\mathrm{m}} = (x_1 : H;\ x_2 : L,\ \mathbf{tt})\}$$
$$\mathcal{P}_{\mathrm{MD}}(2) = \{P_{\mathrm{d}}^1 = (y : L;\ z : H;\ z_1 : H;\ z_2 : L,\ y = 1),$$
$$\qquad\qquad P_{\mathrm{d}}^2 = (y : L;\ z : L;\ z_1 : H;\ z_2 : L,\ y \neq 1)\}$$
$$\mathcal{P}_{\mathrm{MD}}^{\mathrm{ch}} = \{P^{\circ} = (c : L),$$
$$\qquad\quad P_1^{\bullet} = (c.1 : L;\ c.2 : H,\ c.1 : \{1\};\ c.2 : \mathbb{Z}),$$
$$\qquad\quad P_2^{\bullet} = (c.1 : L;\ c.2 : L,\ c.1 : \{2\};\ c.2 : \mathbb{Z})\}$$

For convenience of reference, the policies are named. Take the policy $P_{\mathrm{m}} \in \mathcal{P}_{\mathrm{MD}}(1)$ for example, we have $P_{\mathrm{m}\mathsf{V}} = \mathbf{tt}$ and $P_{\mathrm{m}\mathsf{S}} = [x_1 \mapsto H][x_2 \mapsto L]$. The syntax with colons and semi-colons is used for confidentiality policy components such as $P_{\mathrm{m}\mathsf{S}}$ for conciseness. □

We next define the satisfaction of variable policies by states ($\sigma \models P$), and the satisfaction of channel policies by actions ($\alpha \models_{\rho} P^{\bullet}$). Our concern here is what policies are relevant according to the memory content or communication content. For a vector v, we write $|v|$ for its total number of components, and v_j for the j-th one.

Definition 1 (Satisfaction).

$$\sigma \models P \triangleq \sigma \models P_{\mathsf{V}} \quad (\sigma \text{ is a model of the formula } P_{\mathsf{V}})$$
$$\alpha \models_{\rho} P^{\bullet} \triangleq P^{\bullet} \in \mathcal{P}^{\mathrm{ch}} \wedge \forall c, v : \alpha = c\rho v \Rightarrow \forall j \text{ s.t. } 1 \leq j \leq |v| : v_j \in P_{\mathsf{V}}^{\bullet}(c.j)$$

For channel policies, the satisfaction relation $\models_{\rho}$ is parameterized with a polarity ρ. The intuition is that the check on content is turned on only when the polarity of α is ρ. In this case it is required that the j-th value communicated over the polyadic channel of α should indeed be described by the value component of $P^\bullet$ for the atomic channel $c.j$. If α does not have the polarity ρ, then nothing is required.

5   The Type System

We specify a type system for ensuring that a system Σ respects the information flow policies given by $\mathcal{P}$ (such that $\mathbf{D}_\mathcal{P} = Pid(\Sigma)$) and $\mathcal{P}^{\mathrm{ch}}$. To deal with the value components P_V of policies P, the type system is integrated with a Hoare logic for reasoning about the values of variables [2]. The typing rules for processes and systems are specified in Table 2 in order.

The Typing of Processes. The judgment of the type system for processes has the form $X, l_1 \vdash_\mathcal{K} \{\phi\} S \{\phi'\} : Y, l_2$ where X is a set of variables that may incur implicit flows [11], Y is a set of variables whose information can be leaked through *progress*, $\mathcal{K}$ is the set of variable policies for the process S, and ϕ and ϕ' are the pre- and post-conditions of S in the form of logical formulae over the variables local to S. In addition, l_1 and l_2 are the levels of information that can be leaked through blocked communication attempts (due to inability of synchronization), before reaching S, and within S, respectively. The levels l_1 and l_2 become H when encountering communication channels whose presence levels are H.

In Table 2, $P \preceq P'$ represents $P_\mathsf{S} \sqsubseteq P_\mathsf{S}' \wedge P_\mathsf{V} \Rightarrow P_\mathsf{V}'$, where $P_\mathsf{S} \sqsubseteq P_\mathsf{S}'$ if and only if $\forall u \in \mathbf{D}_{P_\mathsf{S}} \cap \mathbf{D}_{P_\mathsf{S}'} : P_\mathsf{S}(u) \sqsubseteq P_\mathsf{S}'(u)$. We write $P[x \mapsto l]_\mathsf{S}$ for $(P_\mathsf{S}[x \mapsto l], P_\mathsf{V})$, which is an update if $x \in \mathbf{D}_{P_\mathsf{S}}$ and an extension otherwise, $P[u/x]_\mathsf{V}$ for $(P_\mathsf{S}, P_\mathsf{V}[u/x])$ where u is an arithmetic expression or an atomic channel, and $P \wedge f$ for $(P_\mathsf{S}, P_\mathsf{V} \wedge f)$ where f is a logical formula.

The Hoare logic part of the type system is fairly simple since all variables are local. Most typing rules strengthen a precondition ϕ to the formula $\phi \wedge P_\mathsf{V}$ that allows to select the relevant variable policies P using their content information P_V. We elaborate on the rules for assignment, output and input.

The typing rule for assignment requires the existence of a post-policy P' for each selected pre-policy P. This policy P' should satisfy $l \sqcup P_\mathsf{S}[fv(a) \cup X] \sqsubseteq P_\mathsf{S}'(x)$, and for all variables y different than x, $P_\mathsf{S}(y) \sqsubseteq P_\mathsf{S}'(y)$ should hold. Requiring $l \sqsubseteq P_\mathsf{S}'(x)$ and $P_\mathsf{S}[X] \sqsubseteq P_\mathsf{S}'(x)$ is to capture *implicit flows* [11]. On the other hand, under the pre-condition $P_\mathsf{V} \wedge \phi[a/x]$, it is required that $P_\mathsf{V} \Rightarrow P_\mathsf{V}'[a/x]$. In other words, $P_\mathsf{V} \wedge \phi[a/x] \Rightarrow P_\mathsf{V}'[a/x]$ should hold. This guarantees that for a state σ satisfying P and the precondition $\phi[a/x]$, the post state derived from σ after the assignment satisfies the post policy P'.

Example 3. We have $\{y\}, L \vdash_{\mathcal{P}_{\mathrm{MD}}(2)} \{y = 1\} z_1 := z \{y = 1\} : \emptyset, L$ for the assignment $z_1 := z$ in the demultiplexer process S_D of Fig. 1. Essentially, it needs to be shown that no matter if P is instantiated with P_d^1 or P_d^2, we can find an appropriate policy in $\mathcal{P}_{\mathrm{MD}}(2)$ for the instantiation of P', satisfying the side conditions of the typing rule for assignment. First instantiate P with P_d^1. We still use P_d^1 for P',

Table 2. Information flow type system for processes and systems.

$X, l \vdash_{\mathcal{K}} \{\phi\} \, \mathsf{nil} \, \{\phi\} : \emptyset, L$ $X, l \vdash_{\mathcal{K}} \{\phi\} \, \mathsf{skip} \, \{\phi\} : \emptyset, L$

$X, l \vdash_{\mathcal{K}} \{\phi[a/x]\} \, x := a \, \{\phi\} : \emptyset, L$
   if $\forall P \in \mathcal{K} : P_\mathsf{V} \wedge \phi[a/x] \Rightarrow \exists P' \in \mathcal{K} : P[x \mapsto l \sqcup P_\mathsf{S}[fv(a) \cup X]]_\mathsf{S} \preceq P'[a/x]_\mathsf{V}$

$$\frac{X, l \vdash_{\mathcal{K}} \{\phi\} \, S_1 \, \{\rho\} : Y_1, l_1 \quad X \cup Y_1, l \sqcup l_1 \vdash_{\mathcal{K}} \{\rho\} \, S_2 \, \{\psi\} : Y_2, l_2}{X, l \vdash_{\mathcal{K}} \{\phi\} \, S_1; S_2 \, \{\psi\} : Y_1 \cup Y_2, l_1 \sqcup l_2}$$

$$\frac{X \cup fv(b), l \vdash_{\mathcal{K}} \{\phi \wedge b\} \, S_1 \, \{\psi\} : Y_1, l_1 \quad X \cup fv(b), l \vdash_{\mathcal{K}} \{\phi \wedge \neg b\} \, S_2 \, \{\psi\} : Y_2, l_2}{X, l \vdash_{\mathcal{K}} \{\phi\} \, \mathsf{if} \ b \ \mathsf{then} \ S_1 \ \mathsf{else} \ S_2 \, \{\psi\} : Y_1 \cup Y_2 \cup fv(b), l_1 \sqcup l_2}$$

$$\frac{Y, l \vdash_{\mathcal{K}} \{\phi \wedge b\} \, S \, \{\phi\} : Y, l}{X, l \vdash_{\mathcal{K}} \{\phi\} \, \mathsf{while} \ b \ \mathsf{do} \ S \, \{\phi \wedge \neg b\} : Y, l} \quad \text{if } X \cup fv(b) \subseteq Y$$

$X, l \vdash_{\mathcal{K}} \{\phi\} \, c!a \, \{\phi\} : \emptyset, l' \quad \text{if } l \sqsubseteq P^\circ(c) \sqsubseteq l' \text{ and}$
$\forall P \in \mathcal{K} : P_\mathsf{V} \wedge \phi \Rightarrow (P_\mathsf{S}[X] \sqsubseteq P^\circ(c) \wedge \ \exists P' \in \mathcal{K}, P^\bullet \in \mathcal{P}^{\mathrm{ch}} :$
$\qquad P[(c.j \mapsto P_\mathsf{S}(a_j))_j]_\mathsf{S} \preceq (P'_\mathsf{S} \uplus P_\mathsf{S}^\bullet, P'_\mathsf{V} \wedge \bigwedge_j a_j \in P_\mathsf{V}^\bullet(c.j)))$

$X, l \vdash_{\mathcal{K}} \{\forall \boldsymbol{x} : \phi\} \, c?\boldsymbol{x} \, \{\phi\} : \emptyset, l' \quad \text{if } l \sqsubseteq P^\circ(c) \sqsubseteq l' \text{ and}$
$\forall P \in \mathcal{K} : P_\mathsf{V} \wedge (\forall \boldsymbol{x} : \phi) \Rightarrow (P_\mathsf{S}[X] \sqsubseteq P^\circ(c) \wedge \ \forall P^\bullet \in \mathcal{P}^{\mathrm{ch}} : \forall \boldsymbol{v} \ s.t. \bigwedge_j v_j \in P^\bullet(c.j) :$
$\qquad \exists P' \in \mathcal{K} : P[(x_j \mapsto P_\mathsf{S}^\bullet(c.j) \sqcup P^\circ(c))_j]_\mathsf{S} \preceq P'[(v_j/x_j)_j]_\mathsf{V})$

$$\frac{X', l'_1 \vdash_{\mathcal{K}} \{\phi'\} \, S \, \{\psi'\} : Y', l'_2}{X, l_1 \vdash_{\mathcal{K}} \{\phi\} \, S \, \{\psi\} : Y, l_2} \quad \begin{array}{l} \text{if } (\phi \Rightarrow \phi') \wedge (\psi' \Rightarrow \psi) \wedge \\ X \subseteq X' \wedge Y' \subseteq Y \wedge l_1 \sqsubseteq l'_1 \wedge l'_2 \sqsubseteq l_2 \end{array}$$

$$\frac{\emptyset, L \vdash_{\mathcal{K}} \{\phi\} \, S_i \, \{\psi\} : Y, l'}{[i \mapsto \mathcal{K}] \vdash \{[i \mapsto \phi]\} \, i : S_i \, \{[i \mapsto \psi]\}} \text{ if } nip(\mathcal{K}) \qquad \frac{\mathcal{P} \vdash \{\Phi\} \, \Sigma \, \{\Psi\}}{\mathcal{P} \vdash \{\Phi\} \, \Sigma \setminus \Omega \, \{\Psi\}}$$

$$\frac{\mathcal{P}_1 \vdash \{\Phi_1\} \, \Sigma_1 \, \{\Psi_1\} \quad \mathcal{P}_2 \vdash \{\Phi_2\} \, \Sigma_2 \, \{\Psi_2\}}{\mathcal{P}_1 \uplus \mathcal{P}_2 \vdash \{\Phi_1 \uplus \Phi_2\} \, \Sigma_1 || \Sigma_2 \, \{\Psi_1 \uplus \Psi_2\}}$$

---

and the side condition specializes to $y = 1 \Rightarrow P_\mathsf{d}^1[z_1 \mapsto L \sqcup P_\mathsf{dS}^1[\{y, z\}]] \preceq P_\mathsf{d}^1[z/z_1]_\mathsf{V}$. This condition further expands to the following, which holds.

$$\begin{aligned} y = 1 \quad &\Rightarrow ((y : L; z : H; z_1 : H; z_2 : L)[z_1 \mapsto H], \ y = 1) \\ &\preceq ((y : L; z : H; z_1 : H; z_2 : L), \ (y = 1)[z/z_1]). \end{aligned}$$

Next instantiate P with P_d^2. The side condition specializes to $y = 1 \wedge y \neq 1 \Rightarrow ...$, which vacuously holds.   □

The typing rule for output imposes the constraint $l \sqsubseteq P^\circ(c) \sqsubseteq l'$. Here $P^\circ(c) \sqsubseteq l'$ takes care of the possibility for the output to be blocked by the environment (in line with the use of synchronous communication the treatment of output is "symmetric" to that of input; hence the possibility of blocked output is also considered). In more detail, the presence/absence of the output can leak information if the subsequent computation is not kept confidential. This kind of leakage is in a sense analogous to the leakage created by looping. On the other hand, $l \sqsubseteq P^\circ(c)$ takes care of the possibility that a previously blocked communication can be revealed through the indirect blockage (absence) of the current output. Next, the constraint $P_\mathsf{S}[X] \sqsubseteq P^\circ(c)$ is concerned with the implicit flows from conditionals having variables in X to the *presence* of the output. Finally, the seemingly involved constraint $P[(c.j \mapsto P_\mathsf{S}(a_j))_j]_\mathsf{S} \preceq (P'_\mathsf{S} \uplus P^\bullet_\mathsf{S}, P'_\mathsf{V} \wedge \bigwedge_j a_j \in P^\bullet_\mathsf{V}(c.j))$ can be understood by comparing the output $c!\boldsymbol{a}$ to the assignment $c := \boldsymbol{a}$.

The typing rule for input uses constraints about the presence label $P^\circ(c)$ of the channel c in a way similar to the rule for output does. Its last constraint $P[(x_j \mapsto P^\bullet_\mathsf{S}(c.j) \sqcup P^\circ(c))_j]_\mathsf{S} \preceq P'[(v_j/x_j)_j]_\mathsf{V}$, on the other hand, can be understood by comparing the input $c?\boldsymbol{x}$ to the assignment $\boldsymbol{x} := c$. The constraint $P^\circ(c) \sqsubseteq P'_\mathsf{S}(x_j)$ is imposed for all $j \in \{1, 2, ..., |c|\}$, because the presence of the input leads to the modification of the variable x_j.

We remark on the typing rule for if, where the set $fv(b)$ is unioned into the "progress set", resulting in $fv(b) \cup Y_1 \cup Y_2$. This guarantees a noninterference condition where two systems advance in a manner close to "lock-step" execution. Similar treatment of the "termination effect" of the if statement in typing can be found in [5, 29]. We conjecture that this facilitates our articulation of the security guarantees when the execution of the processes is controlled by certain schedulers in the future.

The Typing of Systems. The typing judgments for systems are of the form $\mathcal{P} \vdash \{\varPhi\} \varSigma \{\varPsi\}$. Here $\mathcal{P}$ is a policy environment for the system $\varSigma$, and for each $i \in Pid(\varSigma)$, $\varPhi(i)$ and $\varPsi(i)$ are the pre-condition and post-condition, respectively, for the process with identifier i in $\varSigma$. We also denote by $\mathbf{T}^\varSigma$ the mapping such that $\mathbf{D}_{\mathbf{T}^\varSigma} = Pid(\varSigma)$ and $\forall i \in \mathbf{D}_{\mathbf{T}^\varSigma} : \mathbf{T}^\varSigma(i) = \mathbf{tt}$. The typing rules follow patterns that are fairly straightforward.

The side condition $nip(\mathcal{K})$ of the rule for $i : S_i$ is a "healthiness" constraint saying that the choice of policies cannot be decided by confidential information. This is desirable since confidentiality levels have *access control* implications. A public observer would be able to deduce information about confidential variables based on whether it is allowed to access the values of certain variables, if confidential information had interference on the policies in use.

The predicate $nip(-)$ is expressed with the help of the notations $\sigma_1 \overset{\mathcal{K}}{=} \sigma_2$ and $c\rho' \boldsymbol{v}_1 \overset{\mathcal{K}}{\underset{\rho}{=}} c\rho' \boldsymbol{v}_2$. The notation $\sigma_1 \overset{\mathcal{K}}{=} \sigma_2$ represents that σ_1 and σ_2 have the same domain and map each variable that is *low with respect to every policy in* $\mathcal{K}$ to the same value. Similarly, $c\rho' \boldsymbol{v}_1 \overset{\mathcal{K}}{\underset{\rho}{=}} c\rho' \boldsymbol{v}_2$ says that if ρ is the same as ρ', then the atomic channels of c that are *low with respect to every policy in* $\mathcal{K}$ should communicate the same values.

Definition 2 (Low Equivalence Parameterized by Sets of Policies).

$$\sigma_1 \stackrel{\mathcal{K}}{=} \sigma_2 \;\triangleq\; \mathbf{D}_{\sigma_1} = \mathbf{D}_{\sigma_2} \wedge \forall x \in \mathbf{D}_{\sigma_1} : (\forall P \in \mathcal{K} : P_{\mathsf{S}}(x) = L) \Rightarrow \sigma_1(x) = \sigma_2(x)$$

$$c\rho' \boldsymbol{v}_1 \stackrel{\mathcal{K}}{\underset{\rho}{=}} c\rho' \boldsymbol{v}_2 \;\triangleq\; \forall j : (\rho = \rho' \wedge \forall P \in \mathcal{K} : P_{\mathsf{S}}(c.j) = L) \Rightarrow v_{1j} = v_{2j}$$

Formally, we have:

$$nip(\mathcal{K}) \;\triangleq\; \forall \sigma_1, \sigma_2 : \sigma_1 \stackrel{\mathcal{K}}{=} \sigma_2 \Rightarrow (\forall P \in \mathcal{K} : \sigma_1 \models P \Leftrightarrow \sigma_2 \models P) \;\wedge$$

$$\forall c, \boldsymbol{v}, \boldsymbol{v}' : c!\boldsymbol{v} \stackrel{\mathcal{P}^{\mathrm{ch}}_{\bullet}}{\underset{!}{=}} c!\boldsymbol{v}' \Rightarrow (\forall P^{\bullet} : c!\boldsymbol{v} \models_! P^{\bullet} \Leftrightarrow c!\boldsymbol{v}' \models_! P^{\bullet}).$$

Example 4. The system Σ_{MD} of Example 1 can be typed using the policies given in Example 2. It is not difficult to verify that $nip(\mathcal{P}_{\mathrm{MD}}(1))$ and $nip(\mathcal{P}_{\mathrm{MD}}(2))$ hold, and that $\mathcal{P}_{\mathrm{MD}} \vdash \{\mathbf{T}^{\Sigma_{\mathrm{MD}}}\}\, \Sigma_{\mathrm{MD}}\, \{\mathbf{T}^{\Sigma_{\mathrm{MD}}}\}$ can be established.   □

Subject Reduction. In the subject reduction result of Theorem 1, $\sigma \models \Phi$ represents $\forall i \in \mathbf{D}_\Phi : \sigma \models \Phi(i)$ and all un-quantified symbols are implicitly universally quantified. When an input is performed, the existence of channel policies describing the values received are relied on to ensure the satisfaction of the pre-condition Φ' of the derived system Σ', by the resulting state σ'.

Theorem 1 (Subject Reduction). *If* $\mathcal{P} \vdash \{\Phi\}\, \Sigma\, \{\Psi\}$, $\langle \Sigma; \sigma \rangle \stackrel{\alpha}{\longrightarrow}_\eta \langle \Sigma'; \sigma' \rangle$, $\sigma \models \Phi$, $P \in \mathcal{P}$ *and* $\sigma \models P$, *then*

1. $\exists P^{\bullet} : \alpha \models_! P^{\bullet}$, *and*
2. *if* $\exists P^{\bullet} : \alpha \models_? P^{\bullet}$, *then* $\exists P' \in \mathcal{P}, \Phi' : \mathcal{P} \vdash \{\Phi'\}\, \Sigma'\, \{\Psi\} \wedge \sigma' \models \Phi' \wedge \sigma' \models P'$.

6   Noninterference

We introduce a bisimulation-based, compositional noninterference property that accounts for both the communications performed by a system and the modification of memory states. We prove that this noninterference property is enforced by the information flow type system presented in Sect. 5. Some auxiliary notations are first presented in Fig. 3, where Definitions 1 and 2 from previous sections are used.

We extend our transition labels α with *inaction* ϵ and *suspension* $\square$. We also introduce *action schemas* β where the inputs come with holes rather than data. The idea is that the data to be received is under the environment's control. For transitions, we write $C \stackrel{\alpha}{\rightarrow}_\eta C'$ to represent that there *may be* a transition from the configuration C to the configuration C'; the inability to perform a transition is indicated by $\alpha = \square$.

Low-equivalence of configurations is defined with respect to particular policies $P \in \mathcal{P}$ in Fig. 3. The main constraints are that P should be satisfied by the states of the two configurations, and that the values of variables that are low under P_{S} should be equal.

To be able to relate the communications performed in the two executions in our bisimulation-based property, we introduce a notion of low equivalence $(\stackrel{P^{\bullet}}{\underset{\rho}{\sim}})$

Actions and action schemas:

$$\alpha ::= c!\boldsymbol{v} \mid c?\boldsymbol{v} \mid \tau \mid \epsilon \mid \Box$$
$$\beta ::= c!\boldsymbol{v} \mid c?[\,] \mid \tau \mid \epsilon \mid \Box$$
$$\gamma ::= \alpha \mid \beta$$

Decorated transitions:

$$C \stackrel{\alpha}{\twoheadrightarrow}_\eta C' \triangleq C \stackrel{\alpha}{\longrightarrow}_\eta C' \lor$$
$$\alpha = \epsilon \land C' = C \lor$$
$$(\forall \alpha' : C \stackrel{\alpha'}{\longrightarrow} \Rightarrow h\_prc(\alpha')) \land \alpha = \Box \land C' = C$$
$$h\_prc(\alpha') \triangleq \exists c, \rho, \boldsymbol{v} : \alpha' = c\rho\boldsymbol{v} \land P^\circ(c) = H$$

Low equivalence of configurations:

$$\langle \Sigma_1 ; \sigma_1 \rangle \stackrel{P}{\underset{\mathcal{P}}{=}} \langle \Sigma_2 ; \sigma_2 \rangle \triangleq P \in \mathcal{P} \land Pid(\Sigma_1) = Pid(\Sigma_2) = \mathbf{D}_\mathcal{P} \land$$
$$\sigma_1 \models P \land \sigma_2 \models P \land \sigma_1 \stackrel{\{P\}}{=} \sigma_2$$

Low equivalence of actions and actions/action schemas ($\alpha \stackrel{P^\bullet}{\underset{\rho}{\sim}} \gamma$):

$$c\rho'\boldsymbol{v} \stackrel{P^\bullet}{\underset{\rho}{\sim}} \epsilon \quad \text{if } P^\circ(c) = H \land c\rho'\boldsymbol{v} \models_\rho P^\bullet$$
$$c\rho'\boldsymbol{v}_1 \stackrel{P^\bullet}{\underset{\rho}{\sim}} c\rho'\boldsymbol{v}_2 \quad \text{if } P^\circ(c) = L \land c\rho'\boldsymbol{v}_1 \models_\rho P^\bullet \land c\rho'\boldsymbol{v}_2 \models_\rho P^\bullet \land c\rho'\boldsymbol{v}_1 \stackrel{\{P^\bullet\}}{\underset{\rho}{=}} c\rho'\boldsymbol{v}_2$$
$$\tau \stackrel{P^\bullet}{\underset{\rho}{\sim}} \tau$$
$$\tau \stackrel{P^\bullet}{\underset{\rho}{\sim}} \Box$$

Hole filling ($\beta(\boldsymbol{v}')$):

$$c!\boldsymbol{v}(\boldsymbol{v}') = c!\boldsymbol{v} \qquad c?[\,](\boldsymbol{v}') = c?\boldsymbol{v}' \qquad \beta(\boldsymbol{v}') = \beta, \text{ if } \beta \in \{\tau, \epsilon, \Box\}$$

Fig. 3. Auxiliary definitions for noninterference

between actions α and actions/action schemas γ. The relation $\stackrel{P^\bullet}{\underset{\rho}{\sim}}$ is the smallest one satisfying the rules in Fig. 3. Concerning the "presence" of communication, $\alpha \stackrel{P^\bullet}{\underset{\rho}{\sim}} \gamma$ requires that a communication with confidential presence should correspond to inaction (ϵ), which implies among others the absence of communication on the same channel[2]. It is worth pointing out that the $\boldsymbol{v}_2$ in the same definition can be the unary vector [ ]. Although Definition 1 has not been explicitly

---

[2] This pattern is reminiscent of the "Weak bisimulation up to H" by Focardi and Rossi [14].

extended to take care of holes, the bisimulation to be given in Definition 4 will use $\alpha \overset{P^\bullet}{\underset{\rho}{\sim}} \gamma$ in such a way that the check $[\,] \in P^\bullet_V(c.1)$ can never be reached.

We are now in a position to define our noninterference property, termed *communication-aware security* (CA-security). In Definition 3, $- \overset{com}{\underset{\mathcal{P}}{\sim}} -$ is the union of all *communication-aware bisimulations* (CA-bisimulations) that are in turn characterized in Definition 4.

Definition 3 (CA-Security). $Sec_{com}(\Sigma, \mathcal{P})$ *if and only if for all* σ_1, σ_2, *and* P, *if* $\langle \Sigma; \sigma_1 \rangle \overset{P}{\underset{\mathcal{P}}{=}} \langle \Sigma; \sigma_2 \rangle$, *then* $(\langle \Sigma; \sigma_1 \rangle, P) \overset{com}{\underset{\mathcal{P}}{\sim}} (\langle \Sigma; \sigma_2 \rangle, P)$.

Definition 4 (CA-Bisimulation).
A CA-bisimulation $R_\mathcal{P}$ *is a symmetric relation such that*
$(C_1, P) \; R_\mathcal{P} \; (C_2, P)$ *implies* $C_1 \overset{P}{\underset{\mathcal{P}}{=}} C_2$ *and the following:*

$$\forall \alpha, \eta, C_1' \; s.t. \; C_1 \overset{\alpha}{\longrightarrow}_\eta C_1' :$$
$$\exists P^\bullet_!, \beta : \alpha \overset{P^\bullet_!}{\underset{!}{\sim}} \beta \; \wedge$$
$$\forall P^\bullet_?, \boldsymbol{v} \; s.t. \; \alpha \overset{P^\bullet_?}{\underset{?}{\sim}} \beta(\boldsymbol{v}) :$$
$$\exists C_2', P' : C_2 \overset{\beta(\boldsymbol{v})}{\twoheadrightarrow}_\eta C_2' \; \wedge \; (C_1', P') \, R_\mathcal{P} \, (C_2', P').$$

In prose, a symmetric relation $R_\mathcal{P}$ qualifies as a CA-bisimulation if for a pair (C_1, P) and (C_2, P) related by $R_\mathcal{P}$, and a transition performing action α from C_1, involving processes in η, there exists a policy $P^\bullet_!$ and an action schema β low-equivalent to α concerning output, and for all value vectors $\boldsymbol{v}$ and policies $P^\bullet_?$ such that $\beta(\boldsymbol{v})$ is low-equivalent to α concerning input, there exists a simulation of $\overset{\alpha}{\longrightarrow}_\eta$ by $\overset{\beta(\boldsymbol{v})}{\twoheadrightarrow}_\eta$ from C_2, and a policy P' whose pairings with the configurations reached are still related under $R_\mathcal{P}$.

Example 5. To aid the reader's intuition, we provide a *partial* unfolding of a CA-bisimulation for the system $2 : S_D$. Note that a proof of the CA-security of $2 : S_D$ is *not* the aim here. We represent by $\sigma_{v_1 v_2 v_3 v_4}$ the local state $[y \mapsto v_1][z \mapsto v_2][z_1 \mapsto v_3][z_2 \mapsto v_4]$, and by $\mathcal{P}_D$ the policy environment $[2 \mapsto \mathcal{P}_{MD}(2)]$.

We have $\langle 2 : S_D; \sigma_{2070} \rangle \overset{P^2_d}{\underset{\mathcal{P}_D}{=}} \langle 2 : S_D; \sigma_{2080} \rangle$. Hence one of the conditions that $Sec_{com}(2 : S_D, \mathcal{P}_D)$ calls for is the existence of CA-bisimulation $R_\star$ such that

$$(\langle 2 : S_D; \sigma_{2070} \rangle, P^2_d) \; R_\star \; (\langle 2 : S_D; \sigma_{2080} \rangle, P^2_d).$$

Suppose
$$\langle 2 : S_D; \sigma_{2070} \rangle \overset{\tau}{\longrightarrow}_2 \langle 2 : c?(y,z); \underline{if}; \underline{wh}; \sigma_{2070} \rangle \tag{1}$$

There exist $P^\bullet_!$ and τ, such that $\tau \overset{P^\bullet_!}{\underset{!}{\sim}} \tau$. Pick for instance $P^\bullet_? = P^\bullet_!$ and $\boldsymbol{v} = (0,0)$, for which $\tau \overset{P^\bullet_?}{\underset{?}{\sim}} \tau(0,0)$. Simulation of (1) is required with the action $\tau(0,0) = \tau$.

The only possibility is $\langle 2 : S_D; \sigma_{2080} \rangle \xrightarrow{\tau}_2 \langle 2 : c?(y,z); if; wh; \sigma_{2080} \rangle$. Since $\sigma_{2070} \models P_d^2$ but $\sigma_{2070} \not\models P_d^1$, the following is required:

$$(\langle 2 : c?(y,z); if; wh; \sigma_{2070} \rangle, P_d^2)\ R_\star\ (\langle 2 : c?(y,z); if; wh; \sigma_{2080} \rangle, P_d^2).$$

This further necessitates the condition below, which can be verified easily:

$$\langle 2 : c?(y,z); if; wh; \sigma_{2070} \rangle \overset{P_d^2}{\underset{\mathcal{P}_D}{=}} \langle 2 : c?(y,z); if; wh; \sigma_{2080} \rangle.$$

Suppose

$$\langle 2 : c?(y,z); if; wh; \sigma_{2070} \rangle \xrightarrow{c?(1,k_1)}_2 \langle 2 : if; wh; \sigma_{1k_1 70} \rangle, \tag{2}$$

where k_1 is an integer. There should exist some $P_!^\bullet$ and β such that $c?(1,k_1) \overset{P_!^\bullet}{\underset{!}{\sim}} \beta$.

Since $P^\circ(c) = L$, $\beta = c?[\ ]$. Pick for instance $P_?^\bullet = P_1^\bullet$, and v, $c?(1,k_1) \overset{P_1^\bullet}{\underset{?}{\sim}} c?[\ ](v)$ implies $v_1 = 1$ since $P_1^\bullet(c.1) = L$. Hence a simulation of (2) with action $c?[\ ](1,k_2)$ is required for all $k_2 \in \mathbb{Z}$ ($P_1^\bullet(c.2) = H$). It can only be of the form $\langle 2 : c?(y,z); if; wh; \sigma_{2080} \rangle \xrightarrow{c?(1,k_2)}_2 \langle 2 : if; wh; \sigma_{1k_2 80} \rangle$. And the following is required

$$(\langle 2 : if; wh; \sigma_{1k_1 70} \rangle, P_d^1)\ R_\star\ (\langle 2 : if; wh; \sigma_{1k_2 80} \rangle, P_d^1).$$

This further requires $\langle 2 : if; wh; \sigma_{1k_1 70} \rangle \overset{P_d^1}{\underset{\mathcal{P}_D}{=}} \langle 2 : if; wh; \sigma_{1k_2 80} \rangle$, which holds.

Going through two more "lock steps", the following is required.

$$(\langle 2 : z_1 := z; wh; \sigma_{1k_1 70} \rangle, P_d^1)\ R_\star\ (\langle 2 : z_1 := z; wh; \sigma_{1k_2 80} \rangle, P_d^1)$$

$$(\langle 2 : S_D; \sigma_{1k_1 k_1 0} \rangle, P_d^1)\ R_\star\ (\langle 2 : S_D; \sigma_{1k_2 k_2 0} \rangle, P_d^1) \tag{3}$$

And we still have $\langle 2 : S_D; \sigma_{1k_1 k_1 0} \rangle \overset{P_d^1}{\underset{\mathcal{P}_D}{=}} \langle 2 : S_D; \sigma_{1k_2 k_2 0} \rangle$ as required by (3).

We stop this demonstration here.   □

In CA-bisimulation, the treatment of output and input resembles that of rely-guarantee reasoning [17], and leads to the preservation of security under $||$ — the second compositionality result given below.

Theorem 2 (Compositionality). *For Σ_1 with policy environment $\mathcal{P}_1$, and Σ_2 with policy environment $\mathcal{P}_2$, such that $\mathbf{D}_{\Sigma_1} \cap \mathbf{D}_{\Sigma_2} = \emptyset$,*

1. $Sec_{\mathrm{com}}(\Sigma_1, \mathcal{P}_1) \implies \forall \Omega \subseteq \mathbf{PCh} : Sec_{\mathrm{com}}(\Sigma_1 \setminus \Omega, \mathcal{P}_1)$, *and*
2. $Sec_{\mathrm{com}}(\Sigma_1, \mathcal{P}_1) \wedge Sec_{\mathrm{com}}(\Sigma_2, \mathcal{P}_2) \implies Sec_{\mathrm{com}}(\Sigma_1 || \Sigma_2, \mathcal{P}_1 \uplus \mathcal{P}_2)$.

The most important result of this section, that well-typedness guarantees communication aware security, is formalized in Theorem 3. This soundness result means that our motivating example is noninterfering (Example 6).

Theorem 3 (Soundness). *For all systems Σ with policy environments $\mathcal{P}$, if $\mathcal{P} \vdash \{\mathbf{T}^\Sigma\}\ \Sigma\ \{\mathbf{T}^\Sigma\}$, then $Sec_{\mathrm{com}}(\Sigma, \mathcal{P})$.*

Example 6. Going back to the multiplexer example, by Theorem 3, the well-typedness of the system Σ_{MD} of Example 1 guarantees $Sec_{\mathrm{com}}(\Sigma_{\mathrm{MD}}, \mathcal{P}_{\mathrm{MD}})$.   □

The proof of Theorem 3 is sketched below, where the role played by the compositionality result will also be elucidated. All details of this proof can be found in the Coq development.

We define high/low processes with the help of the type system, following the approach of [30,32]. The non-standard facet is: to take care of content-dependent policies, the memory state σ and policy P satisfied by σ are made explicit in the defined predicates.

Definition 5. *A process S with set $\mathcal{K}$ of variable policies is* high *at state σ, under precondition ϕ and with policy P, written $hi_\phi^{\mathcal{K}}(\langle S; \sigma \rangle, P)$, if*

$$\sigma \models P \ \wedge\ \sigma \models \phi \ \wedge$$
$$\exists X, l, X', l', \psi : \sigma \models \phi \ \wedge\ X, l \vdash_{\mathcal{K}} \{\phi\}\, S\, \{\psi\} : X', l' \ \wedge\ (l = H \vee \exists x \in X : P_{\mathsf{S}}(x) = H)$$

Definition 6. *A process S with set $\mathcal{K}$ of variable policies is* low *at state σ, under precondition ϕ and with policy P, written $lo_\phi^{\mathcal{K}}(\langle S; \sigma \rangle, P)$, if*

$$\sigma \models P \ \wedge\ \sigma \models \phi \ \wedge$$
$$(\exists X, l, X', l', \psi : X, l \vdash_{\mathcal{K}} \{\phi\}\, S\, \{\psi\} : X', l') \ \wedge$$
$$(\forall X, l, X', l', \psi : X, l \vdash_{\mathcal{K}} \{\phi\}\, S\, \{\psi\} : X', l' \Rightarrow (l = L \wedge \forall x \in X : P_{\mathsf{S}}(x) = L))$$

We then define a low-equivalence relation $\stackrel{[i \mapsto \mathcal{K}]}{\simeq}$ concerned with systems of the form $i : S$ in Table 3. For two singleton systems with low processes to be related, the processes they execute need to be the same, and the preconditions used should be identical. In both cases of Table 3, the policies used on both sides of $\stackrel{[i \mapsto \mathcal{K}]}{\simeq}$ are the same (P), and the memory states are required to be low-equivalent under P.

Table 3. The low equivalence relation on singleton systems

(LO$_{\mathrm{EQ}}$)	$\dfrac{\exists \phi : lo_\phi^{\mathcal{K}}(\langle S; \sigma_1 \rangle, P) \wedge lo_\phi^{\mathcal{K}}(\langle S; \sigma_2 \rangle, P) \quad \sigma_1 \stackrel{\{P\}}{=} \sigma_2 \quad nip(\mathcal{K})}{(\langle i : S; \sigma_1 \rangle, P) \stackrel{[i \mapsto \mathcal{K}]}{\simeq} (\langle i : S; \sigma_2 \rangle, P)}$
(HI$_{\mathrm{EQ}}$)	$\dfrac{hi_{\phi_1}^{\mathcal{K}}(\langle S_1; \sigma_1 \rangle, P) \wedge hi_{\phi_2}^{\mathcal{K}}(\langle S_2; \sigma_2 \rangle, P) \quad \sigma_1 \stackrel{\{P\}}{=} \sigma_2 \quad nip(\mathcal{K})}{(\langle i : S_1; \sigma_1 \rangle, P) \stackrel{[i \mapsto \mathcal{K}]}{\simeq} (\langle i : S_2; \sigma_2 \rangle, P)}$

We next build up to the following results:

- $\stackrel{[i \mapsto \mathcal{K}]}{\simeq}$ qualifies as a CA-bisimulation, and

- if $[i \mapsto \mathcal{K}] \vdash \{[i \mapsto \mathbf{tt}]\}\, i : S\, \{[i \mapsto \mathbf{tt}]\}$ holds, and $\langle i : S; \sigma_1 \rangle \overset{P}{\underset{[i \mapsto \mathcal{K}]}{=}} \langle i : S; \sigma_2 \rangle$,

  then $(\langle i : S;\, \sigma_1 \rangle, P) \overset{[i \mapsto \mathcal{K}]}{\simeq} (\langle i : S;\, \sigma_2 \rangle, P)$ holds.

In other words, if $[i \mapsto \mathcal{K}] \vdash \{[i \mapsto \mathbf{tt}]\}\, i : S\, \{[i \mapsto \mathbf{tt}]\}$ can be established, then $Sec_{\mathrm{com}}(i : S, [i \mapsto \mathcal{K}])$ holds. Suppose a system $\Sigma_\star$ has the form $\Sigma_1 \| \Sigma_2$ or $\Sigma' \setminus \Omega$, and the policy environment $\mathcal{P}_\star$. By the typing rule for systems, and compositionality, we can then inductively show that $\mathcal{P}_\star \vdash \{\mathbf{T}^{\Sigma_\star}\}\, \Sigma_\star\, \{\mathbf{T}^{\Sigma_\star}\}$ implies $Sec_{\mathrm{com}}(\Sigma_\star, \mathcal{P}_\star)$.

7   Conclusion and Discussion

This paper studies information flow problems with the use of content-dependent confidentiality policies in a concurrent language. In our language, processes use local variables and communicate along channels with each other and the environment. A bisimulation-based noninterference condition is formulated to characterize security under the selection of different confidentiality policies according to the current memory and communication content. "Presence" and "content" are treated as separate aspects of communication, and a "rely-guarantee" pattern in picking the policies relevant to output and input leads to a compositionality result. The satisfaction of the condition is achieved by a static type system that employs a Hoare logic component, which provides information on the possible memory content at different program points.

A major scenario related to our development is a concurrent system in which the destination of messages depends on their tagging. This is illustrated by our running example involving a communicating pair of multiplexer and demultiplexer, that is shown to be well-typed and secure.

The CA-bisimulation formulated in Sect. 6 has the flavor of the "flat bisimulation" considered in [10] that further goes back to [5]. "Flat bisimulations" consider only memories consistent with the execution and are thus more realistic compared with notions (e.g., in [28]) that range over all memories (irrespective of their reachability) at each step. However, flat bisimulations do not give rise to a compositional notion of security when shared-memory is used, since memory modifications by other concurrent processes are not captured. Nevertheless, our use of local variables with communication rectifies this issue and makes our CA-security compositional. Not surprisingly, this compositionality result allows us to focus on systems with single processes in our soundness proof.

As mentioned in the introduction, several developments [1,6,20] where information flow policies depend on certain conditions exist for *sequential languages*. On the other hand, type/proof systems and noninterference properties have been studied extensively for concurrent systems (e.g., [5,10,21]), using information flow policies from *simple security lattices*.

We have not discussed the security of our concurrent processes under (disjunctive policies and) the control of certain schedulers [22,26,31]. We leave the investigation of the security implications of different types of schedulers in our setting to future work.

References

1. Amtoft, T., Dodds, J., Zhang, Z., Appel, A., Beringer, L., Hatcliff, J., Ou, X., Cousino, A.: A certificate infrastructure for machine-checked proofs of conditional information flow. In: Degano, P., Guttman, J.D. (eds.) Principles of Security and Trust. LNCS, vol. 7215, pp. 369–389. Springer, Heidelberg (2012)
2. Apt, K.R.: Ten years of Hoare's logic: A survey - part 1. ACM Trans. Program. Lang. Syst. **3**(4), 431–483 (1981)
3. Austin, T.H., Flanagan, C.: Efficient purely-dynamic information flow analysis. In: PLAS 2009, pp. 113–124 (2009)
4. Besson, F., Bielova, N., Jensen, T.: Hybrid information flow monitoring against web tracking. In: CSF 2013 (2013)
5. Boudol, G., Castellani, I.: Noninterference for concurrent programs and thread systems. Theoret. Comput. Sci. **281**(1), 109–130 (2002)
6. Broberg, N., Sands, D.: Paralocks: role-based informationflow control and beyond. In: POPL 2010, pp. 431–444 (2010)
7. Clarkson, M.R., Chong, S., Myers, A.C.: Civitas: Toward a secure voting system. In: S&P 2008, pp. 354–368 (2008)
8. Cohen, E.S.: Information transmission in computational systems. In: SOSP 1977 (1977)
9. The Coq Proof Assistant. http://coq.inria.fr
10. Dam, M.: Decidability and proof systems for language-based noninterference relations. In: POPL 2006 (2006)
11. Denning, D.E., Denning, P.J.: Certification of programs for secure information flow. Commun. ACM **20**(7), 504–513 (1977)
12. Eggert, S., van der Meyden, R., Schnoor, H., Wilke, T.: The complexity of intransitive noninterference. In: S&P 2011, pp. 196–211 (2011)
13. Fenton, J.S.: Memoryless subsystems. Comput. J. **17**(2), 143–147 (1974)
14. Focardi, R., Rossi, S.: Information flow security in dynamic contexts. In: (CSFW 2002), pp. 307–319 (2002)
15. Hedin, D., Birgisson, A., Bello, L., Sabelfeld, A.: JSFlow: tracking information flow in javascript and its APIs. In: SAC 2014, pp. 1663–1671 (2014)
16. Hedin, D., Sabelfeld, A.: A perspective on information-flow control. In: Software Safety and Security - Tools for Analysis and Verification, pp. 319–347 (2012)
17. Jones, C.B.: Development Methods for Computer Programs including a Notion of Interference. Ph.D. thesis, Oxford University, June 1981
18. Jovanovic, N., Kruegel, C., Kirda, E.: Pixy: A static analysis tool for detecting web application vulnerabilities, p. 6 (2006)
19. Kobayashi, N.: Type-based information flow analysis for the pi-calculus. Acta Inf. **42**(4–5), 291–347 (2005)
20. Lourenço, L., Caires, L.: Dependent information flow types. In: POPL 2015 (2015)
21. Mantel, H., Sabelfeld, A.: A unifying approach to the security of distributed and multi-threaded programs. J. Comput. Secur. **11**(4), 615–676 (2003)
22. Mantel, H., Sudbrock, H.: Flexible scheduler-independent security. In: Gritzalis, D., Preneel, B., Theoharidou, M. (eds.) ESORICS 2010. LNCS, vol. 6345, pp. 116–133. Springer, Heidelberg (2010)
23. Milner, R.: Communication and Concurrency, vol. 84. Prentice hall, Upper Saddle River (1989)
24. Rafnsson, W., Sabelfeld, A.: Compositional information-flow security for interactive systems. In: CSF 2014, pp. 277–292 (2014)

25. Rushby, J.: Separation and integration in MILS (the MILS constitution). Computer Science Laboratory SRI International, Technical Report (2008)
26. Sabelfeld, A.: Confidentiality for multithreaded programs via bisimulation. In: Broy, M., Zamulin, A.V. (eds.) PSI 2003. LNCS, vol. 2890, pp. 260–274. Springer, Heidelberg (2004)
27. Sabelfeld, A., Myers, A.C.: Language-based information-flow security. IEEE J. Sel. Areas Commun. 21(1), 5–19 (2003)
28. Sabelfeld, A., Sands, D.: Probabilistic noninterference for multi-threaded programs. In: CSFW 2000, pp. 200–214 (2000)
29. Smith, G.: Improved typings for probabilistic noninterference in a multi-threaded language. J. Comput. Secur. 14(6), 591–623 (2006)
30. Smith, G., Volpano, D.M.: Secure information flow in a multi-threaded imperative language. In: POPL 1998, pp. 355–364 (1998)
31. van der Meyden, R., Zhang, C.: Information flow in systems with schedulers, part I: definitions. Theor. Comput. Sci. 467, 68–88 (2013)
32. Volpano, D.M., Irvine, C.E., Smith, G.: A sound type system for secure flow analysis. J. Comput. Secur. 4(2/3), 167–188 (1996)

Near-Optimal Scheduling for LTL with Future Discounting

Shota Nakagawa and Ichiro Hasuo$^{(\boxtimes)}$

University of Tokyo, Tokyo, Japan
ichiro@is.s.u-tokyo.ac.jp

Abstract. We study the search problem for optimal schedulers for the *linear temporal logic (LTL) with future discounting*. The logic, introduced by Almagor, Boker and Kupferman, is a quantitative variant of LTL in which an event in the far future has only discounted contribution to a truth value (that is a real number in the unit interval [0, 1]). The precise problem we study—it naturally arises e.g. in search for a scheduler that recovers from an internal error state as soon as possible—is the following: given a Kripke frame, a formula and a number in [0, 1] called a *margin*, find a path of the Kripke frame that is optimal with respect to the formula up to the prescribed margin (a truly optimal path may not exist). We present an algorithm for the problem; it works even in the extended setting with propositional quality operators, a setting where (threshold) model-checking is known to be undecidable.

1   Introduction

In the field of *formal methods* where a mathematical approach is taken to modeling and verifying systems, the conventional theory is built around the Boolean notion of truth: if a given system satisfies a given specification, or not. This *qualitative* theory has produced an endless list of notable achievements from hardware design to communication protocols. Among many techniques, *automata-based* ones for verification and synthesis have been particularly successful in serving engineering needs, by offering a specification method by temporal logic and push button-style algorithms. See e.g. [20, 23].

However, trends today in the use of computers—computers as part of more and more *heterogeneous* systems—have pushed researchers to turn to *quantitative* consideration of systems, too. For example, in an *embedded system* where a microcomputer controls a bigger system with mechanical/electronic components, concerns include *real-time properties*—if an expected task is finished within the prescribed deadline—and *resource consumption* e.g. with respect to electricity, memory, etc.

Quantities in formal methods can thus arise from a specification (or an *objective*) that is quantitative in nature. Another source of quantities are systems that are themselves quantitative, such as one with probabilistic behaviors.

An extended version of the current paper, with further details and proofs, is found at [19].

© Springer International Publishing Switzerland 2016
P. Ganty and M. Loreti (Eds.): TGC 2015, LNCS 9533, pp. 112–130, 2016.
DOI: 10.1007/978-3-319-28766-9_8

Besides, quantities can arise simply via *refinement* of the Boolean notion of satisfaction. For example, consider the usual interpretation of the *linear temporal logic (LTL)* formula $\mathsf{F}\varphi$—it is satisfied by a sequence $s_0 s_1 \ldots$ if there exists i such that $s_i \models \varphi$. It has the following natural quantitative refinement, where the modality F is replaced with a *discounted* modality $\mathsf{F}_{\exp\frac{1}{2}}$:

$$[\![s_0 s_1 \ldots, \mathsf{F}_{\exp\frac{1}{2}}\varphi]\!] = (\tfrac{1}{2})^i, \quad \text{where } i \text{ is the least index such that } s_i \models \varphi. \quad (1)$$

This value $[\![s_0 s_1 \ldots, \mathsf{F}_{\exp\frac{1}{2}}\varphi]\!] \in [0,1]$ is a quantitative *truth value* and is like *utility* in the game-theoretic terminology. Such refinements allow quantitative reasoning about so-called *quality of service (QoS)*, specifically "how soon φ becomes true" in this example. Another example is a variation $\mathsf{G}_{\exp\frac{1}{2}}\varphi$ of $\mathsf{G}\varphi$, where $[\![s_0 s_1 \ldots, \mathsf{G}_{\exp\frac{1}{2}}\varphi]\!] = 1 - (\tfrac{1}{2})^i$—where i is the least index such that $s_i \not\models \varphi$— meaning that violation of φ in the far future only has a small negative impact.

$\mathrm{LTL}^{\mathrm{disc}}[\mathcal{D}, \mathcal{F}]$: **LTL with Future Discounting.**   The last examples are about quantitative refinement of temporal specifications. An important step in this direction is taken in the recent work [3]. There various useful quantitative refinements in LTL—including the last examples—are unified under the notion of *future discounting*, an idea first presented in [12] in the field of formal methods. They introduce a clean syntax of the logic $\mathrm{LTL}^{\mathrm{disc}}[\mathcal{D}, \mathcal{F}]$—called *LTL with discounting*—that combines: (1) a "discounting until" operator U_η; (2) the usual features of LTL such as the non-discounting one U; and (3) so-called propositional quality operators such as the (binary) average operator $\oplus$, in addition to $\wedge$ and $\vee$. In [3] they define its semantics; and importantly, they show that usual automata-theoretic techniques for verification and synthesis (e.g. from [20,23]) mostly remain applicable.

Probably the most important algorithm in [3] is for the *threshold model-checking problem*: given a Kripke structure $\mathcal{K}$, a formula φ and a *threshold* $v \in [0,1]$, it asks if $[\![\mathcal{K}, \varphi]\!] > v$, i.e. the worst case truth value of a path of $\mathcal{K}$ is above v or not. The core idea of the algorithm is what we call an *event horizon*: assuming that a discounting function η in U_η tends to 0 as time goes by, and that $v > 0$, there exists a time beyond which nothing is significant enough to change the answer to the threshold model-checking problem. In this case we can approximate an infinite path by its finite prefix.

Our Contribution: Near-Optimal Scheduling for $\mathrm{LTL}^{\mathrm{disc}}[\mathcal{D}, \mathcal{F}]$.   Now that a temporal formula φ assigns quantitative *truth* or *utility* $[\![\xi, \varphi]\!]$ to each path ξ, a natural task is to find a path ξ_0 in a given Kripke structure $\mathcal{K}$ that achieves the optimal. On the ground that the logic $\mathrm{LTL}^{\mathrm{disc}}[\mathcal{D}, \mathcal{F}]$ from [3] is capable of expressing many common specifications encountered in real-world problems, finding an optimal path—i.e. resolving nondeterminism in the best possible way—must have numerous applications. The situation is similar to one with *timed automata*, for which optimal scheduling problems are studied e.g. in [1].

It turns out, however, that a (truly) optimal path need not exist (Example 4.1): $v_0 = \sup_{\xi \in \mathrm{path}(\mathcal{K})} [\![\xi, \varphi]\!]$ is obviously a limit point but no ξ_0 achieves $[\![\xi_0, \varphi]\!] = v_0$. This leads us to the following *near*-optimal scheduling problem:

Near-optimal scheduling. Given a Kripke structure $\mathcal{K}$, an $\mathrm{LTL}^{\mathrm{disc}}[\mathcal{D}, \mathcal{F}]$ formula φ and a *margin* $\varepsilon \in (0, 1)$, find a path $\xi_0 \in \mathrm{path}(\mathcal{K})$ that is ε-*optimal*, that is, $\sup_{\xi \in \mathrm{path}(\mathcal{K})} [\![\xi, \varphi]\!] - \varepsilon \le [\![\xi_0, \varphi]\!]$.

We study automata-theoretic algorithms for this problem. In the basic setting where there are no propositional quality operators, we can find a straightforward algorithm that conducts binary search using the model-checking algorithm from [3]. Our main contribution, however, is an alternative algorithm that takes the usual workflow: it constructs, from a formula φ and a margin ε, an automaton $\mathcal{A}_{\varphi, \varepsilon}$ with which we combine a system model $\mathcal{K}$; running a nonemptiness check-like algorithm to the resulting automaton then yields an answer.

On the one hand, our (alternative) algorithm resembles the one in [3]. In particular it relies on the idea of event horizon: a margin ε in our setting plays the role of a threshold v in [3] and enables us to ignore events in the far future.

On the other hand, a major difference from [3] is that we translate a specification (φ, ε) into an automaton that is itself quantitative (what we call a $[0, 1]$-*acceptance values automaton*, with Boolean branching and $[0, 1]-$*acceptance values*). This is unlike [3] where the target automaton is totally Boolean. An advantage of $[0, 1]$-acceptance automata is that they allow optimal path search much like emptiness of Büchi automata is checked (via lasso computations). Applied to our current problem, this enables us to directly find a near-optimal path for $\mathrm{LTL}^{\mathrm{disc}}[\mathcal{D}, \mathcal{F}]$ without knowing the optimal value $\sup_{\xi \in \mathrm{path}(\mathcal{K})} [\![\xi, \varphi]\!]$.

Presence of $\oplus$ and Other Propositional Quality Operators. Notably, our (alternative) algorithm is shown to work even in the presence of any propositional quality operators that are *monotone* and *continuous* (in the sense we will define later; an example is the average operator $\oplus$). Those operators makes the logic more complex: indeed [3] shows that, in presence of the average operator $\oplus$, the model-checking problem for the logic $\mathrm{LTL}^{\mathrm{disc}}[\mathcal{D}, \mathcal{F}]$ becomes undecidable. The binary-search algorithm mentioned earlier (that repeats model checking) ceases to work for this reason; our alternative algorithm works, nevertheless.

We analyze the complexity of the proposed algorithm, focusing on a subclass of the logic $\mathrm{LTL}^{\mathrm{disc}}[\mathcal{D}, \mathcal{F}]$ (Sect. 4.3). Furthermore we present our prototype implementation and some experimental results (see the extended version [19]). They all seem to suggest the following: addition of propositional quality operators (like the average operator $\oplus$) does incur substantial computational costs—as is expected from the fact that $\oplus$ makes model checking undecidable; still our automata-theoretic approach is a viable approach, potentially applicable to optimization problems in the field of model-based system design.

The significance of the average operator $\oplus$ in envisaged applications is that it allows one to *superpose* multiple objectives. For example, one would want an event φ as soon as possible, but at the same time avoiding a different event ψ as long as possible. This is a trade-off situation and the formula $F_\eta\varphi \oplus G_{\eta'}\neg\psi$—with suitable discounting functions η, η'—represents a 50-50 trade-off. Other trade-off ratios can be represented as (monotone and continuous) proportional quality operators, too, and our algorithm accommodates them.

Related Work. Quantitative temporal logics and their decision procedures have been a very active research topic [2,3,7,12,14]. We shall lay them out along a basic taxonomy. We denote by $\mathcal{K}$ (the model of) the system against which a specification formula φ is verified (or tested, synthesized, etc.).

Quantitative vs. Boolean System Models. Sometimes we need quantitative considerations just because the system $\mathcal{K}$ itself is quantitative. This is the case e.g. when $\mathcal{K}$ is a Markov chain, a Markov decision process, a timed or hybrid automaton, etc. In the current work $\mathcal{K}$ is a Kripke structure and is Boolean.

Quantitative vs. Boolean Truth Values. The previous distinction is quite orthogonal to whether a formula φ has truth values from $[0, 1]$ (or another continuous domain), or from $\{tt, ff\}$. For example, the temporal logic PCTL [15] for reasoning about probabilistic systems has modalities like $\mathcal{P}_{>v}\psi$ ("ψ with a probability $> v$") and has Boolean interpretation. In $\mathrm{LTL}^{\mathrm{disc}}[\mathcal{D}, \mathcal{F}]$ studied here, truth values are from $[0, 1]$.

Linear Time vs. Branching Time. This distinction is already there in the qualitative/Boolean setting [22]—its probabilistic variant is studied in [11]—and gives rise to temporal logics with the corresponding flavors (LTL vs. CTL, CTL*). In fact the idea of future discounting is first introduced to a branching-time logic in [12], where an approximation algorithm for truth values is presented.

Future Discounting vs. Future Averaging. The temporal quantitative operators in $\mathrm{LTL}^{\mathrm{disc}}[\mathcal{D}, \mathcal{F}]$ are *discounting*—an event's significance tends to 0 as time proceeds—a fact that benefits model checking via event horizons. Different temporal quantitative operators are studied in [7], including the *long-run average* operator $\widetilde{G}\psi$. Presence of $\widetilde{G}$, however, makes most common decision problems undecidable [7].

Let us discuss a few other related works. In [14] LTL (without additional quantitative operators) is interpreted over the unit interval $[0, 1]$, and its model-checking problem against quantitative systems $\mathcal{K}$ is shown to be decidable. In this setting—where the LTL connectives are interpreted by idempotent operators min and max—the variety of truth values arises only from a finite-state quantitative system $\mathcal{K}$, hence is finite.

In [3, Theorem 4] the *threshold synthesis* problem is shown to be feasible for the logic $\mathrm{LTL}^{\mathrm{disc}}[\mathcal{D}, \emptyset]$ (see Definition 2.4). This problem asks: given a partition of atomic propositions into the input and output signals, an $\mathrm{LTL}^{\mathrm{disc}}[\mathcal{D}, \emptyset]$ formula φ and $v \in [0, 1]$, to come up with a transducer (i.e. a finite-state strategy) that makes the truth value of φ at least v. We remark that this is different from the near-optimal scheduling problem that we solve in this paper. The *synthesis* problem in [2, Sect. 2.2], without a threshold, is closer to ours.

Automata- (or game-) theoretic approaches are taken in [6,8] to the synthesis of controllers or programs with better quantitative performance, too. In these papers, a specification is given itself as an automaton, instead of a temporal formula in the current work. Another difference is that, in [6,8], utility is computed along a path by limit-averaging, not future discounting. The algorithms in [6,8] therefore rely on those which are known for mean-payoff games, including the ones in [10].

More and more diverse quantitative measures of systems' QoS are studied recently: from best/worst case probabilities and costs, to quantiles, conditional probabilities and ratios. See [5] and the references therein. Study of such in $\text{LTL}^{\text{disc}}[\mathcal{D}, \mathcal{F}]$ is future work.

In [9] so-called *cut-point languages* of weighted automata are studied. Let $L : \Sigma^\omega \to \mathbb{R}$ be the quantitative language of a weighted automata $\mathcal{A}$. For a threshold η, the cut-point language of $\mathcal{A}$ is the set of all words w such that $L(w) \geq \eta$. In [9] it is proved that the cut-point languages of deterministic limit-average automata and those of discounted-sum automata are ω-regular if the threshold η is *isolated*, that is, there is no word w such that $L(w)$ is close to η. We expect that similar properties for the logic $\text{LTL}^{\text{disc}}[\mathcal{D}, \mathcal{F}]$ are not hard to establish, although details are yet to be worked out.

Discounting in temporal logics/automata/MSOs has also been used as a technical tool for forcing certain convergence properties in the setting of infinite words. See e.g. [13].

Organization of the Paper. In Sect. 2 we review the logic $\text{LTL}^{\text{disc}}[\mathcal{D}, \mathcal{F}]$ and known results on threshold model checking and satisfiability, all from [3]. We introduce quantitative variants of (alternating) Büchi automata, called (alternating) [0, 1]-acceptance automata, in Sect. 3, with auxiliary observations on their relation to *fuzzy automata* [21]. These automata play a central role in Sect. 4 where we formalize and solve the near-optimal scheduling problem for the logic $\text{LTL}^{\text{disc}}[\mathcal{D}, \mathcal{F}]$ (under certain assumptions on $\mathcal{D}$ and $\mathcal{F}$). We also study complexities, focusing on the average operator $\oplus$ as the only propositional quality operator. in Sect. 5 we conclude, citing some future work. Omitted proofs and further details are found in the extended version [19] of the current paper.

Notations and Terminologies. We shall fix some notations and terminologies, mostly following [3]. They are all standard.

The powerset of a set X is denoted by $\mathcal{P}X$. We fix the set AP of *atomic propositions*. A *computation* (over AP) is an infinite sequence $\pi = \pi_0\pi_1 \ldots \in (\mathcal{P}(AP))^\omega$ over the alphabet $\mathcal{P}(AP)$. For $i \in \mathbb{N}$, $\pi^i = \pi_i\pi_{i+1} \ldots$ denotes the suffix of π starting from its i-th element.

A *Kripke structure* over AP is a tuple $\mathcal{K} = (W, R, \lambda)$ of: a finite set W of states; a transition relation $R \subseteq W^2$ that is left-total (meaning that $\forall s \in W. \exists s' \in W. (s, s') \in R$), and a labeling function $\lambda : W \to \mathcal{P}(AP)$. We follow [17] and call an infinite sequence $\xi = s_0s_1 \ldots$ of states $s_i \in W$, such that $(s_i, s_{i+1}) \in R$ for each $i \in \mathbb{N}$, a *path* of a Kripke structure $\mathcal{K}$. The set of paths of $\mathcal{K}$ is denoted by path($\mathcal{K}$). A path $\xi = s_0 s_1 \ldots \in W^\omega$ gives rise to a computation $\lambda(s_0) \lambda(s_1) \ldots \in (\mathcal{P}(AP))^\omega$; the latter is denoted by $\lambda(\xi)$.

Given a set X, $\mathcal{B}^+(X)$ denotes, as usual, the set of positive propositional formulas (using $\wedge, \vee, \top, \bot$) over $x \in X$ as atomic propositions.

2 The Logic LTL$^{\mathrm{disc}}[\mathcal{D}, \mathcal{F}]$, and its Threshold Problems

Here we recall from [2,3] our target logic, and some existing (un)decidability results.

The logic LTL$^{\mathrm{disc}}[\mathcal{D}, \mathcal{F}]$ extends LTL with: (1) propositional quality operators [2] like the average operator $\oplus$; and (2) discounting in temporal operators [3]. In [3] the two extensions have been studied separately because their coexistence leads to undecidability of the (threshold) model-checking problem; here we put them altogether.

The logic LTL$^{\mathrm{disc}}[\mathcal{D}, \mathcal{F}]$ has two parameters: a set $\mathcal{D}$ of discounting functions; and a set $\mathcal{F}$ of propositional connectives, called propositional quality operators.

Definition 2.1 (Discounting Function [3]**).** A *discounting function* is a strictly decreasing function $\eta : \mathbb{N} \to [0,1]$ such that $\lim_{i\to\infty} \eta(i) = 0$. A special case is an *exponential discounting function* $\exp_\lambda$, where $\lambda \in (0,1)$, that is defined by $\exp_\lambda(i) = \lambda^i$.
The set $\mathcal{D}_{\mathrm{exp}} = \{\exp_\lambda \mid \lambda \in (0,1) \cap \mathbb{Q}\}$ is that of exponential discounting functions.

Definition 2.2 ((Monotone and Continuous) Propositional Quality operator [2]**).** Let $k \in \mathbb{N}$ be a natural number. A k-ary *propositional quality operator* is a function $f : [0,1]^k \to [0,1]$.

We will eventually restrict to propositional quality operators that are *monotone* (wrt. the usual order between real numbers) and *continuous* (wrt. the usual Euclidean topology). The set of such monotone and continuous operators is denoted by $\mathcal{F}_{\mathrm{mc}}$.

Example 2.3. A prototypical example of a propositional quality operator is the *average operator* $\oplus: [0,1]^2 \to [0,1]$, defined by $v_1 \oplus v_2 = (v_1 + v_2)/2$. (Note that $\oplus$ is a "propositional" average operator and is different from the "temporal" average operator $\tilde{\mathsf{U}}$ in [7]). The operator $\oplus$ is monotone and continuous. Other (unary) examples from [4] include: $\triangledown_\lambda(v) = \lambda \cdot v$ and $\blacktriangledown_\lambda(v) = \lambda \cdot v + (1 - \lambda)$ (they are explained in [4] to express *competence* and *necessity*, respectively). The conjunction and disjunction connectives $\wedge, \vee$, interpreted by infimums and supremums in $[0, 1]$, can also be regarded as binary propositional quality operators. They are monotone and continuous, too.

Recall that the set AP is that of atomic propositions.

Definition 2.4. ($\text{LTL}^{\text{disc}}\mathcal{D}, \mathcal{F}$) Given a set $\mathcal{D}$ of discounting functions and a set $\mathcal{F}$ of propositional quality operators, the *formulas* of $\text{LTL}^{\text{disc}}[\mathcal{D}, \mathcal{F}]$ are defined by the grammar: $\varphi ::= \text{True} \mid p \mid \neg\varphi \mid \varphi \wedge \varphi \mid X\varphi \mid \varphi \cup \varphi \mid \varphi \cup_\eta \varphi \mid f(\varphi, \dots, \varphi)$, where $p \in AP$, $\eta \in \mathcal{D}$ is a discounting function and $f \in \mathcal{F}$ is a propositional quality operator (of a suitable arity). We adopt the usual notation conventions: $F\varphi = \text{True}\, U\varphi$ and $G\varphi = \neg F \neg\varphi$. The same goes for discounting operators: $F_\eta \varphi = \text{True}\, U_\eta \varphi$ and $G_\eta \varphi = \neg F_\eta \neg\varphi$.

As we have already discussed, the logic $\text{LTL}^{\text{disc}}[\mathcal{D}, \mathcal{F}]$ extends the usual LTL with: (1) discounted temporal operators like U_η (cf. (1)); and (2) propositional quality operators like $\oplus$ that operate, on truth values from $[0, 1]$ that arise from the discounted modalities, in the ways other than $\wedge$ and $\vee$ do. The precise definition below closely follows [2,3].

Definition 2.5 (Semantics of $\text{LTL}^{\text{disc}}[\mathcal{D}, \mathcal{F}]$ [2,3]). Let $\pi = \pi_0 \pi_1 \dots \in (\mathcal{P}(AP))^\omega$ be a computation (see Sect. 1), and φ be an $\text{LTL}^{\text{disc}}[\mathcal{D}, \mathcal{F}]$ formula. The *truth value* $[\![\pi, \varphi]\!]$ of φ in π is a real number in $[0, 1]$ defined as follows. Recall that $\pi^i = \pi_i \pi_{i+1} \dots$ is a suffix of π.

$$[\![\pi, \text{True}]\!] = 1 \qquad\qquad\qquad [\![\pi, p]\!] = 1 \quad (\text{if } p \in \pi_0); 0 \quad (\text{if } p \notin \pi_0)$$
$$[\![\pi, \neg\varphi]\!] = 1 - [\![\pi, \varphi]\!] \qquad\qquad [\![\pi, \varphi_1 \wedge \varphi_2]\!] = \min\{\, [\![\pi, \varphi_1]\!], [\![\pi, \varphi_2]\!] \,\}$$
$$[\![\pi, X\varphi]\!] = [\![\pi^1, \varphi]\!]$$
$$[\![\pi, \varphi_1 U \varphi_2]\!] = \sup_{i \in \mathbb{N}} \{\, \min\{ [\![\pi^i, \varphi_2]\!], \min_{0 \leq j < i} [\![\pi^j, \varphi_1]\!] \} \,\}$$
$$[\![\pi, \varphi_1 U_\eta \varphi_2]\!] = \sup_{i \in \mathbb{N}} \{\, \min\{ \eta(i)[\![\pi^i, \varphi_2]\!], \min_{0 \leq j < i} \eta(j)[\![\pi^j, \varphi_1]\!] \} \,\}$$
$$[\![\pi, f(\varphi_1, \dots, \varphi_k)]\!] = f([\![\pi, \varphi_1]\!], \dots, [\![\pi, \varphi_k]\!])$$

Compare the semantics of $\varphi_1 U \varphi_2$ and that of $\varphi_1 U_\eta \varphi_2$. The former is a straightforward quantitative analogue of the usual Boolean semantics; the latter additionally includes "discounting" by $\eta(i), \eta(j) \in [0, 1]$. Recall that a discounting function η is deemed to be strictly decreasing; this allows us to express intuitions like in (1).

Proposition 2.6. *The truth value $[\![\pi, \varphi_1 U_\eta \varphi_2]\!]$ lies between 0 and $\eta(0)$.* □

Definition 2.7. Let $\mathcal{K}$ be a Kripke structure and ξ be a path of $\mathcal{K}$. The truth value $[\![\xi, \varphi]\!]$ of φ in the path ξ is defined by $[\![\xi, \varphi]\!] = [\![\lambda(\xi), \varphi]\!]$, where $\lambda(\xi) \in (\mathcal{P}(AP))^\omega$ is the computation induced by ξ (see Sect. 1). The truth value $[\![\mathcal{K}, \varphi]\!]$ of φ in $\mathcal{K}$ is defined by $[\![\mathcal{K}, \varphi]\!] = \inf_{\xi \in \text{path}(\mathcal{K})} [\![\xi, \varphi]\!]$.

Remark 2.8. In this paper we restrict to propositional quality operators that are monotone and continuous, i.e. $\text{LTL}^{\text{disc}}[\mathcal{D}, \mathcal{F}]$ with $\mathcal{F} \subseteq \mathcal{F}_{\text{mc}}$. Such a logic can nevertheless express some non-monotonic operators with the help of negation. For example, the function $f_0 \colon [0, 1] \to [0, 1], f_0(v) = |v - \frac{1}{2}|$ can be expressed as a combination $f_0(v) = \max\{1 - f_1(v), f_2(v)\}$, using $f_1(v) = \min\{v + \frac{1}{2}, 1\}$ and $f_2(v) = \max\{v - \frac{1}{2}, 0\}$ (note that $f_1, f_2 \in \mathcal{F}_{\text{mc}}$)—i.e. as the semantics of the formula $(\neg f_1 \varphi) \vee (f_2 \varphi)$. A nonexample is the function $f_3(v) = v \cdot \sin \frac{1}{v}$ that oscillates infinitely often in $[0, 1]$.

The following "threshold" problems are studied in [3,4]. It is shown that the logic $\text{LTL}^{\text{disc}}[\mathcal{D}, \emptyset]$—i.e. without propositional quality operators other than $\wedge, \vee$—has those problems decidable. Adding the average operator $\oplus$ makes them undecidable [3], while adding ∇_λ (Example 2.3) maintains decidability [4]. Here the complexities are in terms of a suitable notion $|\langle\varphi\rangle|$ of the size of φ (see [3]).

Theorem 2.9 ([3]). *The threshold model-checking problem for $LTL^{\mathrm{disc}}[\mathcal{D},\emptyset]$ is: given a Kripke structure $\mathcal{K}$, an $LTL^{\mathrm{disc}}[\mathcal{D},\emptyset]$ formula φ and $v \in [0,1]$, decide whether $[\![\mathcal{K},\varphi]\!] \geq v$. It is decidable; when restricted to $LTL^{\mathrm{disc}}[\mathcal{D}_{\mathrm{exp}},\emptyset]$ and $v \in \mathbb{Q}$, the problem is in PSPACE in $|\langle\varphi\rangle|$ and in the description of v, and in NLOGSPACE in the size of $\mathcal{K}$. The threshold satisfiability problem for $LTL^{\mathrm{disc}}[\mathcal{D},\emptyset]$ is: given an $LTL^{\mathrm{disc}}[\mathcal{D},\emptyset]$ formula φ, $v \in [0,1]$ and $\sim \in \{<,>\}$, decide whether there exists a computation $\pi \in (\mathcal{P}(AP))^\omega$ such that $[\![\pi,\varphi]\!] \sim v$. This is decidable; when restricted to $LTL^{\mathrm{disc}}[\mathcal{D}_{\mathrm{exp}},\emptyset]$ and $v \in \mathbb{Q}$, the problem is in PSPACE in $|\langle\varphi\rangle|$ and in the description of v.* $\qquad\square$

Theorem 2.10 ([3]). *For $LTL^{\mathrm{disc}}[\mathcal{D},\{\oplus\}]$ where $\mathcal{D} \neq \emptyset$, both the threshold model-checking problem and the threshold satisfiability problem are undecidable.* $\qquad\square$

3 $[0,1]$-Acceptance Büchi Automata

Our algorithm for near-optimal scheduling relies on a certain notion of quantitative automaton—called $[0,1]$-*acceptance Büchi automaton*, see Definition 3.1—and an algorithm for its optimal value problem (Lemma 3.2). The notion is not extensively studied in the literature, to the best of our knowledge. In a $[0,1]$-acceptance Büchi automaton a state has a value $v \in [0,1]$, instead of $b \in \{\mathtt{tt},\mathtt{ff}\}$, of acceptance. Note that branching is Boolean (i.e. nondeterministic) and not $[0,1]$-weighted.

Definition 3.1 ($[0,1]$-**Acceptance Automaton**). A $[0,1]$-*acceptance Büchi automaton*—or simply a $[0,1]$-*acceptance automaton* henceforth—is $\mathcal{A} = (\Sigma, Q, I, \delta, F)$, where Σ is a finite alphabet, Q is a finite set of states, $I \subseteq Q$ is a set of initial states, $\delta : Q \times \Sigma \to (\mathcal{P}(Q) \setminus \{\emptyset\})$ is a transition function and $F : Q \to [0,1]$ is a function that assigns an *acceptance value* to each state. We define the (weighted) language $\mathcal{L}(\mathcal{A}) : \Sigma^\omega \to [0,1]$ of $\mathcal{A}$ by

$$\mathcal{L}(\mathcal{A})(w) \;=\; \max\{F(q) \mid \exists \rho \in \mathrm{run}(w).\, q \in \mathrm{Inf}(\rho)\} \quad \text{for each } w \in \Sigma^\omega, \qquad (2)$$

where the sets $\mathrm{run}(w)$ and $\mathrm{Inf}(\rho)$ are defined as usual.

Note that, when we restrict to Boolean acceptance values (i.e. $F(q) \in \{0,1\}$), the acceptance value in (2) precisely coincides with the one in the usual notion of Büchi automaton. Note also that, in (2), we take the maximum of finitely many values (the state space Q is finite).

The following observation, though not hard, is a key fact for our search algorithm. It is a quantitative analogue of emptiness check in usual (Boolean) automata.

Lemma 3.2 (The Optimal Value Problem for $[0, 1]$-Acceptance Automata). *Let $\mathcal{A}$ be a $[0, 1]$-acceptance Büchi automaton. There exists the maximum $\max_{w \in \Sigma^\omega} \mathcal{L}(\mathcal{A})(w)$ of $\mathcal{L}(\mathcal{A})$. Moreover, there is an algorithm that computes the value $\max_{w \in \Sigma^\omega} \mathcal{L}(\mathcal{A})(w)$ as well as a run $\rho_{max} = q_0 a_0 q_1 a_1 \ldots \in (\Sigma \times Q)^\omega$ that realizes the maximum.* □

The algorithm is much like for emptiness check of (ordinary) Büchi automata, searching for a suitable lasso computation.

We first translate a formula into an *alternating* $[0, 1]$-acceptance automata.

Definition 3.3 (Alternating $[0, 1]$-Acceptance Automaton). An *alternating $[0, 1]$-acceptance (Büchi) automaton* is a tuple $\mathcal{A} = (\Sigma, Q, I, \delta, F)$, where Σ is a finite alphabet, Q is a finite set of states, $I \subseteq Q$ is a set of initial states, $\delta : Q \times \Sigma \to \mathcal{B}^+(Q \cup [0, 1])$ is a transition function and $F : Q \to [0, 1]$ gives acceptance values. Recall (Sect. 1) that $\mathcal{B}^+(Q \cup [0, 1])$ is the set of positive propositional combinations of $q \in Q$ and $v \in [0, 1]$. We define the (weighted) language $\mathcal{L}(\mathcal{A}) : \Sigma^\omega \to [0, 1]$ of $\mathcal{A}$ by $\mathcal{L}(\mathcal{A})(w) = \max_{\tau \in \mathrm{run}_\mathcal{A}(w)} \min_{\rho \in \mathrm{path}_{\mathcal{A}, w}(\tau)} F^\infty(\rho)$, where *runs*, *paths* and the function F^∞ are formally defined much like with the usual alternating automaton.

Precise definitions of runs, paths and F^∞ are found in the extended version [19]. In the above we used max and min (not sup or inf) since $\{F(q) \mid q \in Q\}$ is a finite set.

Proposition 3.4. *Let $\mathcal{A} = (\Sigma, Q, I, \delta, F)$ be an alternating $[0, 1]$-acceptance automaton. There exists a $[0, 1]$-acceptance automaton $\mathcal{A}'$ such that $\mathcal{L}(\mathcal{A}) = \mathcal{L}(\mathcal{A}')$.* □

The construction of $\mathcal{A}'$ is a quantitative adaptation of the one in [18] that turns an alternating ω-automaton into a nondeterministic one. In our adaptation we use what we call *exposition flags*, an idea that is potentially useful in other settings with Büchi-type acceptance conditions, too. See Appendix B.1 (of the extended version [19]) for details of the proof and the construction therein.

Later we will also use the fact that $[0, 1]$-acceptance automata are closed under monotone propositional quality operators (Definition 2.2).

Proposition 3.5. *Let $f : [0, 1]^k \to [0, 1]$ be monotone, and $\mathcal{A}_1, \ldots, \mathcal{A}_k$ be $[0, 1]$-acceptance automata over a common alphabet Σ. There is a $[0, 1]$-acceptance automaton $f(\mathcal{A}_1, \ldots, \mathcal{A}_k)$ such that $\mathcal{L}(f(\mathcal{A}_1, \ldots, \mathcal{A}_k))(w) = f(\mathcal{L}(\mathcal{A}_1)(w), \ldots, \mathcal{L}(\mathcal{A}_k)(w))$ for each w.* □

A generalization of $[0, 1]$-acceptance automaton is naturally obtained by making transitions also $[0, 1]$-weighted. The result is called *fuzzy automaton* and studied e.g. in [21]. In Appendix C of the extended version [19] we show that this generalization does not add expressivity. In fact we prove a more general result there, parametrizing $[0, 1]$ into a suitable semiring $\mathbb{K}$.

4   Near-Optimal Scheduling for LTL$^{\text{disc}}[\mathcal{D}, \mathcal{F}_{\text{mc}}]$

In [3,4] the threshold model-checking problem for the logic LTL$^{\text{disc}}[\mathcal{D}, \mathcal{F}]$ is studied. In this paper, instead, we are interested in the following problem: what path of a given Kripke structure $\mathcal{K}$ is the best for a given LTL$^{\text{disc}}[\mathcal{D}, \mathcal{F}]$ formula φ.

In general, however, there does not exist an optimal path ξ_0 of $\mathcal{K}$, i.e. one that achieves $[\![\xi_0, \varphi]\!] = \sup_{\xi \in \text{path}(\mathcal{K})} [\![\xi, \varphi]\!]$.

Example 4.1 (Optimality not Achievable). Take a formula $\varphi = \mathsf{G}_\eta \mathsf{F} p$ and the Kripke structure $\mathcal{K}$ shown in the above. This example illustrates that the existence of an optimal path is not guaranteed in general: indeed, whereas $\sup_{\xi' \in \text{path}(\mathcal{K})} [\![\xi', \varphi]\!] = 1$ in this example, there is no path ξ that achieves $[\![\xi, \varphi]\!] = 1$.

More specifically: we first note that, in each path ξ of the Kripke structure, p is true at most once. The later the state s_1 occurs in a path ξ, the bigger the truth value $[\![\xi, \varphi]\!]$ is; moreover the value $[\![\xi, \varphi]\!]$ tends to 1 (since η tends to 0). However there is no path ξ that achieves exactly $[\![\xi, \varphi]\!] = 1$: if p is postponed indefinitely, no state in ξ satisfies p, in which case $\mathsf{F}p$ is everywhere false and hence $[\![\xi, \varphi]\!] = 0$.

Definition 4.2. The *near-optimal scheduling* problem for LTL$^{\text{disc}}[\mathcal{D}, \mathcal{F}]$ is: given a Kripke structure $\mathcal{K} = (W, R, \lambda)$, an LTL$^{\text{disc}}[\mathcal{D}, \mathcal{F}]$ formula φ and a positive real number $\varepsilon \in (0, 1)$, to find a path $\xi_0 \in \text{path}(\mathcal{K})$ such that $[\![\xi_0, \varphi]\!] \geq \sup_{\xi \in \text{path}(\mathcal{K})} [\![\xi, \varphi]\!] - \varepsilon$.

Ultimately we will show that the problem in the above is decidable (Theorem 4.14), when all the propositional quality operators are monotone and continuous ($\mathcal{F} \subseteq \mathcal{F}_{\text{mc}}$).

We first note that, in the special case for LTL$^{\text{disc}}[\mathcal{D}, \emptyset]$ (i.e. no propositional quality operators), there is a straightforward binary search algorithm that relies on the (threshold) model-checking algorithm in [3] (Theorem 2.9). Specifically, the binary search algorithm repeatedly conducts threshold model-checking for: the threshold $v = \frac{1}{2}$ in the first round; $v = \frac{1}{4}$ or $\frac{3}{4}$ in the second round, depending on the outcome of the first round; then for $v = \frac{1}{8}, \ldots, \frac{6}{8}$ or $\frac{7}{8}$, depending on the outcome of the second round; and so on. Given a margin $\varepsilon \in (0, 1)$, this way, we need $-\log \varepsilon$ rounds. This binary search algorithm is rather effective (see Sect. 5 of the extended version [19]).

However the binary search algorithm does not work in presence of the average operator $\oplus$, simply because the threshold model-checking problem is undecidable (Theorem 2.10). Our main contribution is a novel algorithm for near-optimal scheduling that works even in this case (and more generally for the logic LTL$^{\text{disc}}[\mathcal{D}, \mathcal{F}_{\text{mc}}]$). Our algorithm first translates a formula φ and a margin $\varepsilon \in (0, 1)$ to an alternating $[0, 1]$-acceptance automaton $\mathcal{A}_{\varphi, \varepsilon}$, which is further turned into a $[0, 1]$-acceptance automaton (Proposition 3.4). The resulting automaton—after taking the product with $\mathcal{K}$—is amenable to optimal value search (Lemma 3.2), yielding a solution to the original problem.

In the rest of the section we describe our algorithm. We shall however first restrict to the logic $\text{LTL}^{\text{disc}}[\mathcal{D}, \emptyset]$ for the sake of presentation (although this basic fragment allows binary search). After describing the basic algorithm for $\text{LTL}^{\text{disc}}[\mathcal{D}, \emptyset]$ in Sect. 4.1, in Sect. 4.2 we explain how it can be modified to accommodate propositional quality operators.

4.1   Our Algorithm, When Restricted to $\text{LTL}^{\text{disc}}[\mathcal{D}, \emptyset]$

Our translation of φ and $\varepsilon \in (0, 1)$ to an automaton $\mathcal{A}_{\varphi, \varepsilon}$ is an extension of the standard translation from LTL formulas to alternating Büchi automata (e.g. in [23]), with: (1) incorporation of quantities—accumulation of discount factors, more specifically—by means of what we call *discount sequences*; and (2) cutting off those events which are far in the future—the idea of *event horizon* from [3]. The extension is not complicated on the conceptual level. Its details need care, however, especially in handling negations and alternation of greatest and least fixed points.

As preparation, we recall some definitions and notations from [3].

Definition 4.3 (η^{+k}, $xcl(\varphi)$ [3]). Let $\eta : \mathbb{N} \to [0, 1]$ be a discounting function. We define a discounting function $\eta^{+k} : \mathbb{N} \to [0, 1]$ by $\eta^{+k}(i) = \eta(i + k)$ for each $k \in \mathbb{N}$. For an $\text{LTL}^{\text{disc}}[\mathcal{D}, \mathcal{F}]$ formula φ, the *extended closure* $xcl(\varphi)$ of φ [3] is defined by $xcl(\varphi) = \text{Sub}(\varphi) \cup \{\varphi_1 \mathsf{U}_{\eta^{+k}} \varphi_2 \mid k \in \mathbb{N}, \varphi_1 \mathsf{U}_\eta \varphi_2 \in \text{Sub}(\varphi)\}$, where $\text{Sub}(\varphi)$ denotes the set of subformulas of φ.

Discounting Sequences. We go on to technical details. In the alternating $[0, 1]$-acceptance automaton $\mathcal{A}_{\varphi, \varepsilon}$ that we shall construct, a state is a pair $(\psi, \vec{d})$ of a formula ψ and a *discount sequence* $\vec{d} \in [0, 1]^+$.

Definition 4.4 (Discount Sequence). A *discount sequence* is a sequence $\vec{d} = d_1 d_2 \ldots d_n \in [0, 1]^+$ of real numbers with a nonzero length ($d_i \in [0, 1]$ for each i).

The notion of discount sequence is a quantitative extension of that of *priority* in parity automata. Specifically, the length n of a discount sequence $\vec{d} = d_1 d_2 \ldots d_n$ corresponds to a priority—i.e. the alternation depth of greatest and least fixed points. Each real number d_i in the sequence, in turn, stands for the accumulated discount factor in each level of fixed-point alternation. For example, the formula $\mathsf{F}_{\exp\frac{1}{2}} \mathsf{G}_{\exp\frac{2}{3}} \mathsf{F}_{\exp\frac{3}{4}} p$ will induce a discount sequence $((\frac{1}{2})^{n_1}, (\frac{2}{3})^{n_2}, (\frac{3}{4})^{n_3})$ of length 3—where n_1, n_2 and n_3 are the numbers of steps for which the three discounting temporal operators F_{η_1}, G_{η_2} and F_{η_3} "have waited," respectively.

We use three operators $\odot, :, \boxtimes$ that act on discount sequences; the intuitions are as follows. The first two are for accumulating discount factors: we use $\odot$ in case there is no alternation of greatest and least fixed points; and we use : in case there is. Examples are: $\left((\frac{1}{2})^2, (\frac{2}{3})^3, \frac{3}{4}\right) \odot \frac{4}{5} = \left((\frac{1}{2})^2, (\frac{2}{3})^3, \frac{3}{4} \cdot \frac{4}{5}\right) = \left((\frac{1}{2})^2, (\frac{2}{3})^3, \frac{3}{5}\right)$ and $\left((\frac{1}{2})^2, (\frac{2}{3})^3, \frac{3}{4}\right) : \frac{4}{5} = \left((\frac{1}{2})^2, (\frac{2}{3})^3, \frac{3}{4}, \frac{4}{5}\right)$. Note that in the former the length is preserved, while in the latter the sequence gets longer by one.

Definition 4.5 ($\vec{d} \odot d'$, $\vec{d}{:}d'$). The operator $\odot$ takes a discount sequence $\vec{d}$ and a discount factor $d' \in [0, 1]$ as arguments, and multiplies the last element of $\vec{d}$ by d'. That is, $(d_1 d_2 \ldots d_n) \odot d' = d_1 d_2 \ldots d_{n-1}(d_n \cdot d') \in [0,1]^+$. The operator : is simply the concatenation operator: given $\vec{d} = d_1 d_2 \ldots d_n$ and $d' \in [0, 1]$, the sequence $\vec{d}{:}d'$ is $d_1 d_2 \ldots d_n d'$ of length $n + 1$.

We use the operator $\boxtimes$ in $\vec{d} \boxtimes v$ to let a discount sequence $\vec{d}$ act on a truth value $v \in [0, 1]$.

Definition 4.6 ($\vec{d} \boxtimes v$). The operator $\boxtimes$ takes $\vec{d} \in [0, 1]^+$ and $v \in [0, 1]$ as arguments. The value $\vec{d} \boxtimes v \in [0, 1]$ is defined inductively by:

$$d \boxtimes v = dv , \qquad \vec{d}d' \boxtimes v = \vec{d} \boxtimes (1 - d'v) . \quad \text{Explicitly:} \tag{3}$$

$$(d_1 d_2 \ldots d_n) \boxtimes v = \\ d_1 - d_1 d_2 + d_1 d_2 d_3 - \cdots + (-1)^n d_1 d_2 \ldots d_{n-1} + (-1)^{n+1} d_1 d_2 \ldots d_n v . \tag{4}$$

The intuition behind the action $\vec{d} \boxtimes v$ is most visible in (3), where dv and $d'v$ denote multiplication of real numbers. Given a discount sequence $\vec{d}d'$: (1) we apply the final discount factor d' to the truth value v, obtaining $d'v$; (2) the alternation between greatest and least fixed points is taken into account, by taking the negation $1 - d'v$ (cf. Definition 2.5); and (3) we apply the remaining sequence $\vec{d}$ inductively and obtain $\vec{d} \boxtimes (1 - d'v)$. An example is $\left(\frac{3}{4}, \frac{1}{3}, \frac{2}{5}\right) \boxtimes 1 = \left(\frac{3}{4}, \frac{1}{3}\right) \boxtimes \left(1 - \frac{2}{5} \cdot 1\right) = \left(\frac{3}{4}, \frac{1}{3}\right) \boxtimes \frac{3}{5} = \left(\frac{3}{4}\right) \boxtimes \left(1 - \frac{1}{3} \cdot \frac{3}{5}\right) = \left(\frac{3}{4}\right) \boxtimes \frac{4}{5} = \frac{3}{5}$.

Table 1. Transition function δ of $\mathcal{A}^{p}_{\varphi,\varepsilon}$

$$\delta\big((\mathtt{True}, \vec{d}), \sigma\big) = \vec{d} \boxtimes 1 \qquad \delta\big((p, \vec{d}), \sigma\big) = \begin{cases} \vec{d} \boxtimes 1 & \text{if } p \in \sigma, \\ \vec{d} \boxtimes 0 & \text{otherwise.} \end{cases}$$

$$\delta\big((\mathsf{X}\psi, \vec{d}), \sigma\big) = (\psi, \vec{d}) \qquad \delta\big((\neg\psi, \vec{d}), \sigma\big) = \delta\big((\psi, \vec{d}{:}1), \sigma\big) \tag{5}$$

$$\delta\big((\psi_1 \wedge \psi_2, \vec{d}), \sigma\big) = \begin{cases} \delta\big((\psi_1, \vec{d}), \sigma\big) \wedge \delta\big((\psi_2, \vec{d}), \sigma\big) & \text{if } |\vec{d}| \text{ is odd,} \\ \delta\big((\psi_1, \vec{d}), \sigma\big) \vee \delta\big((\psi_2, \vec{d}), \sigma\big) & \text{otherwise.} \end{cases}$$

$$\delta\big((\psi_1 \mathsf{U} \psi_2, \vec{d}), \sigma\big) = \begin{cases} \delta\big((\psi_2, \vec{d}), \sigma\big) \vee \big(\delta\big((\psi_1, \vec{d}), \sigma\big) \wedge (\psi_1 \mathsf{U} \psi_2, \vec{d})\big) & \text{if } |\vec{d}| \text{ is odd,} \\ \delta\big((\psi_2, \vec{d}), \sigma\big) \wedge \big(\delta\big((\psi_1, \vec{d}), \sigma\big) \vee (\psi_1 \mathsf{U} \psi_2, \vec{d})\big) & \text{otherwise.} \end{cases}$$

For $\delta\big((\psi_1 \mathsf{U}_\eta \psi_2, \vec{d}), \sigma\big)$ we make cases. Let $\vec{d} = d_1 \ldots d_n$. If $\eta(0) \cdot \prod_{i=1}^{n} d_i \le \varepsilon$:

$$\delta\big((\psi_1 \mathsf{U}_\eta \psi_2, \vec{d}), \sigma\big) = \begin{cases} \vec{d} \boxtimes 0 & \text{if } |\vec{d}| \text{ is odd,} \\ \vec{d} \boxtimes \eta(0) & \text{otherwise;} \end{cases} \tag{6}$$

otherwise, i.e. if $\eta(0) \cdot \prod_{i=1}^{n} d_i > \varepsilon$:

$$\delta\big((\psi_1 \mathsf{U}_\eta \psi_2, \vec{d}), \sigma\big) = \\ \begin{cases} \delta\big((\psi_2, \vec{d} \odot \eta(0)), \sigma\big) \vee \big(\delta\big((\psi_1, \vec{d} \odot \eta(0)), \sigma\big) \wedge (\psi_1 \mathsf{U}_{\eta+1} \psi_2, \vec{d})\big) & \text{if } |\vec{d}| \text{ is odd,} \\ \delta\big((\psi_2, \vec{d} \odot \eta(0)), \sigma\big) \wedge \big(\delta\big((\psi_1, \vec{d} \odot \eta(0)), \sigma\big) \vee (\psi_1 \mathsf{U}_{\eta+1} \psi_2, \vec{d})\big) & \text{otherwise.} \end{cases} \tag{7}$$

The following relationship between $\odot$ and $\boxtimes$ is easily seen to hold: $(\vec{d} \odot d') \boxtimes v = \vec{d} \boxtimes (d' \cdot v)$. The three operators $\odot, :, \boxtimes$ defined in the above will be used shortly, in the construction of the automaton $\mathcal{A}_{\varphi,\varepsilon}$. Their roles are briefly discussed after Definition 4.7.

Construction of $\mathcal{A}_{\varphi,\varepsilon}$. We describe the construction of $\mathcal{A}_{\varphi,\varepsilon}$, for a formula φ of $\mathrm{LTL}^{\mathrm{disc}}[\mathcal{D}, \emptyset]$ and a margin ε. We subsequently discuss ideas behind it, comparing the definition with other known constructions.

We first define $\mathcal{A}_{\varphi,\varepsilon}^{\mathrm{p}}$ that is infinite-state, and obtain $\mathcal{A}_{\varphi,\varepsilon}$ as the reachable part. The latter will be shown to be finite-state (Lemma 4.8).

Definition 4.7 (The Automata $\mathcal{A}_{\varphi,\varepsilon}^{\mathrm{p}}, \mathcal{A}_{\varphi,\varepsilon}$). Let φ be an $\mathrm{LTL}^{\mathrm{disc}}[\mathcal{D}, \emptyset]$ formula and $\varepsilon \in (0,1)$. We define an alternating $[0, 1]$-acceptance automaton $\mathcal{A}_{\varphi,\varepsilon}^{\mathrm{p}} = (\mathcal{P}(AP), Q, I, \delta, F)$ as follows. Its state space Q is $xcl(\varphi) \times [0,1]^+$; hence a state is a pair $(\psi, \vec{d})$ of a formula and a discount sequence. The transition function $\delta : Q \times \mathcal{P}(AP) \to \mathcal{B}^+(Q \cup [0,1])$ is defined as in Table 1, where we let $\vec{d} = d_1 d_2 \ldots d_n \in [0,1]^+$ and $\sigma \in \mathcal{P}(AP)$.

The set I of the initial states of $\mathcal{A}_{\varphi,\varepsilon}^{\mathrm{p}}$ is $\{(\varphi, 1)\}$. The acceptance function F is

$$F(\psi, \vec{d}) = \begin{cases} 1 & \text{if } \psi = \psi_1 \mathsf{U} \psi_2 \text{ and } |\vec{d}| \text{ is even} \\ 0 & \text{otherwise.} \end{cases} \tag{8}$$

The alternating $[0, 1]$-acceptance automaton $\mathcal{A}_{\varphi,\varepsilon}$ is defined to be the restriction of $\mathcal{A}_{\varphi,\varepsilon}^{\mathrm{p}}$ to the states that are reachable from the initial state $(\varphi, 1)$.

Examples of $\mathcal{A}_{\varphi,\varepsilon}$ are in Figs. 1–2, where $(\varphi, \varepsilon) = (\mathsf{G}_{\exp\frac{1}{2}} \mathsf{F}_{\exp\frac{2}{5}} p, \frac{1}{3})$ and $(\mathsf{F}_{\exp\frac{1}{2}} \mathsf{G} p, \frac{1}{3})$. There a discount sequence $d_1 \ldots d_n$ is denoted by $\langle d_1, \ldots, d_n \rangle$ for readability.

Some remarks on Definition 4.7 are in order.

In Absence of Discounting (Sanity Check). If the formula φ contains no discounting operator U_η, then the construction essentially coincides the usual one in [23] that translates a (usual) LTL formula to an alternating Büchi automaton. To see it, recall that the length $|\vec{d}|$ of a discount sequence plays the role of a priority in parity automata (Sect. 4.1). Therefore in the first case of (8), $|\vec{d}|$ being even means that we are in fact dealing with a greatest fixed point. This makes the state accepting (in the Büchi sense), much like in [23].

$\mathcal{A}_{\varphi,\varepsilon}$ is Quantitative. The acceptance values of the states of $\mathcal{A}_{\varphi,\varepsilon}$ are Boolean (see (8)). Nevertheless the automaton is quantitative, in that non-Boolean values from $[0, 1]$ appear as atomic propositions in the range $\mathcal{B}^+(Q \cup [0,1])$ of the transition δ (they occur at the leaves in Figs. 1–2). Once we transform $\mathcal{A}_{\varphi,\varepsilon}$ to a non-alternating automaton (Proposition 3.4), these non-Boolean propositional values give rise to non-Boolean acceptance values.

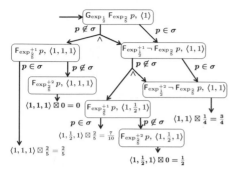

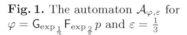

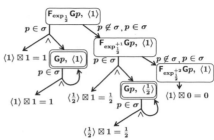

Fig. 1. The automaton $\mathcal{A}_{\varphi,\varepsilon}$ for $\varphi = \mathsf{G}_{\exp\frac{1}{2}}\mathsf{F}_{\exp\frac{2}{5}}p$ and $\varepsilon = \frac{1}{3}$

Fig. 2. The automaton $\mathcal{A}_{\varphi,\varepsilon}$ for $\varphi = \mathsf{F}_{\exp\frac{1}{2}}\mathsf{G}p$ and $\varepsilon = \frac{1}{3}$. The double-lined nodes have the acceptance value 1.

Event Horizon. A fundamental idea from [3] is the following. A discounting operator, in presence of a threshold (in [3]) or a nonzero margin (here), allows an exact representation by a (finitary) formula without a fixed point operator. The latter means, for example:

$$[\![\pi, \mathsf{F}_{\exp\frac{1}{2}}\varphi]\!] \geq \tfrac{1}{4} \quad \Longleftrightarrow \quad \pi \models \varphi \vee \mathsf{X}\varphi \vee \mathsf{XX}\varphi \ , \quad \text{and} \tag{9}$$

$$[\![\pi, \mathsf{G}_{\exp\frac{1}{2}}\varphi]\!] \geq \tfrac{3}{4} \quad \Longleftrightarrow \quad \pi \models \varphi \wedge \mathsf{X}\varphi \wedge \mathsf{XX}\varphi \ , \tag{10}$$

and so on. Note that in (9), whatever happens after two time units has contributions less than $(\frac{1}{2})^2 = \frac{1}{4}$ and therefore never enough to make up the threshold. The example (10) is similar, with events in the future having only negligible negative contributions. In other words: fixed point operators with discounting have an *event horizon*—in the above examples (9–10) it lies between $t = 2$ and 3—nothing beyond which matters.

This idea of event horizon is used in the distinction between (6) and (7). The value $\eta(0) \cdot \prod_{i=1}^{n} d_i$ is, as we shall see, the greatest contribution to a truth value that the events henceforth potentially have. In case it is smaller than the margin ε we can safely ignore the *positive* contribution henceforth and take the smallest possible truth value 0—much like the disjunct $\mathsf{X}^3\varphi \vee \mathsf{X}^4\varphi \vee \cdots$ is truncated in (9). This is what is done in the first case in (6). The second case in (6) is about a greatest fixed point and we truncate the *negative* contributions of the events beyond the event horizon—this is much like the obligation $\mathsf{X}^3\varphi \wedge \mathsf{X}^4\varphi \wedge \cdots$ is lifted in (10). In this case we use the greatest truth value possible, namely $\eta(0)$. This is what is done in (6).

Use of Discount Sequences. Discount sequences $\vec{d}$ are used for two purposes. Firstly, as we already described, its length $|\vec{d}|$ indicates the alternation between positive and negative views on a formula—observe that a discount sequence gets longer in (5). Consequently many clauses in the definition of δ distinguish cases according to the parity of $|\vec{d}|$. Secondly it records all the discount factors that have been encountered. See (7), where the last element of $\vec{d}$ is multiplied by the newly encountered factor $\eta(0)$ and updated to $\vec{d} \odot \eta(0)$. Such accumulation $\vec{d}$ of discount factors acts on a truth value via the $\boxtimes$ operator, like in (6) and in the definition of $\delta\big((\mathtt{True}, \vec{d}), \sigma\big)$.

Lemma 4.8. *The automaton $\mathcal{A}_{\varphi,\varepsilon}$ has only finitely many states.*   □

The following "correctness lemma" claims that $\mathcal{A}_{\varphi,\varepsilon}$ conducts the expected task.

Lemma 4.9. *Let φ be an $LTL^{\mathrm{disc}}[\mathcal{D}, \emptyset]$ formula and $\varepsilon \in (0,1)$ be a positive real number. For each computation $\pi \in (\mathcal{P}(AP))^{\omega}$, we have $[\![\pi, \varphi]\!] - \varepsilon \leq \mathcal{L}(\mathcal{A}_{\varphi,\varepsilon})(\pi) \leq [\![\pi, \varphi]\!]$*   □

The Algorithm. After the construction of $\mathcal{A}_{\varphi,\varepsilon}$, the algorithm proceeds in the following manner. We first translate $\mathcal{A}_{\varphi,\varepsilon}$ to a (non-alternating) $[0, 1]$-acceptance automaton (relying on Proposition 3.4).

Corollary 4.10. *Let φ be an $LTL^{\mathrm{disc}}[\mathcal{D}, \emptyset]$ formula and $\varepsilon \in (0,1)$ be a positive real number. There exists a (non-alternating) $[0, 1]$-acceptance automaton $\mathcal{A}_{\varphi,\varepsilon}^{\mathrm{na}}$ such that $[\![\pi, \varphi]\!] - \varepsilon \leq \mathcal{L}(\mathcal{A}_{\varphi,\varepsilon}^{\mathrm{na}})(\pi) \leq [\![\pi, \varphi]\!]$ for each computation $\pi \in (\mathcal{P}(AP))^{\omega}$.*   □

Towards the solution of the near-optimal scheduling problem (Definition 4.2), we construct the *product* of $\mathcal{A}_{\varphi,\varepsilon}^{\mathrm{na}}$ in Corollary 4.10 and the given Kripke structure $\mathcal{K}$. Since transitions of $[0, 1]$-acceptance automata are nondeterministic, this product can be defined just as usual.

Definition 4.11. *Let $\mathcal{A} = (\mathcal{P}(AP), Q, I, \delta, F)$ be a $[0, 1]$-acceptance automaton and $\mathcal{K} = (W, R, \lambda)$ be a Kripke structure. Their product $\mathcal{A} \times \mathcal{K}$ is a $[0, 1]$-acceptance automaton $(1, Q', I', \delta', F')$—over a singleton alphabet $1 = \{\bullet\}$—defined by: $Q' = Q$; $I' = I \times W$; $\delta'\big((q, s), \bullet\big) = \big\{ (q', s') \mid q' \in \delta(q, \lambda(s)), (s, s') \in R \big\}$; and $F'(q, s) = F(q)$.*

Lemma 4.12. *Let $(q_0, s_0) \bullet (q_1, s_1) \bullet \ldots$ be an optimal run of the automaton $\mathcal{A} \times \mathcal{K}$ (that necessarily exists by Lemma 3.2). The path $s_0 s_1 \ldots \in \mathrm{path}(\mathcal{K})$ realizes the optimal value of $\mathcal{A}$, that is, $\mathcal{L}(\mathcal{A})\big(\lambda(s_0)\lambda(s_1)\ldots\big) = \max_{\xi \in \mathrm{path}(\mathcal{K})} \mathcal{L}(\mathcal{A})\big(\lambda(\xi)\big)$.*   □

Theorem 4.13 (Optimal Scheduling for ($\mathbf{LTL}^{\mathrm{disc}}[\mathcal{D}, \emptyset]$). *Assume the setting of Definition 4.2, and that $\mathcal{F} = \emptyset$ (i.e. the formula φ contains no propositional quality operators). Let $(q_0, s_0) \bullet (q_1, s_1) \bullet \ldots$ be an optimal run (computed by Lemma 3.2) for the $[0, 1]$-acceptance automaton $\mathcal{A}_{\varphi,\varepsilon}^{\mathrm{na}} \times \mathcal{K}$ constructed as in Definition 4.7, Corollary 4.10 and Definition 4.11. Then the path $s_0 s_1 \ldots \in \mathrm{path}(\mathcal{K})$ is a solution to the near-optimal scheduling problem (Definition 4.2).*

Moreover, the solution $s_0 s_1 \ldots$ can be chosen to be ultimately periodic.   □

4.2   Our General Algorithm for LTL$^{\text{disc}}[\mathcal{D}, \mathcal{F}_{\text{mc}}]$

Our general algorithm works in the setting of LTL$^{\text{disc}}[\mathcal{D}, \mathcal{F}_{\text{mc}}]$—i.e. in the presence of monotone and continuous propositional quality operators like $\oplus$—where threshold model checking is potentially undecidable [3] and therefore the binary-search algorithm (described after Definition 4.2) may not work.

The general algorithm is a (rather straightforward) adaptation of the one we described for LTL$^{\text{disc}}[\mathcal{D}, \emptyset]$ (Sect. 4.1). Here we construct the alternating [0, 1]-acceptance automaton $\mathcal{A}_{\varphi,\varepsilon}$ *inductively* on the construction on the formula φ: (1) when the outermost connective is other than a propositional quality operator, the construction is much like in Definition 4.7; (2) when the outermost connective is a propositional quality operator, we rely on Proposition 3.5. The rest of the algorithm (i.e. the part described in Sect. 4.1) remains unchanged. An extensive description of the details of the construction is deferred to Appendix A of [19].

Theorem 4.14 (Main Theorem, Optimal Scheduling for LTL^{disc} $[\mathcal{D}, \mathcal{F}_{\text{mc}}]$). *In the setting of Definition 4.2, assume that $\mathcal{F} \subseteq \mathcal{F}_{\text{mc}}$ (i.e. all the operators in φ are monotone and continuous). Then the near-optimal scheduling problem is decidable.*   □

4.3   Complexity

The two parameters $\mathcal{D}$ and $\mathcal{F}$ in LTL$^{\text{disc}}[\mathcal{D}, \mathcal{F}]$—i.e. discounting functions (Definition 2.1) and propositional quality operators (Definition 2.2)—are both relevant to the complexity of our algorithm. Formulating a complexity result is hard when these parameters are left open. We therefore restrict to: (1) exponential discounting functions (Definition 2.1), i.e. $\mathcal{D} = \mathcal{D}_{\text{exp}} = \{\exp_\lambda \mid \lambda \in (0,1) \cap \mathbb{Q}\}$, as is done in [3]; and (2) the average operator $\oplus$, i.e. $\mathcal{F} = \{\oplus\}$. We use the definition $|\langle\varphi\rangle|$ of the size of a formula φ, which is from [3]: it reflects the description length of $\lambda \in \mathbb{Q}$ that appears in discounting functions, as well as the length of φ as an expression.

Proposition 4.15 (Size of $\mathcal{A}_{\varphi,\varepsilon}$). *Let φ be an LTL$^{\text{disc}}[\mathcal{D}_{\text{exp}}, \{\oplus\}]$ formula and $\varepsilon \in (0,1) \cap \mathbb{Q}$ be a positive rational number. The size of the state space of the alternating [0, 1]-acceptance automaton $\mathcal{A}_{\varphi,\varepsilon}$ is singly exponential in $|\langle\varphi\rangle|$ and in the length of the description of ε.*   □

Theorem 4.16 (Complexity for LTL$^{\text{disc}}[\mathcal{D}_{\text{exp}}, \{\oplus\}]$). *The near-optimal scheduling problem for LTL$^{\text{disc}}[\mathcal{D}_{\text{exp}}, \{\oplus\}]$ is: in EXPSPACE in $|\langle\varphi\rangle|$ and in the description length of ε; and in NLOGSPACE in the size of $\mathcal{K}$.*   □

In case of absence of propositional quality operators (i.e. LTL$^{\text{disc}}[\mathcal{D}_{\text{exp}}, \emptyset]$), we can further optimize the complexity by using a heuristic and avoiding the exponential blowup from $\mathcal{A}_{\varphi,\varepsilon}$ to $\mathcal{A}_{\varphi,\varepsilon}^{\text{na}}$. This yields the following complexity result, which is also achievable by the binary-search algorithm.

Theorem 4.17 (Complexity for LTL$^{\text{disc}}[\mathcal{D}_{\text{exp}}, \emptyset]$). *The near-optimal scheduling problem for LTL$^{\text{disc}}[\mathcal{D}_{\text{exp}}, \emptyset]$ is: in PSPACE in $|\langle\varphi\rangle|$ and in the description length of ε; and in NLOGSPACE in the size of $\mathcal{K}$.*   □

We implemented our algorithm in Sect. 4 that solves the near-optimal scheduling for $\mathrm{LTL}^{\mathrm{disc}}[\mathcal{D}_{\mathrm{exp}}, \{\oplus\}]$. There are some experimental results in the extended version [19].

5   Conclusions and Future Work

For the quantitative logic $\mathrm{LTL}^{\mathrm{disc}}[\mathcal{D}_{\mathrm{exp}}, \mathcal{F}]$ with future discounting [3], we formulated a natural problem of near-optimal scheduling, and presented an algorithm. The latter relies on: the existing idea of *event horizon* exploited in [3] for the threshold model checking problem, as well as a supposedly widely-applicable technique of translation to $[0, 1]$-acceptance automata and a lasso-style optimal value algorithm for them.

Here are several directions of future work.

Controller Synthesis for Open Systems. We note that the current results are focused on *closed* systems. For *open* or *reactive* systems (like a server that responds to requests that come from the environment) we would wish to synthesize a *controller*—formally a *strategy* or a *transducer*—that achieves a near-optimal performance.

An envisaged workflow, following the one in [23], is as follows. We will use the same automaton $\mathcal{A}_{\varphi,\varepsilon}$ (Definition 4.7). It is then: (1) determinized, (2) transformed into a tree automaton that accepts the desired strategies, and (3) the optimal value of the tree automaton is checked, much like in Lemma 3.2. While the step (2) will be straightforward, the steps (1) and (3) (namely: determinization of $[0, 1]$-acceptance automata, and the optimal value problem for "$[0, 1]$-acceptance Rabin automata") are yet to be investigated. Another possible workflow is by an adaptation of the Safraless algorithm [16].

Probabilistic Systems and $\mathbf{LTL}^{\mathrm{disc}}[\mathcal{D}_{\mathrm{exp}}, \mathcal{F}]$. Here and in [3] the system model is a Kripke structure that is nondeterministic. Adding probabilistic branching will gives us a set of new problems to be solved: for Markov chains the threshold model-checking problem can be formulated; for Markov decision processes, we have both the threshold model-checking problem and the near-optimal scheduling problem. Furthermore, another axis of variation is given by whether we consider the expected value or the worst-case value. In the latter case we would wish to exclude truth values that arise with probability 0. All these variations have important applications in various areas.

Acknowledgments. Thanks are due to Shaull Almagor, Shuichi Hirahara, and the anonymous referees, for useful discussions and comments. The authors are supported by Grants-in-Aid No. 24680001, 15KT0012 and 15K11984, JSPS.

References

1. Abdeddaïm, Y., Asarin, E., Maler, O.: Scheduling with timed automata. Theor. Comput. Sci. **354**(2), 272–300 (2006)

2. Almagor, S., Boker, U., Kupferman, O.: Formalizing and reasoning about quality. In: Fomin, F.V., Freivalds, R., Kwiatkowska, M., Peleg, D. (eds.) ICALP 2013, Part II. LNCS, vol. 7966, pp. 15–27. Springer, Heidelberg (2013)
3. Almagor, S., Boker, U., Kupferman, O.: Discounting in LTL. In: Ábrahám, E., Havelund, K. (eds.) TACAS 2014 (ETAPS). LNCS, vol. 8413, pp. 424–439. Springer, Heidelberg (2014)
4. Almagor, S., Boker, U., Kupferman, O.: Formalizing and reasoning about quality. Extended version of [2], preprint (private communication) (2014)
5. Baier, C., Dubslaff, C., Klüppelholz, S.: Trade-off analysis meets probabilistic model checking. In: Henzinger, T.A., Miller, D. (eds.), CSL-LICS 2014, p. 1. ACM (2014)
6. Bloem, R., Chatterjee, K., Henzinger, T.A., Jobstmann, B.: Better quality in synthesis through quantitative objectives. In: Bouajjani, A., Maler, O. (eds.) CAV 2009. LNCS, vol. 5643, pp. 140–156. Springer, Heidelberg (2009)
7. Bouyer, P., Markey, N., Matteplackel, R.M.: Averaging in LTL. In: Baldan, P., Gorla, D. (eds.) CONCUR 2014. LNCS, vol. 8704, pp. 266–280. Springer, Heidelberg (2014)
8. Černý, P., Chatterjee, K., Henzinger, T.A., Radhakrishna, A., Singh, R.: Quantitative synthesis for concurrent programs. In: Gopalakrishnan, G., Qadeer, S. (eds.) CAV 2011. LNCS, vol. 6806, pp. 243–259. Springer, Heidelberg (2011)
9. Chatterjee, K., Doyen, L., Henzinger, T.A.: Expressiveness and closure properties for quantitative languages. Logical Methods Comput. Sci. **6**(3), 1–23 (2010)
10. Chatterjee, K., Henzinger, T.A., Jurdzinski, M.: Mean-payoff parity games. In: LICS 2005, pp. 178–187. IEEE Computer Society (2005)
11. Cheung, L., Stoelinga, M., Vaandrager, F.W.: A testing scenario for probabilistic processes. J. ACM **54**(6) (2007). Article No. 29
12. de Alfaro, L., Henzinger, T.A., Majumdar, R.: Discounting the future in systems theory. In: Baeten, J.C.M., Lenstra, J.K., Parrow, J., Woeginger, G.J. (eds.), ICALP 2003, volume 2719 of LNCS, pp. 1022–1037. Springer (2003)
13. Droste, M., Rahonis, G.: Weighted automata and weighted logics with discounting. Theor. Comput. Sci. **410**(37), 3481–3494 (2009)
14. Faella, M., Legay, A., Stoelinga, M.: Model checking quantitative linear time logic. Electr. Notes Theor. Comput. Sci. **220**(3), 61–77 (2008)
15. Hansson, H., Jonsson, B.: A logic for reasoning about time and reliability. Formal Asp. Comput. **6**(5), 512–535 (1994)
16. Kupferman, O., Piterman, N., Vardi, M.Y.: Safraless compositional synthesis. In: Ball, T., Jones, R.B. (eds.) CAV 2006. LNCS, vol. 4144, pp. 31–44. Springer, Heidelberg (2006)
17. Kupferman, O., Vardi, M.Y., Wolper, P.: An automata-theoretic approach to branching-time model checking. J. ACM **47**(2), 312–360 (2000)
18. Miyano, S., Hayashi, T.: Alternating finite automata on omega-words. Theor. Comput. Sci. **32**, 321–330 (1984)
19. Nakagawa, S., Hasuo, I.: Near-optimal scheduling for LTL with future discounting (2015). CoRR, abs/1410.4950
20. Pnueli, A., Rosner, R.: On the synthesis of a reactive module. In: Conference Record of the Sixteenth Annual ACM Symposium on Principles of Programming Languages, Austin, Texas, USA, January 11–13, 1989, pp. 179–190. ACM Press (1989)
21. Rahonis, G.: Infinite fuzzy computations. Fuzzy Sets Syst. **153**(2), 275–288 (2005)

22. van Glabbeek, R.J.: The linear time-branching time spectrum I; the semantics of concrete, sequential processes. In: Bergstra, J.A., Ponse, A., Smolka, S.A. (eds.), Handbook of Process Algebra, chapter 1, pp. 3–99. Elsevier (2001)
23. Vardi, M.Y.: An automata-theoretic approach to linear temporal logic. In: Logics for Concurrency: Structure Versus Automata, vol. 1043 of LNCS, pp. 238–266. Springer-Verlag (1996)

A Switch, in Time

Lenore D. Zuck[1] and Sanjiva Prasad[2]([✉])

[1] University of Illinois at Chicago, Chicago, USA
lenore@cs.uic.edu
[2] Indian Institute of Technology Delhi, New Delhi, India
sanjiva@cse.iitd.ac.in

Abstract. Communication networks are quintessential concurrent and distributed systems, posing verification challenges concerning network protocols, reliability, resilience and fault-tolerance, and security. While techniques based on logic and process calculi have been employed in the verification of various protocols, there is a mismatch between the abstractions used in these approaches and the essential structure of networks. In particular, the formal models do not accurately capture the organization of networks in terms of (fast but dumb) table-based switches forwarding structured messages, with intelligence/control located only at the endpoints.

To bridge this gap, we propose an extension of the axiomatic basis of communication proposed by Karsten et al. In this paper, a simple model of abstract switches and table-based prefix rewriting is characterized axiomatically using temporal logic. This formulation is able to address reconfigurations over time of the network. We illustrate our framework with simple examples drawn from SDNs, IPv6 mobility and anonymous routing protocols.

Keywords: Abstract switches · Network protocols · Data plane · Control · Time-dependent behavior · Correctness

1 Introduction

Communication networks are quintessential concurrent and distributed systems. Apart from issues pertaining to scale and efficient implementation, networks pose challenging verification and validation problems such as the correctness of protocols, reliability, resilience and fault-tolerance, and security. Indeed, the correct operation of most distributed systems depends on the correctness of networks and their protocols.

Networks are organized as a "stack" of several protocol layers, from the physical to application (and beyond), with the workhorse being the network layer and the suite of IP protocols configured as a reticulum of fast (but "dumb") table-based routers/switches that forward packets. "Intelligence" is confined to

---

This work was partially supported by a grant from Microsoft Research to the first author, and NSF CCS-1228697 to the second author.

© Springer International Publishing Switzerland 2016
P. Ganty and M. Loreti (Eds.): TGC 2015, LNCS 9533, pp. 131–146, 2016.
DOI: 10.1007/978-3-319-28766-9_9

the peripheries of the data forwarding network [5]. Much of the robustness and efficiency of the Internet derives from this architecture. Proposals to embed greater intelligence into the data network often (i) suffer from inefficiency, (ii) are difficult to deploy, configure and maintain, and (iii) may introduce potential vulnerabilities.

Several formal techniques have been used to model and verify different aspects of a wide variety of network protocols. Approaches based on automata and temporal logic have traditionally been used to reason about fundamental protocols. Modal logics (particularly of knowledge) have been used to formulate protocol correctness [10,12]. However, verifying whether a system satisfies a given property usually requires considerable expertise since one has to formalize within the framework the behavior of all agents, including that of the adversary/environment.

The AVISPA project [3] and subsequent lines of research, e.g. [4,7] comprise a large body of work involving the automated validation of internet security protocols. Several security properties have been expressed using LTL with a "sometime in the past" operator [17], following which model-checking techniques have been used to verify or detect errors in a large number of widely used protocols. Such *Safety Temporal Properties* are of the form $\Box(P \to \Diamond Q)$, which roughly states: *"For any reachable state satisfying a property P, there was a past state satisfying Q."*

An alternative approach uses process calculi to provide a formal operational model of the system, and where the adversarial context is mapped to the generic notion of an observer. For example, CCS has been used for modeling the alternating bit protocol [6,18]; the π-calculus for mobile handover protocols [19]; and the applied π-calculus for security protocols [1]. While the process calculus approach is attractive as it comes equipped with notions of equivalence such as bisimulation and their associated proof techniques, stating logical properties about the protocols is not always easy.

Although these approaches have been successful in formally modeling and verifying various network protocols, they have done so by abstracting away much of the essential structure of communication networks. There is a mismatch between the structure of networks and the manner in which they are represented in these *ad hoc* (used in the original, non-pejorative sense) abstract models. While the hierarchical structure of the network stack presents apparently abstract and modular structures, these do not correlate well with the formal notions of abstraction and refinement. When attempting to refine the elegant abstract models to account for the nitty-gritty details of network structure and behavior, the formal approaches often end up "over-modeling" mundane or irrelevant details about, say, data delivery. Another issue is the lack of modularity when combining different analyses (e.g., routing and security) that were independently modeled and verified under assumptions of orthogonality, and often in quite different formalisms.

We therefore posit that it is important to have a simple modular framework for reasoning about the delivery of data messages that corresponds well with the actual structures of communication networks over which other analyses may be formalized. A presentation that is general enough to capture the complexities of existing data networks which is also compatible with existing formal operational and logical models (for modeling and specification) will facilitate robust proofs of correctness. Indeed, we hope that many analyses in the literature can be adapted and refined to work in a modular fashion with such a framework.

In this paper, we propose a framework in which data communication network structures and behavior may be represented at *any* appropriate level of detail. The framework naturally admits *refinements* in the description of the network elements as well as in the *logical specification* of their behavior. An organizing principle in our treatment is a systematic separation between the data and control planes. This factoring of network structure and function into a data plane and control plane has gained far greater importance with the advent of *Software Defined Networks* (SDNs) [15], which are motivated by the need to respond to the dynamics of network events and to enforce policies in continuously changing environments.

The main contribution of this paper is an abstract presentation of the structure and operational behavior of the data plane. The description of the data plane is (in logical terms) an extension of the formal model of abstract switches presented in [14]. The advantages of choosing that framework lie in (1) its ability to formalize fundamental network concepts (names, addresses, links, scopes, etc.) at all layers of the so-called network stack as well as across layers; (2) its operational simplicity (being based on table-based prefix rewriting); (3) its axiomatic treatment of arbitrarily complex multi-layer forwarding systems [14]; (4) its natural support for refinement and compositionality [21]; (5) that it can be easily interfaced with process calculi, typically for expressing the control protocols.

The new contribution of this paper is a reformulation of the axiomatic basis for communication [14,21] using temporal logic (Sect. 2). This presentation enables a clearer exposition of time-varying routing behavior and associated properties, as seen in, e.g., SDNs and Mobile IP. It also supports a more natural form of reasoning about network invariants, abstracting from detailed reasoning about topological structure. The version of LTL that we employ in this paper is expressive enough for stating the desired time-dependent properties, and admits hierarchical reasoning about the model [16].

We illustrate our approach by presenting a fresh and concise analysis of the IPv6 mobility model using temporal logic (Sect. 3). This is in contrast to the detailed process calculus model of [2], where the correctness properties were not explicitly stated, and the correctness of the protocol was expressed as barbed equivalence [22] to a simpler reference system. Next, we present an extension that allows switches perform transformations on messages, including cryptographic operations (Sect. 4). We model an anonymizing network service such as TOR [8], and outline how one may reason about the correctness of the design of such anonymizing network services by using knowledge modalities. We conclude in Sect. 5 with a recapitulation of the main ideas of this paper, and some directions for future work. In our exposition of the framework and approach, we have attempted to convey the intuitions, restricting the formalism to the bare essentials.

2   The Model

The architecture of our model reflects ideas from *Software Defined Networks* (SDNs). The network's operation is decoupled into a *data plane* — a collection of fast (unintelligent) table-based switching elements that relay messages — and a *control plane*, the part of a network that carries signaling traffic and is responsible for routing. The occurrence of *events* in the data plane triggers the control plane to initiate changes in switches/routers in the data plane. We describe here the structure and behavior of the data plane, which is designed to be a generic message delivery architecture, agnostic to the control operations. The data plane can be seen as a massive distributed system, with many orders of magnitude more messages than those in the control plane. The purpose of most control plane protocols is to configure or make changes in the data plane, which should continue to operate concurrently while those changes are effected. Network protocols in the control plane may be described in any of a variety of process calculi or other formalisms. The examples in this paper do not focus on the specification and operation of the control protocols, but model their effects on the data plane. While our account omits the precise interface between the two planes, we believe this would be relatively straightforward to specify.

2.1   The Data Plane Model

The data plane is a directed graph the *nodes* of which are *abstract switches* (ASs), denoted as $A, B, C, \ldots X, Y, Z$. Switches represent *any* kind of processing elements — hardware or software — at *any* level of the network stack. Each AS (Fig. 1) has a number of named input and output *ports*. These ports are the endpoints of simplex directed *edges* (written $e(A, B)$) between adjacent ASs. We use the notation A^B and $_AB$ to denote the output port at A directly connected to B, and the input port at B with an incoming edge from A. We write $_?B$ and $A^?$ when we wish to leave unspecified a port's connection. Generic ports are denoted x, y, z.

The ASs send *messages* along the edges. Messages are represented as *strings of identifiers* drawn from an arbitrary alphabet Σ. Typical messages are denoted

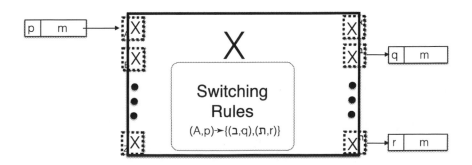

Fig. 1. Schematic view of an abstract switch

$m, m', \ldots$ and *prefixes* of messages are usually denoted as $p, p', \ldots$ The presence of a message m at a port x is denoted as $m@x$. Creation and consumption of messages may be internalized within the system as follows: The *creation* of a message m at B is modeled as m being at a (virtual logical) port $_0B$, and its *consumption* as it being at the (virtual logical) port B^0.

An AS maintains a local *switching table*. The switching table at AS B, denoted as S_B, contains mappings of the form $\langle A, p \rangle \mapsto \{\langle C_i, p_i' \rangle\}$ (S_B maps an AS-prefix pair to a *set of AS-prefix pairs*). The table represents a *finite-domain function*, which may not be defined for several $\langle A, p \rangle$ pairs. The switching table specifies a local prefix rewriting system at that AS. We assume that switching table entries are *exact matches*, i.e., if $\mathsf{S}_B[A, p] \neq \emptyset$, then for no prefix p' of p is $\mathsf{S}_B[A, p'] \neq \emptyset^1$. The correctness of computer network protocols crucially hinges on the *distributed state of the switching tables collectively satisfying and maintaining* certain properties that ensure deliverability of messages.

Informally, the operation of model is: When a message pm appears on the input port $_AB$ such that S_B has an entry $\langle A, p \rangle \mapsto \{\langle C_i, p_i' \rangle\}$, then for each i, a message $p_i'm$ is placed on the output port B^{C_i}. Note that the switching tables at different ASs may be quite different.

Definition 1. *A message m arriving at an input port $_xA$ is called a* barb, *written $m@_xA \uparrow$, if $\mathsf{S}_A[X, p] = \emptyset$ for each prefix p of m.*

Barbs are the *observables* of the data plane, which occur when a switch is unable to handle an incoming message. Barbs can form the basis for an operational account of the data plane's behavior. In this paper, instead, we provide a logical account of the behavior.

2.2 Axioms

The following axiom schema specify the behavior of edges and switches.

RT1. (Direct Communication)

$$e(A, B) \wedge m@A^B \Rightarrow \Diamond (m@_AB)$$

RT2. (Local Switching)

$$pm@_AB \wedge \langle C, p' \rangle \in \mathsf{S}_B[A, p] \Rightarrow \Diamond (p'm@B^C)$$

Axiom RT1 describes direct communication between ASs. If there is a direct edge from A to B, a message on output port A^B eventually appears on the input port $_AB$. Axiom RT2 expresses the lookup and switching capability of an AS. If a message with prefix p is at an input port of B and the switching table

---

[1] This assumption is to keep the model simple; more complex matching rules such as matching with the maximal prefix, or allowing for priorities among potential prefixes may be viewed as practical optimizations.

there indicates that a message with this prefix at that input port should have its prefix rewritten to p' and placed on output port C, then the transformed message eventually appears at that port. Note that RT2 also covers any form of multi-recipient forwarding, such as multicast, since $S_B[A, p]$ may have multiple elements.

These axiom schema capture a notion of *deliverability*, and apply to message transmission between ASs at *any* two levels in the protocol stack in the data plane. For simplicity of exposition, we assume that messages do not get lost or corrupted at ASs or at edges. Note that loss and corruption of messages may be explicitly simulated within the model by using suitably defined ASs. The model naturally permits message reordering. The model is completely distributed: ASs may operate concurrently and independent of one another, and even the operations on messages at the same/different ports of an AS may be concurrent.

We write $m@x \rightsquigarrow m'@y$ (read *relays-to*[2]) as convenient shorthand for $m@x \Rightarrow \Diamond m'@y$. We abbreviate, e.g., $m@x \Rightarrow \Diamond m'@y \land m'@y \Rightarrow \Diamond m''@z$ by writing $m@x \rightsquigarrow m'@y \rightsquigarrow m''@z$. The relays-to relation helps define a number of well-known communication concepts.

Let A and B be ASs and $p \neq \epsilon$. We then define:

Name. Prefix p *is a name for B at A* if

$$\exists X, Y, Z: \quad \exists p' \neq \epsilon: \quad \forall m : pm@_X A \rightsquigarrow p'm@_Y B \rightsquigarrow m@B^Z.$$

The name for an AS B at another AS A is a non-empty prefix that is removed when a message is transmitted from A to B. By default, names are local and their meaning is *relative* to the AS where they are interpreted. Note that p can be a name at A for multiple ASs, and that the ASs denoted by a name can vary with changes to switching tables. The condition $p' \neq \epsilon$ ensures that B is indeed the AS where the prefix or any residual of it is removed.

Address. Prefix p *is an address for B at A* if

$$\forall X: \exists Y, Z: \forall m: \quad pm@_X A \rightsquigarrow pm@_Y B \rightsquigarrow m@B^Z.$$

An address is a special kind of name whose meaning is independent of the input port, and which does not change along the path traversed by a message (though the ASs between A and B may add prefixes to pm). Note that p can be an address for multiple ASs.

Tunnel. There is a *tunnel from A to B* if

$$\exists W, X, Y, Z : \exists p, p' \neq \epsilon : \forall m: \quad m@_W A \rightsquigarrow pm@A^X \rightsquigarrow p'm@_Y B \rightsquigarrow m@B^Z$$

A tunnel from A to B takes a message at A, "wraps" it with a prefix, and delivers it to B where it is unwrapped. Tunnels provide a means for abstracting away the series of intermediate edges that establish the connection between two

---

[2] In [14], this relation was inductively defined using four axiom schema, two of which – reflexivity and transitivity — are implicit in temporal logic.

nodes. Let $tunnel(_wA, B^z)$ denote the existence of a tunnel between A and B with entry and exit ports at W, Z.

Tunnels can be composed (by connecting the output port of the first to the input port of the second):

Lemma 1 (Tunnel Composition). *If* $tunnel(_wA, B^x)$ *and* $tunnel(_yB, C^z)$, *then (by linking* B^x *to* $_yB$*),* $tunnel(_wA, C^z)$.

2.3 Table Updates

Network events necessitate dynamic updates to switching tables. New entries can be added and existing entries modified or deleted. Updates to switching tables occur relatively infrequently and are atomic. Consequently, we may safely assume that at each point in the execution, the tables are stable and well defined.

An update S_B^1 of S_B is *monotone* if for every $\langle C, p' \rangle \in S_B[A, p]$, $\langle C, p' \rangle \in S_B^1[A, p]$. The update S_B^1 *preserves a name for* A *at* C if the name is not disturbed by the update. Similarly, the update S_B^1 *preserves a tunnel from* A *to* C if this tunnel is not disturbed by the update.

Lemma 2. *Monotone updates preserve names and tunnels.*

Example: Routing updates in SDNs. The occurrence of a barb in the data plane indicates that at some AS there is no switching rule for handling a message that arrived there. This may indicate an error in the protocol. However, if the tables have been properly configured (as presumed), the barb is an event that necessitates action on part of the control plane to update the switching tables. Such an event may occur, for instance, when a new device has been introduced into the network, and messages addressed to it need to be forwarded. Typically, the control plane responds by placing output messages at some output ports and performing a *monotone update* to the switching table of that AS. Lemma 2 implies that such SDN updates preserve names and tunnels.

Corollary 1. *Routing updates in SDNs preserve names and tunnels.*

Routing updates, being monotone, preserve deliverability of messages. Note though, that while they are intended to remove the barbs that triggered them, they may introduce new barbs at other nodes.

Further, they may introduce forwarding cycles, which cause messages to traverse cycles. A message m is said to traverse a *cycle* if for some A, p, p', p'', X, Y, Z, $pm@_xA \rightsquigarrow p'm@A^Y \rightsquigarrow p''m@_zA$. Note that a message traversing a cycle does not necessarily imply that it will remain in that loop indefinitely — by returning to A at a different input port, and/or with a different prefix p'', it may be switched differently the second time around. Another way that forwarding cycles may be broken is via updates to a switching table.

3   IP Mobility

Changes in the network topology may disrupt the "relays-to" relation, resulting in the invalidation of certain names or a change in their meaning. This may be repaired by updates to one or more switching tables. A good example of such updates occurs in IPv6 mobility [20], the essence of which we model here.

3.1   Tunnel Maintenance

Recall that tunnels allow us to abstract from the details of all nodes and direct edges in the network graph. Thus we can focus on only IP layer nodes and tunnels between them. For each node A, let n_A be its universal address (a "well-known address" in networks parlance). We write $tunnel^{(n_B)}(X, Y)$ to indicate that at AS X the switching tables are configured to tunnel any message with prefix n_B to Y.

IPv6 support for mobility is based on a proxy architecture, where a mobile node B is associated with

- its *identifying* IP address n_B;
- its home router, denoted $H(B)$, which never changes;
- its current location, denoted $h(B)$, which may change over time. At any point in time, B is "hosted by" at most one router.

We assume that if a message intended for B reaches $h(B)$, it will eventually be delivered to B.

$$\textbf{(mIP)} \quad n_B m @_? h(B) \Rightarrow \Diamond (m @ B^?)$$

In a stable state of the network, a sender sends a message to a mobile node B by either

1. tunneling it to B's home router $H(B)$ (B's default location); (a) if B is at home ($h(B) = H(B)$), the message will be delivered to B. (b) if B is away ($h(B) \neq H(B)$), $H(B)$ tunnels it to $h(B)$, which $H(B)$ presumably knows.
2. alternatively, if the sender knows $h(B)$, it may tunnel the message to $h(B)$.

In all the above cases, Lemma 1 and (mIP) ensure that the message will be delivered to B.

However, when B moves, we cannot assume that $h(B)$ will be known to nodes, in particular to $H(B)$, wishing to communicate with it. With a small number of *control messages* that eventually lead to (re)establishing correct forwarding tables, the IPv6 mobility protocol achieves correct forwarding of messages. We focus here only on the effects of the control messages on the switching tables. It is the control protocol's responsibility to ensure that table update messages received out-of-order are ignored (this can be achieved using sequence numbers).

We assume that initially for every $X \neq H(B)$, $tunnel^{(n_B)}(X, H(B))$. Moreover, at any time, if nodes X and Y are not in $\{H(B), h(B)\}$

and $tunnel^{(n_B)}(Y,X)$ exists, this tunnel can be removed and replaced by $tunnel^{(n_B)}(Y, H(B))$ (a "time-out reset"). Once registered at $h(B)$, B (or $h(B)$ on its behalf) may send control messages to any correspondent node A not necessarily involved in the move, telling A of its current location, in which case A *may* update to $tunnel^{(n_B)}(Y, h(B))$. The only possible other n_B-tunnel changes are triggered by B's moves, with the associated mandatory updates summarized in Fig. 2.

Move	Remove Tunnels	Create Tunnel
$H(B)$ to F_1	$tunnel^{(n_B)}(F_1, X)$, $tunnel^{(n_B)}(H(B), X)$ $X \neq F_1$	$tunnel^{(n_B)}(H(B), F_1)$
F_1 to $H(B)$	$tunnel^{(n_B)}(F_1, X)$ $X \neq H(B)$ $tunnel^{(n_B)}(H(B), X)$	$tunnel^{(n_B)}(F_1, H(B))$
F_1 to F_2	$tunnel^{(n_B)}(F_2, X)$ $tunnel^{(n_B)}(H(B), F_1)$	$tunnel^{(n_B)}(H(B), F_2)$ exactly one of $tunnel^{(n_B)}(F_1, F_2)$ or $tunnel^{(n_B)}(F_1, H(B))$

Fig. 2. Tunnel updating on moves

The IPv6 protocol implementation is assumed to ensure that *control messages will get delivered*, especially to the home network, and consequently that there are no ways of creating $tunnel^{(n_B)}(X,Y)$ other than those in Fig. 2, or by "timing out". We assume that the removal and creation of tunnels at a single AS happens atomically. Observe that the updates mentioned are *not monotonic*.

3.2   Properties

By induction on the tunnel update moves, we can prove the following properties:

Tunnel Endpoint. Tunnels only end at previously visited hosts.

$$\forall X.\ tunnel^{(n_B)}(X,Y) \ \Rightarrow\ (Y = H(B) \vee \diamondsuit(Y = h(B))$$

No Wandering. Messages (at tunnel end-points) can only visit their sender, receiver, the receiver's home or any node that hosted it: For every message m from sender A to receiver B,

$$\forall X. n_B m@_? X \ \Rightarrow\ (X = A \vee X = B \vee X = H(B) \vee \diamondsuit(X = h(B)))$$

Note that all tunnels created in response to control messages involve a router that has been visited earlier.

No Forwarding Cycles. Tunnels do not form a true cycle[3]. Let $(tunnel^*)^{(n_B)}$ be the transitive closure of $tunnel^{(n_B)}$ as per Lemma 1.

$$\forall X :\ \neg((tunnel^*)^{(n_B)}(X,X))$$

---

[3] Actually, this property can be weakened to one requiring only that any such forwarding cycle will eventually get broken (see [23] for details).

Lemma 3. *If the mobile node settles at its home, eventually there is permanent tunnel from all other nodes to its home.*

$$\Box(h(B) = H(B)) \Rightarrow \forall Y \neq H(B).\Diamond \Box tunnel^{(n_B)}(Y, H(B))$$

Proof. Let σ be a computation satisfying $\Box(h(B) = H(B))$ and let $Y \notin \{B, H(B)\}$. Initially $tunnel^{(n_B)}(Y, H(B))$; from the "time-out" action or if B moves, it follows from the rules of Fig. 2 that there exists a suffix σ' of σ where $tunnel^{(n_B)}(Y, H(B))$. Now, since B remains at $H(B)$, Y creates no other tunnel for n_B. Thus, σ' satisfies $\Box(tunnel^{(n_B)}(Y, H(B)))$.

Of course, there may be points in a computation where a n_B-tunnel does not exist to B's location. However, by the eventual delivery of control messages, or by time-out, such a tunnel will be constructed. Observe that the model does not place any buffer-space limitations or delivery-order restrictions on messages, so in an implementation, their deliverability relies on buffering them until a tunnel is (re-)constructed. The next lemma addresses n_B-tunnels when B settles at a non-home node.

Lemma 4. *If the mobile node settles at a place, there is a tunnel from home to that place, and a tunnel from every previously visited node to either home or to that permanent host. The proof is similar to that of Lemma 3.*

$$\forall X, Y.\Box(h(B) = X \land X \neq H(B) \land Y \notin \{h(B), H(B)\}) \Rightarrow$$
$$\Diamond \Box \left(\begin{array}{l} tunnel^{(n_B)}(H(B), h(B)) \\ \land (tunnel^{(n_B)}(Y, h(B)) \lor tunnel^{(n_B)}(Y, H(B))) \end{array} \right)$$

Theorem 1 establishes that if a node remains at a single host for sufficiently long, then it will receive every message sent to it.

Theorem 1. *If a mobile node settles, any message addressed to it eventually gets delivered.*

$$\Box(h(B) = X) \Rightarrow (n_B m@_?A \Rightarrow \Diamond (m@B^?))$$

Proof. Let σ be a computation satisfying $\Box(h(B) = X)$, and assume $n_B m@_?A$ holds. From Lemmas 3 and 4 it follows that there exists a suffix σ' of σ such that $\sigma' \models \Box(tunnel^{(n_B)}(Y, X)$ for every $Y \notin \{X, H(B), B\}$. The No Wandering property establishes that at the initial state of σ', m has either already reached its destination B or is at some other node. In the latter case, once in σ', m will be forwarded through the permanent tunnel to X, and eventually reach B by (mIP).

The theorem does not (incorrectly) claim that messages cannot go into a cycle. The No Forwarding Cycles property guarantees it does not stay in a cycle if the mobile node settles (rendered as "ever after" in LTL) at a host. However, if a mobile node B does not stay "long enough" at any node, a message may forever keep chasing it without ever catching up with it.

This theorem has been validated for a finite version of the model using TLV [23].

4   Security Primitives: The TOR Example

In addition to routing, security is an important issue in network protocols. Encryption and decryption operations on messages motivate an extension to the model of Sect. 2 by allowing switches to perform cryptographic and other functional transformations on messages. We illustrate the extension by presenting the essence of the TOR [8] architecture, which is designed to support anonymous communication. Formal notions of anonymity have always been among the hardest security properties to capture [13].

We modify the Local Switching axiom to

RT2′ $pm@_AB \wedge \langle C, p', f_{ABC} \rangle \in \mathsf{S}_B[A, p] \Rightarrow \Diamond (p'm'@B^C)$ $(m' = f_{ABC}(p, m))$

Mappings of the form $\langle A, p \rangle \mapsto \{\langle C, p', f_{ABC} \rangle\}$ now populate S_B, the switching table at AS B, where C and p' are as before, and f_{ABC} is a function that transforms messages. A message placed on an output port is a functional transformation of the incoming message, where the function may depend on the switch B and on the input and output ports. This generalization permits expressing a variety of operations, such as encryption, hashing, route recording, etc.

4.1   TOR

TOR (The Onion Router) is a low-latency anonymous communication service. To send an anonymous message, a client chooses at least three intermediate routers to be used as a chain of relays to the recipient. The client establishes shared secret session keys with each of the intermediate TOR nodes, and encrypts the message successively with these keys in the inverse order with respect to the routers through which the message will pass. The TOR routers are only aware of their successor and predecessor nodes in the relay chain. The protocol is designed to ensure that none of the intermediate routers are aware of both the sender and receiver of the message.

For example, suppose sender $A \in \mathcal{A}$, where $\mathcal{A}$ is the set of potential senders, wishes to sends a message m to receiver $B \in \mathcal{B}$ ($\mathcal{B}$ is the set of potential destinations) via TOR nodes $X; Y; Z$. To simplify the presentation, we connect Z to an extra (non-TOR) "fan-out" router W to communicate with the actual recipient of the message. (See Fig. 3, where for simplifying the exposition, we depict the tunnels between the routers as direct links).

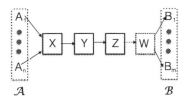

Fig. 3. Schematic view of TOR

Client node A sends to the first TOR router X the message

$$m_A = n_X \, E_X(n_Y \, E_Y(n_Z \, \underbrace{\underbrace{\underbrace{E_Z(n_B m_B)))}_{m_Z}}_{m_Y}}_{m_Z}$$

where $E_i(m')$ is the cipher text obtained by encrypting m' with the key shared between A and i; each n_i is the "well-known" address of i. Upon receipt of a message each TOR node decrypts it using the shared key, and transmits the result to the next node in the chain. Here anonymity implies that neither Y nor Z is able to learn the identity of sender A, and neither X nor Y can learn the identity of receiver B from a set of potential senders and receivers of the message.

The TOR protocol involves a very special version of switching, where the switching decisions are *not* made based on the prefixes of the messages but rather are effected based on the *decrypted content* of the messages. Moreover, the function f_{ABC} at TOR nodes depends only on B (in fact on the key shared by B with the TOR client): for every A' and C', $f_{A'BC'} = f_{ABC}$. We therefore refer to the switch transformation function as f_B.

Suppose X is the ingress TOR router, with input messages from possible sources $A_1, \ldots A_k$. The switching table at the ingress router X has entries of the form:

$$\langle A_i, n_X \rangle \mapsto \langle Y, \epsilon, E_X^{-1} \rangle$$

where E_X^{-1} is the decryption function using the key shared with the client and X. When X receives the message $n_X E_X(n_Y m_Y)$, it places $n_Y m_Y$ on the output port to Y. Note that since X does not have the keys shared between A and Y, it cannot learn that the message is intended for B. At the intermediate TOR router Y, with predecessor X and successor Y, the switching table has entries of the form:

$$\langle X, n_Y \rangle \mapsto \langle Z, \epsilon, E_Y^{-1} \rangle$$

When Y receives the message $n_Y m_Z$, it places $n_Z m_Z$ on the output port to Z. Since Y does not have the keys shared between A, Z, it cannot learn that the message is intended for B, nor does it know the source A of this message, since the message was from the input port from X. At the TOR router Z, with predecessor Y and a single egress router W which connects to nodes in $\mathcal{B}$, the switching table is:

$$\langle Y, n_Z \rangle \mapsto \langle W, \epsilon, E_Z^{-1} \rangle$$

When Z receives the message $n_Z E_Z(n_B m_B)$, it places $n_B m_B$ on the output port to W. Router Z does not have any indication of the source A of this message, since all messages were on the input port from Y.

4.2   Proving Some TOR Properties

Our main technique for proving correctness of TOR is derived from the *strand* formalism in [11], which supports a representation of the execution of a protocol in terms of local views of principals and the messages exchanged in that execution.

Security protocols are cast as cryptoalgebras in [11], where to decrypt an encrypted term $t = E_P(m)$, an adversary needs to have received prior messages from which E_P can be derived. Though the Dolev-Yao model [9] abstracts from more realistic assumptions regarding message structure and cryptographic schemes addressed by [11] (e.g., bounds on message length, the particular encryption/decryption functions, and ability to guess keys and ciphers), it is considered a standard adversarial model for formal security analysis. For the purpose of this section, we restrict to the Dolev-Yao model. Recall that a Dolev-Yao adversary can only encrypt/decrypt messages whose keys it possesses.

Following terminology roughly influenced by formal reasoning about knowledge (see, e.g., [10,12]), let $K_i(z)$ denote that a participant i knows the value of a variable z. Initially, every participant P knows the names of all participants and the encryption/decryption keys to which it is privy, i.e., $K_P(n_Q)$ for every participant P and Q, and $K_P(E_P)$. The adversary may know additional keys, but we assume that it knows at most two of the three keys A shares with X, Y, and Z. During the course of the protocol, the adversary may decrypt any messages whose encryption keys it knows, as well as send messages that may be encrypted with keys known to it. Moreover, for every honest participant P, the encryption key E_P can never be derived, that is, honest participants never send any information that reveals their keys. In particular, if the adversary does not initially know E_i and cannot derive it from any message it had seen, then it cannot decrypt any message encrypted with E_i.

We assume that every participant knows the sets $\mathcal{A}$ and $\mathcal{B}$. For TOR message m, let $src(m) \in \mathcal{A}$ be its source and $dest(m) \in \mathcal{B}$ be its intended destination. Thus, when a TOR message m is received, for every participant P, $K_P(src(m) \in \mathcal{A})$ and $K_{adv}(dest(m) \in \mathcal{B})$. Moreover, for every honest participant P, $\neg K_{adv}(E_P)$.

Our goal is to show that no participant, but for the source and destination, get to learn both source and destination of a TOR message even if adversary knows all but one key of an intermediate node.

Theorem 2. *For every TOR message m_A and every participant $P \neq A, B$,*

$$\Box \neg (K_P(src(m_A)) \ \wedge \ K_P(dest(m_A)))$$

even if two of X, Y, and Z are compromised.

Proof (Proof Outline). We present the most commonly studied case, where X and Z are compromised, but not Y. Initially $K_{adv}(E_X)$ and $K_{adv}(E_Z)$. When $m_A = n_X m_Y @_? X$, the adversary can learn $src(m_A)$. We have to show that it never learns $dest(m_A)$. From our assumption it follows that $\Box \ \neg K_{adv}(E_Y)$. In the protocol, X sends the message m_Y, thus eventually $m_X = n_Y m_Y @_?Y$. While the adversary may know $m_X @_?Y$, from our assumptions it follows that it cannot decipher m_Y, and hence, cannot associate the event $m_Z = n_Z m_Z @Y^?$ with the message m_A. That is, it cannot derive that $m_Z = n_Y E_Y(m_Z)$. From here the adversary cannot determine that $m_Z @Y^?$ implies that $\Diamond m_A @_?X$, from which the claim follows.

5 Conclusions

The disparity between the structure and behavior of computer networks and the abstract formal models used for modeling and verifying protocols motivated us to present a modular logical account of the data plane of networks. By separating the data plane from control protocol descriptions, we hope that formal analyses of various control protocols (routing, security, etc.) can be performed independently of modeling the details of message delivery within a given abstract framework. Our framework provides a general model of message relay at multiple layers of the network stack, thereby supporting formal analyses using appropriate abstractions that accurately capture real network behavior. By ensuring that the data plane model is presented in a manner that naturally admits refinements, both in temporal logical specifications and in the hierarchical structure, we claim that the resultant framework can support more robust proofs of correctness. In this paper, we have accounted for changes in the routing and forwarding topologies, and can specify and model network structure and behavior that changes over time.

To our knowledge there are few formal models of networks, and fewer that account for dynamic changes to network structure. The example we chose to illustrate our approach, i.e., modeling IPv6 mobility shows how one can construct concise and abstract proofs of correctness of a protocol, without modeling too many operational details of the protocol and the network. Our analysis is minimalist in that it does not mistakenly claim stronger properties than are necessary. For example, some formal analyses of IPv6 mobility claimed (incorrectly) that the protocol does not allow data messages traverse cycles, or that forwarding cycles are never created. The correctness of the protocol, however, hinges on a far weaker property: that any temporarily created message or forwarding cycles will be broken ("sooner or later" – though this argument is made without explicitly reasoning about time).

The other generalization made in this paper is to endow switches with the ability to perform functional transformations on messages. This supports the modeling of a large variety of security protocols within the data plane. We are unaware of any earlier formal logical account of the correctness of the TOR protocol in providing anonymity.

In this paper, the two extensions — dealing with dynamic changes in the forwarding topologies and providing switches with the ability to transform messages — have been treated orthogonally. We believe that there are a large number of time-dependent security protocols that can fruitfully be explored in a combination of these extensions, for instance, whether the TOR protocol provides *perfect forward secrecy* or *perfect forward anonymity*. Indeed, the notion of anonymity merits further investigation.

Acknowledgements. The authors thank the anonymous referees for their valuable suggestions.

References

1. Abadi, M., Fournet, C.: Private authentication. Theor. Comput. Sci. **322**(3), 427–476 (2004)
2. Amadio, R.M., Prasad, S.: Modelling IP mobility. In: Sangiorgi, D., de Simone, R. (eds.) CONCUR 1998. LNCS, vol. 1466, pp. 301–316. Springer, Heidelberg (1998)
3. Armando, A., et al.: The AVISPA tool for the automated validation of internet security protocols and applications. In: Etessami, K., Rajamani, S.K. (eds.) CAV 2005. LNCS, vol. 3576, pp. 281–285. Springer, Heidelberg (2005)
4. Armando, A., Basin, D.A., Cuéllar, J., Rusinowitch, M., Viganò, L.: Automated reasoning for security protocol analysis. J. Autom. Reason. **36**(1–2), 1–3 (2006)
5. Clark, D.: The design philosophy of the DARPA internet protocols. In: Proceedings of SIGCOMM 1988: ACM Conference on Applications, Technologies, Architectures, and Protocols for Computer Communications, vol. 8, pp. 106–114. ACM (1988)
6. Cleaveland, R., Parrow, J., Steffen, B.: The concurrency workbench. In: Sifakis, J. (ed.) Automatic Verification Methods for Finite State Systems. LNCS, vol. 407, pp. 24–37. Springer, Heidelberg (1989)
7. Delzanno, G., Ganty, P.: Automatic verification of time sensitive cryptographic protocols. In: Jensen, K., Podelski, A. (eds.) TACAS 2004. LNCS, vol. 2988, pp. 342–356. Springer, Heidelberg (2004)
8. Dingledine, R., Mathewson, N., Syverson, P.F.: Tor: The second-generation onion router. In: Proceedings of 13th USENIX Security Symposium, SSYM 2004, pp. 303–320. USENIX Association (2004)
9. Dolev, D., Yao, A.C.C.: On the security of public key protocols. IEEE Trans. Inf. Theor. **29**(2), 198–207 (1983)
10. Fagin, R., Halpern, J.Y., Moses, Y., Vardi, M.Y.:Knowledge-based programs. In: Proceedings of PODC 1995: 14th Annual ACM Symposium on Principles of Distributed Computing, pp. 153–163. ACM (1995)
11. Guttman, J.D., Thayer, F.J., Zuck, L.D.: The faithfulness of abstract protocol analysis: message authentication. J. Comput. Secur. **12**(6), 865–891 (2004)
12. Halpern, J.Y., Zuck, L.D.: A little knowledge goes a long way: Knowledge-based derivations and correctness proofs for a family of protocols. J. ACM **39**(3), 449–478 (1992)
13. Hughes, D.J.D., Shmatikov, V.: Information hiding, anonymity and privacy: a modular approach. J. Comput. Secur. **12**(1), 3–36 (2004)
14. Karsten, M., Keshav, S., Prasad, S., Beg, M.: An axiomatic basis for communication. In: Proceedings of SIGCOMM 2007:ACM Conference on Applications, Technologies, Architectures, and Protocols for Computer Communications, pp. 217–228. ACM (2007)

15. Kreutz, D., Ramos, F.M.V., Veríssimo, P.J.E., Esteve Rothenberg, C., Azodol-molky, S., Uhlig, S.: Software-defined networking: a comprehensive survey. Proc. IEEE **103**(1), 14–76 (2015)
16. Lamport, L.: What good is temporal logic? In: Information Processing 83 - Proceedings of WCC 1983: 9th IFIP World Computer Congress, pp. 657–668. North-Holland/IFIP (1983)
17. Lichtenstein, O., Pnueli, A., Zuck, L.D.: The glory of the past. In: Parikh, R. (ed.) Logic of Programs. LNCS, vol. 193, pp. 196–218. Springer, Heidelberg (1985)
18. Milner, R.: Communication and Concurrency. PHI Series in Computer Science. Prentice Hall, Upper Saddle River (1989)
19. Milner, R., Parrow, J., Walker, D.: A calculus of mobile processes I. Inf. Comput. **100**(1), 1–40 (1992)
20. Perkins, C.E., Johnson, D.B.: Mobility support in IPv6. In: Proceedings of Mobi-Com 1996: 2nd Annual International Conference on Mobile Computing and Networking, pp. 27–37, New York, NY, USA. ACM (1996)
21. Prasad, S.: Abstract switches: A distributed model of communication and computation. In: Perspectives in Concurrency Theory. CRC Press (2009)
22. Sangiorgi, D., Walker, D.W.: On barbed equivalences in π-Calculus. In: Larsen, K.G., Nielsen, M. (eds.) CONCUR 2001. LNCS, vol. 2154, pp. 292–304. Springer, Heidelberg (2001)
23. Zuck, L.D., Prasad, S.: Limited mobility, eventual stability. In: Piterman, N., et al. (eds.) HVC 2015. LNCS, vol. 9434, pp. 139–154. Springer, Heidelberg (2015). doi:10.1007/978-3-319-26287-1_9

Verification of Component-Based Systems via Predicate Abstraction and Simultaneous Set Reduction

Wang Qiang[⊠] and Simon Bliudze

École Polytechnique Fédérale de Lausanne, Lausanne, Switzerland
qiang.wang@epfl.ch

Abstract. This paper presents a novel safety property verification approach for component-based systems modelled in BIP (Behaviour, Interaction and Priority), encompassing multiparty synchronisation with data transfer and priority. Our contributions consist of: (1) an on-the-fly lazy predicate abstraction technique for BIP; (2) a novel explicit state reduction technique, called simultaneous set reduction, that can be combined with lazy predicate abstraction to prune the search space of abstract reachability analysis; (3) a prototype tool implementing all the proposed techniques. We also conduct thorough experimental evaluation, which demonstrates the effectiveness of our proposed approach.

1   Introduction

BIP [2] is a component-based rigorous system design framework, that advocates the methodology of correctness-by-construction. Rigorous system design can be understood as a formal, accountable and coherent process for deriving trustworthy implementations from high-level system models, which aims at guaranteeing the essential properties of a design at the earliest possible design phase, and then automatically generating correct implementations by a sequence of property preserving model transformations progressively refining the models with details specific to the target platforms [22].

BIP supports the rigorous design flow with the well-defined BIP modelling language and an associated tool-set. To model complex systems, the BIP language advocates the principle of separation of concerns (i.e. computation and coordination), and provides a three-layered mechanism for this purpose, i.e. Behaviour, Interaction, and Priority. Behaviour is characterised by a set of atomic components, defined as automata extended with linear arithmetic. Interaction represents the multiparty synchronisation of atomic components, among which data transfer may take place. Priority can be used to schedule the interactions or resolve conflicts when several interactions are enabled simultaneously.

This work was carried out within the D-MILS project, which is partially funded under the European Commission's Seventh Framework Programme (FP7).

P. Ganty and M. Loreti (Eds.): TGC 2015, LNCS 9533, pp. 147–162, 2016.
DOI: 10.1007/978-3-319-28766-9_10

In the BIP framework, DFinder [4] is the dedicated tool for automatic invariant generation and safety properties verification. DFinder computes an invariant in a compositional manner: it first computes a component invariant for each component over-approximating its behaviour and then computes the interaction invariant characterising the coordination constraint of all components. The invariant of the global system is then the conjunction of component invariants and the interaction invariant. However, DFinder does not handle system models with data transfer. This limitation hampers the practical application of DFinder and of the BIP framework, since data transfer is necessary and common in the design of real-life systems. Besides, it is not clear in DFinder how to refine the abstraction automatically when the inferred invariant fails to justify the property.

Some other works on automatic verification of BIP models exist, but they all suffer from certain limitations. The VCS [14] tool translates a BIP model into a symbolic transition system and then performs the bounded model checking. It handles data transfer among components, but only deals with finite domain variables. In [23], a timed BIP model is translated into Timed Automata and then verified with Uppaal [3]. The translation handles data transfers, but it is limited to BIP models with finite domain data variables. In [18], the authors show an encoding of a BIP model into Horn Clauses, which are verified with ELDARICA [17], but they do not handle data transfers on interactions.

In [5], the authors instantiate the ESST (Explicit Scheduler Symbolic Thread) framework [8] for BIP, where a dedicated BIP scheduler is developed to orchestrate the abstract reachability analysis, and partial order reduction techniques [11] are applied to further boost the analysis. Although being closely related, our approach is tailored for BIP and leverages its operational semantics to define the necessary minimal notion of abstract state, as opposed to that of ESST, where additional component status information and primitive functions have to be stored to account for the BIP scheduler.

Our approach is inspired by the idea of separation of computation and coordination, advocated by BIP three-layered modelling mechanism. In brief, we propose to decompose the verification of component-based systems into two levels by taking advantage of the structure features of such systems. Thus, we handle the computation of components and the coordination among components separately. On the computation level, we exploit the state-of-the-art counterexample guided abstraction refinement technique (e.g. lazy abstraction [15,16]) to analyse the behaviour of components; while on the coordination level, we deal with the redundant interleavings by a novel explicit state reduction technique, called simultaneous set reduction. The basic idea is that when two concurrent actions are enabled at the same time, instead of taking into account all the possible interleavings, we may consider executing them simultaneously. To this end, we make the following contributions in this paper: (1) we propose an on-the-fly lazy predicate abstraction technique for the verification of BIP models; (2) we propose a novel explicit state reduction technique (i.e. simultaneous set reduction) to reduce the search space when performing the abstract reachability analysis; (3) we have implemented the proposed techniques in our prototype tool and conducted thorough experimental evaluation, which shows the proposed techniques are promising for verifying generic BIP models.

2   BIP Framework

In this section we introduce the syntax and semantics of a subset of the BIP language, which encompasses the multiparty synchronisation and data transfer.

2.1   BIP Modelling Language

We use symbol Var to denote a finite set of variables with both finite and infinite domains. A guard (or predicate) is a boolean expression over Var. An operation is either an assignment or a sequence of assignments of the form $x := exp$, where $x \in Var$ and exp is an expression in linear arithmetic over Var. We denote by $Guard$ and Op the set of guards and operations over Var respectively, and Op includes a special operation $skip$, which has no effect on variables in Var. Symbols can be indexed to refer to a specific component.

Definition 1 (Atomic Component). *An atomic component is a tuple $B_i = (Var_i, Loc_i, Port_i, Trans_i, l_{0_i})$, where:*

1. *Var_i is a finite set of variables;*
2. *Loc_i is a finite set of control locations;*
3. *$Port_i$ is a finite set of ports, which are labels on the transitions;*
4. *$Trans_i \subseteq Loc_i \times Guard_i \times Port_i \times Op_i \times Loc_i$ is a set of transitions with guards and operations over Var_i.*
5. *$l_{0_i} \in Loc_i$ is the initial control location.*

The values of atomic component variables can be transfered to other components upon interaction (see Definition 2 below). However, they cannot be modified by the receiving components.

Transitions are labelled by ports, which form the interface of atomic components, and are used for defining the interactions. A port is enabled iff the transition labelled by this port is enabled.

Given a set of atomic components $\{B_i\}_{i=1}^n$, we denote $Port = \bigcup_{i=1}^n Port_i$ the set of all the ports and $Var = \bigcup_{i=1}^n Var_i$ the set of all the variables belonging to the components $\{B_i\}_{i=1}^n$. Notice that we assume that all $Port_i$

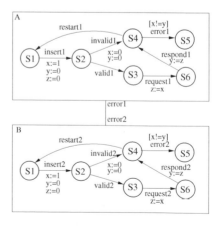

Fig. 1. An example BIP model

and all Var_i, for $i = 1, ..., n$, are pairwise disjoint. Thus, in particular, the scope of a variable can be considered to be the component, to which it belongs. The model in Fig. 1 has six variables: x, y and z in each of the two components A and B.

Composition of a set of atomic components is then specified by a set of interactions.

Definition 2 (Interaction). *An interaction γ is a tuple (g, u, op), where $u \subseteq$ Port such that $|u \cap Port_i| \leq 1$, $\forall i \in [1, n]$, and $g \in Guard$, $op \in Op$.*

Intuitively, an interaction γ specifies a guarded synchronisation among the participating components: the synchronisation and the corresponding operation (i.e. data transfer) op can take place only when the guard g is satisfied, and all the ports in u are enabled. When an interaction is taken, the transitions labelled by these ports are taken synchronously, i.e. the execution of all the operations associated to the interaction and the involved transitions constitutes a single atomic operation. When several interactions are enabled at the same time, priority can be used to schedule the ones to be executed.

Definition 3 (Priority Model). *Given a set of interactions Γ, a priority model π is a strict partial order on Γ. For $\gamma, \gamma' \in \Gamma$, we write $\gamma < \gamma'$ if and only if $(\gamma, \gamma') \in \pi$, which means that interaction γ' has a higher priority than γ.*

Given a set of atomic components $\{B_i\}_{i=1}^n$, a set of interactions $\Gamma = \{\gamma_i\}_{i=1}^m$, and a priority model π, we denote by $\Gamma_\pi(B_1, ..., B_n)$ the system model constructed by composing atomic components with Γ and π.

Example 1. To give an intuitive understanding of the BIP modelling language, we show a simple BIP model with two components A and B in Fig. 1. Each component has three integer variables and may enter a deadlock state $S5$ by taking transition $error1$ or $error2$ when the guard $x \neq y$ is true. There is one binary interaction $\gamma = (true, \{error1, error2\}, skip)$ synchronising the two transitions labelled by ports $error1$ and $error2$, and all the other transitions form singleton interactions (e.g. $(true, \{invalid1\}, x := 0; y := 0)$). No data transfer or priority is defined in this model.

2.2 Operational Semantics of BIP

To define the operational semantics of BIP, we first introduce the notion of configuration.

Definition 4 (Configuration of a BIP Model). *Given a BIP model $\Gamma_\pi(B_1, ..., B_n)$, a configuration is a tuple $c \triangleq ((l_1, \boldsymbol{x}_1), ..., (l_n, \boldsymbol{x}_n))$, where each l_i is a control location of component B_i, and $\boldsymbol{x}_i$ is a valuation of variables in Var_i of B_i.*

An interaction $\gamma = (g, u, op)$ is enabled in a configuration $c = ((l_1, \mathbf{x}_1), ..., (l_n, \mathbf{x}_n))$, if the following two conditions are satisfied: (1) the guard g is satisfied by $(\mathbf{x}_i)_{i=1}^n$; and (2) for each component B_i such that $u \cap Port_i = \{p_i\}$, there is a transition $(l_i, g_i, p_i, op_i, l_i') \in Trans_i$ starting from l_i and labelled by p_i, such that guard g_i is satisfied by $\mathbf{x}_i$.

Definition 5 (Operational Semantics of BIP). *Given a BIP model* $\Gamma_\pi(B_1, ..., B_n)$, *there is a transition from* $c = ((l_1, \boldsymbol{x}_1), ..., (l_n, \boldsymbol{x}_n))$ *to* $c' = ((l'_1, \boldsymbol{x}'_1), ..., (l'_n, \boldsymbol{x}'_n))$ *if there is an interaction* $\gamma = (g, u, op)$, *such that*

1. γ *is enabled in* c *;*
2. *for each component* B_i *such that* $u \cap Port_i = \{p_i\}$, *there is a transition* $(l_i, g_i, p_i, op_i, l'_i) \in Trans_i$ *and* $\boldsymbol{x}'_i = op_i\big(op(\boldsymbol{x}_i)\big)$ *;*
3. *for each component* B_j *such that* $u \cap Port_j = \emptyset$, *we have* $(l'_j, \boldsymbol{x}'_j) = (l_j, \boldsymbol{x}_j)$ *;*
4. *there does not exist an interaction* γ', *such that* γ' *is enabled in* c *and* $\gamma' > \gamma$.

Whenever there is a transition from configuration c to c', we use the notation $c \xrightarrow{\gamma} c'$ to indicate that this transition is triggered by the interaction γ. Notation $op(\mathbf{x})$ denotes the application of operation op to the expression $\mathbf{x}$. When op is an assignment of form $x := exp$, its semantics can be given by substitution $\mathbf{x}[exp/x]$ denoting the valuation of variables, where the valuation of x is substituted by exp.

We say that configuration $c_0 = ((l_1, \mathbf{x}_1), \ldots, (l_n, \mathbf{x}_n))$ is an *initial configuration* if $l_i = l_{0_i}$, for all $1 \leq i \leq n$. A trace is then a sequence of transitions $c_0 \xrightarrow{\gamma_1} c_1 \xrightarrow{\gamma_2} \cdots \xrightarrow{\gamma_k} c_k$. A configuration c is *reachable* if and only if there exists a trace that starts from the initial configuration and ends in c.

To encode a safety property, we identify a set of *error locations* (which are also deadlock locations, e.g. location $S5$ in Fig. 1), such that a BIP model is safe if and only if no error locations are reachable. Notice that every safety property verification problem can be encoded into a reachability problem with additional transitions, interactions and error locations in the BIP model.

3   On-the-fly Lazy Predicate Abstraction of BIP

In this section, we present our key verification algorithm for BIP which is based on lazy abstraction [15, 16] and features an on-the-fly exploration of the abstract reachable states.

3.1   Verification Algorithm

The main function of our verification algorithm is shown in Algorithm 1. The algorithm takes a BIP model with the encoding of safety property as input, and explores its reachable state space by constructing an abstract reachability tree (ART). The verification procedure is sound and complete: the lazy abstraction approach consists in verifying the most abstract model sufficient to establish a definite result (safe or unsafe). Abstraction is refined every time a spurious counterexample is found.

Our algorithm constructs the ART by expanding the ART nodes progressively, starting from the initial one. Whenever an error node is encountered, it generates a counterexample (line 8) and checks if the counterexample is real (line 9). If the counterexample is real, the algorithm stops and reports the model is unsafe and a counterexample is found (line 10). Otherwise, the algorithm will refine the abstraction and restart the exploration (line 12). An ART node is expanded when it cannot be covered by another one and all its children will be pushed into the worklist (lines 16 and 17). When a node is covered, the algorithm stops the expansion from this node by marking it as covered (line 14).

Algorithm 1. Main function

Input: a BIP model $B = \Gamma_\pi(B_1, ..., B_n)$ with encoding of safety property
Output: Either B is safe, or B is unsafe with a counterexample cex
1: create an ART node $node_0$ from the initial state
2: create an ART art with $node_0$ being the root
3: create a worklist wl of ART nodes
4: push $node_0$ into wl
5: **while** $wl \neq \emptyset$ **do**
6:      $node \leftarrow \text{pop}(wl)$
7:      **if** $node$ is an error node **then**
8:          $cex \leftarrow \text{CounterExample}(node)$
9:          **if** cex is real **then**
10:             **return** B is unsafe with a real counterexample cex
11:         **else**
12:             Refine(art, cex)
13:     **else if** $node$ is covered **then**
14:         mark $node$ as covered
15:     **else**
16:         Expand($node$)
17:         push all children of $node$ into wl
18: **return** B is safe

Definition 6 (ART Node). *Given a BIP model $B = \Gamma_\pi(B_1, ..., B_n)$, an ART node is a tuple $\big((l_1, \phi_1), ..., (l_n, \phi_n), \phi\big)$, where (l_i, ϕ_i) is the local region consisting of the control location l_i and the abstract data region ϕ_i of component B_i, and ϕ is the global data region.*

A data region is a formula that over-approximates the concrete valuations of variables. We maintain a global data region ϕ to keep track of all the variables that are used in data transfer. An ART node is an error node if at least one of the control location l_i is an error location and the data regions are consistent, i.e. $\phi \wedge \bigwedge_{i=1}^{n} \phi_i$ is satisfiable.

Definition 7 (Node Covering). *An ART node $\big((l_1, \phi_1), ..., (l_n, \phi_n), \phi\big)$ is covered by another node $\big((l'_1, \phi'_1), ..., (l'_n, \phi'_n), \phi'\big)$ if $l_i = l'_i$ and the implication $\phi_i \Rightarrow \phi'_i$ is valid for all $i \in [1, n]$, and $\phi \Rightarrow \phi'$ is valid.*

We say that an ART is safe when all the nodes are either fully expanded or covered, and there are no error nodes.

Node Expansion. The node expansion procedure is shown in Algorithm 2. The procedure first computes the set of enabled interactions on this node (function EnabledInteraction in line 2). We say that an interaction $\gamma = (u, g, op)$ is *enabled* on an ART node $((l_1, \phi_1), ..., (l_n, \phi_n), \phi)$ if for each component B_i such that $u \cap Port_i = \{p_i\}$, there is a transition $(l_i, g_i, p_i, op_i, l_i') \in Trans_i$ starting from l_i and labelled by p_i. Notice that the interaction enabledness on an ART node is different from the one on a BIP configuration. We do not check the satisfiability of the guards on the ART node, since we are doing lazy abstraction: if an interaction is disabled on the ART node, the successor node will be inconsistent.

For each enabled interaction γ, the procedure creates a new successor ART node with dummy elements, which will be updated accordingly (line 4). To update the abstract data region of B_i, that participates in γ (line 7), the procedure calls ExtractTransition($Trans_i, l_i, p_i$) in line 8 to extract the participating transition starting from l_i and labelled by port p_i from the set of transitions $Trans_i$, and then builds a sequential composition (denoted by symbol $\bullet$) of the guard and operation of this transition (line 11). The new abstract data region ϕ_i' is then obtained by applying the abstract strongest post-condition $SP_{o\hat{p}_i}^{\pi_{l_i'}}(\phi_i)$ to the previous data region ϕ_i (line 12). Our algorithm maintains precisions for both control location (e.g. l_i') and global region, denoted by $\pi_{l_i'}$ and π respectively. A precision is a set of predicates, over which the predicate abstraction is performed. We refer to [16] for more details. For other components, which do not participate in this interaction, their local regions and control locations will stay the same (line 15 and 16).

To update the global region, we need to consider all the participating transitions, since they may also modify component variables. For this purpose, the procedure creates two temporary variables g' and op' (line 5). Variable g' is the conjunction of interaction guard and all the participating transition guards (line 9), and op' is the sequential composition of the data transfer and all the participating transitions (line 10). Notice that, since the operations associated to the transitions modify only variables local to the respective components, the order of composition is irrelevant. The new global region ϕ is then updated by applying the abstract strongest post-condition $SP_{o\hat{p}}^{\pi}(\phi)$ to the previous global region ϕ (line 18), where $o\hat{p}$ is the guarded operation composed of g' and op'. If all abstract strongest post-condition computations succeed, the new ART node is inserted as the child of *node* and the edge is labelled by interaction γ (function AddChild in line 21). Otherwise, this new successor node does not represent any concrete reachable configurations, thus will be ignored.

Counterexample Analysis and Abstraction Refinement. If an error node is encountered during the exploration of abstract state space, we check if this error is reachable or not in the concrete state space in two steps. First, our algorithm constructs a counterexample by backtracking the ART from the error node to the root (function CounterExample in Algorithm 1). In BIP, we denote a counterexample *cex* by a sequence of interactions, labelling the path from the root to the error node. Then, our algorithm builds a sequential execution tr_{cex}

Algorithm 2. Node expansion procedure

1: **procedure** EXPAND($node = ((l_1, \phi_1), ..., (l_n, \phi_n), \phi)$)
2: $interactions \leftarrow$ EnabledInteraction($node$)
3: **for** $\gamma = (g, u, op) \in interactions$ **do**
4:   $node' \leftarrow ((l_1'', \phi_1'), ..., (l_n'', \phi_n'), \phi')$
5:   $g' \leftarrow g;\ op' \leftarrow op$
6:   **for** $B_i \in B = \Gamma_\pi(B_1, ..., B_n)$ **do**
7:    **if** $Port_i \cap u = \{p_i\}$ **then**
8:     $(l_i, g_i, p_i, op_i, l_i') \leftarrow$ ExtractTransition($Trans_i, l_i, p_i$)
9:     $g' \leftarrow g' \wedge g_i$
10:     $op' \leftarrow op' \bullet op_i$
11:     $\hat{op}_i \leftarrow g_i \bullet op_i$
12:     $\phi_i' = SP_{\hat{op}_i}^{\pi_{l_i'}}(\phi_i);\ l_i'' = l_i'$
13:     **if** ϕ_i' is false **then**
14:      goto 3
15:    **else if** $Port_i \cap u = \emptyset$ **then**
16:     $l_i'' = l_i;\ \phi_i' = \phi_i$
17:   $\hat{op} \leftarrow g' \bullet op'$
18:   $\phi' = SP_{\hat{op}}^{\pi}(\phi)$
19:   **if** ϕ' is false **then**
20:    goto 3
21:   AddChild(γ, $node'$)

---

of the counterexample cex, such that the counterexample cex is real if and only if $SP_{tr_{cex}}(true)$ is satisfiable.

Formally, given a counterexample $cex = \gamma_1 \gamma_2 \ldots \gamma_k$, where for each $i \in [1, k]$, interaction $\gamma_i = (u_i, g_i, op_i)$, $u_i = \{p_1^i, \ldots, p_t^i\}$, our algorithm constructs a sequence tr_{γ_i} of transitions $g_i \bullet op_i \bullet op_{j_1}^i \bullet \ldots \bullet op_{j_t}^i$, where the sequence of indices $j_1, \ldots, j_t$ is an arbitrary permutation of $\{1, \ldots, t\}$, and $op_{j_1}^i$ is the operation of transition labelled by port $p_{j_1}^i$. Then the sequential execution of counterexample cex is the sequential composition of all tr_{γ_i}, i.e. $tr_{cex} = tr_{\gamma_1} \bullet \ldots \bullet tr_{\gamma_k}$.

If the analysis reveals that the encountered error location is unreachable in the concrete state space, the precisions of the abstract analysis must be refined to eliminate the spurious counterexample by adding new predicates (function Refine in Algorithm 1). Our algorithm discovers new predicates from the interpolants of trace formula of tr_{cex}. If a predicate involves only variables that are not used in the data transfer, it is added to the precisions associated to the corresponding control locations. A predicate involving variables that are used in the data transfer is added to the global precision.

Once the precisions are refined, our algorithm will remove the sub-tree that contains the spurious counterexample, and then restart the expansion using the refined precisions. We refer to [15] for more details and the correctness of this abstraction refinement approach.

3.2   Correctness Proof

To prove the correctness of Algorithm 1, we need to relate the construction of ART with BIP operational semantics. We first show that the node expansion procedure creates successor nodes that cover (or over-approximate) the corresponding reachable configurations.

Let $B = \Gamma_\pi(B_1, ..., B_n)$ be a BIP model, and $c = ((l_1, \mathbf{x}_1), ..., (l_n, \mathbf{x}_n))$ be a configuration of B. Let $node = ((l'_1, \phi_1), ..., (l'_n, \phi_n), \phi)$ be an ART node. We say that configuration c satisfies ART node $node$ (or $node$ covers c), denoted by $c \models node$, if and only if, for all $i \in [1, n]$, we have $l_i = l'_i$ and $\mathbf{x}_i \models \phi_i$, and $(\mathbf{x}_i)_{i=1}^n \models \phi$.

Lemma 1. *Let node be an ART node for a BIP model $B = \Gamma_\pi(B_1, ..., B_n)$ and node' be its successor. Let c be a configuration such that $c \models node$. If node' is obtained by performing interaction γ, then for any configuration c' such that $c \xrightarrow{\gamma} c'$, we have $c' \models node'$.*

Proof. Suppose $c = ((l_1, \mathbf{x}_1), ..., (l_n, \mathbf{x}_n))$, and $node = ((l_1, \phi_1), ..., (l_n, \phi_n), \phi)$, where $\mathbf{x}_i \models \phi_i$, for each $i \in [1, n]$, and $(\mathbf{x}_i)_{i=1}^n \models \phi$, since $c \models node$. Suppose the successor configuration following $\gamma = (g, u, op)$ is $c' = ((l'_1, \mathbf{x}'_1), ..., (l'_n, \mathbf{x}'_n))$, and the successor node is $node' = ((l''_1, \phi'_1), ..., (l''_n, \phi'_n), \phi')$. To prove $c' \models n'$, we have to show that $l'_i = l''_i$ and $\mathbf{x}'_i \models \phi'_i$, for all $i \in [1, n]$, and $(\mathbf{x}'_i)_{i=1}^n \models \phi'$.

Consider a component B_i, such that $u \cap Port_i = \{p_i\}$, and let the corresponding transition in $Trans_i$ be $(l_i, g_i, p_i, op_i, l'_i)$. Then we have $\mathbf{x}_i \models g_i$ and $\mathbf{x}'_i = op_i(op(\mathbf{x}_i))$. According to Algorithm 2, we have $l''_i = l'_i$ and $\phi'_i = SP_{\hat{op}_i}(\phi_i)$, where $\hat{op}_i$ denotes $g_i \bullet op_i$. Based on the semantics of strongest post-condition, the fact that $\mathbf{x}_i \models \phi_i$ and $\phi_i \wedge g_i$ is satisfiable, we have $\mathbf{x}'_i \models \phi'_i$. Following a similar argument, we can prove $(\mathbf{x}'_i)_{i=1}^n \models \phi'$.

For each component B_i such that $u \cap Port_i = \emptyset$, since it does not participate the interaction, its state is unchanged. Thus, the satisfaction relation trivially holds. $\quad\square$

Theorem 1 (Correctness of On-the-fly Lazy Predicate Abstraction of BIP). *Given a BIP model B, and for every terminating execution of Algorithm 1, we have the following properties:*

1. if Algorithm 1 returns a real counterexample path cex, then there is a concrete execution $c \xrightarrow{cex} c'$ from an initial configuration c and an error configuration c' in B;
2. if Algorithm 1 returns a safe ART, then for every reachable configuration c of B, there is an ART node that covers this configuration.

Proof. (Sketch) In the safe case, the conclusion follows from Lemma 9 and an induction proof on the execution path to the reachable configuration c. In the unsafe case, the conclusion holds because the counterexample analysis boils down to a symbolic simulation. $\quad\square$

4   Simultaneous Set Reduction for BIP

In this section, we present a novel reduction technique, which can be combined with on-the-fly lazy predicate abstraction to reduce the search space of reachability analysis. The idea is based on the observation that in component-based systems, when two concurrent interactions are enabled at the same time (e.g. interactions $\{insert1\}$ and $\{insert2\}$ in Fig. 1), we may consider executing them simultaneously instead of taking into account all the possible interleavings in the reachability analysis. First of all, we have to formalise the constraints imposed on the set of interactions, which can be executed simultaneously, in order to make sure no error location is missed during the reachability analysis.

4.1   Simultaneous Set Constraints

Two interactions can be executed simultaneously only when they are independent.

Definition 8 (Independent Interactions). *Two interactions γ_1 and γ_2 are independent if for every configuration c, the following conditions hold:*

1. if γ_1 is enabled in c, then γ_2 is enabled in c iff γ_2 is enabled in c', where $c \xrightarrow{\gamma_1} c'$.
2. if γ_1 and γ_2 are both enabled in c, then $c'_1 = c'_2$, where $c \xrightarrow{\gamma_1;\gamma_2} c'_1$, and $c \xrightarrow{\gamma_2;\gamma_1} c'_2$.

Since independence relation is a global property, in the sequel we will instead use the valid dependence relation.

Definition 9 (Valid Dependency Relation). *A valid dependence relation D over a set of interactions Γ is a symmetric, reflexive relation such that for every $(\gamma_1, \gamma_2) \notin D$, the interactions γ_1 and γ_2 are independent interactions.*

In BIP context, we can compute a valid dependency relation statically from the specifications: two interactions are *dependent* if they share one common component. It is worthy to notice that our independency and dependency relations also work for abstract analysis.

However, independency is not enough. For instance, in the example BIP model in Fig. 1, suppose we want to expand the node $((S_3, \phi_A), (S_4, \phi_B), \phi)$, where component A is in control location S_3 and component B is in control location S_4. The set of enabled interactions is $\{\{request1\}, \{restart2\}\}$. Notice that interaction $\{error1, error2\}$ is disabled since port $error1$ is disabled. The two interactions $\{request1\}$ and $\{restart2\}$ are independent, however, if we execute them simultaneously we will miss the following (fragment) counterexample from this node: $\{request1\}, \{respond1\}, \{error1, error2\}$. This observation tells us to take into account the future executions when firing interactions simultaneously.

Definition 10 (Simultaneous Set). *A set of interactions SSet on configuration c is called a simultaneous set if the following two constraints are satisfied:*

1. all the interactions in SSet are independent;

2. for each $\alpha \in SSet$, let $c \xrightarrow{\alpha} c_1 \xrightarrow{\beta_1} \ldots \xrightarrow{\beta_n} c_{n+1}$ be a finite execution fragment starting with α, then for each $\alpha' \in SSet$, such that $\alpha' \neq \alpha$, all β_i are independent of α'.

Intuitively, the second constraint means that whatever one does from the simultaneous set should still be independent from the others in the set. We remark that simultaneous set is different from the ample set [10] in that members in ample set are interdependent, and interleavings should be taken into account.

We use notation A_G to represent the full reachable state space, and A_R to represent reduced reachable state space. A transition in A_R is denoted by $c \xrightarrow{SSet(c)} c'$, where $SSet(c)$ is a simultaneous set on c. A trace in A_R is then labelled by a sequence of simultaneous sets, e.g. $c_0 \xrightarrow{SSet(c_0)} c_1 \xrightarrow{SSet(c_1)} \ldots \xrightarrow{SSet(c_{k-1})} c_k$. Similarly, we say that a configuration c is *reachable* in A_R if and only if there exists a trace that starts from the initial configuration and ends up with c. However, a trace in A_R is not a trace of A_G, but a representation of several equivalent traces.

Definition 11 (Semantics of Simultaneous Set). *Given a configuration c, a transition $c \xrightarrow{SSet(c)} c'$ in A_R denotes a set of transition sequences $\{c \xrightarrow{\gamma_1} \ldots \xrightarrow{\gamma_k} c' | \forall i \in [1,k], \gamma_i \in SSet(c) \text{ and } |SSet(c)| = k\}$ in A_G.*

Each transition sequence $c \xrightarrow{\gamma_1} \ldots \xrightarrow{\gamma_k} c'$ is a representation of $c \xrightarrow{SSet(c)} c'$. Inductively, we can also define the representation of a trace in A_R. Based on the definition of simultaneous set, it is easy to see that each representation of a trace in A_R is a trace in A_G.

The correctness of simultaneous set reduction for deadlock state reachability analysis is stated in the following theorem.

Theorem 2 (Correctness of Simultaneous Set Reduction). *Let e be an error configuration. If there is a trace ρ_g leading to e in A_G, then there is also a trace ρ_r leading to e in A_R.*

Proof. Assume $\rho_g = c_0 \xrightarrow{\gamma_0} \ldots \xrightarrow{\gamma_{n-2}} c_{n-1}$, where $c_{n-1} = e$. The proof proceeds by using complete induction on the number of configurations in ρ_g. For the base case $|\rho_g| = 1$, the result trivially holds since the initial configuration is also the error one. Assume the theorem holds for all the cases $|\rho_g| <= n$, where $n >= 1$, then we prove it also holds for $|\rho_g| = n + 1$.

Assume $\rho_g = c_0 \xrightarrow{\gamma_0} c_1 \xrightarrow{\gamma_1} \ldots \xrightarrow{\gamma_{n-2}} c_{n-1} \xrightarrow{\gamma_{n-1}} c_n$, where $c_n = e$, and the simultaneous set on configuration c_0 that contains interaction γ_0 is $SSet(c_0)$. If $SSet(c_0)$ is a singleton set, then ρ_r is ρ_g. If $SSet(c_0) = \{\beta_i | i \in [1,k]\} \cup \{\gamma_0\}$, according to the definition of simultaneous set, β_i is independent of γ_j, for all $i \in [1,k]$, and $j \in [1, n-1]$, then β_i should be enabled on configuration c_n, which contradicts with the fact that c_n is a deadlock state. Thus, all β_i should be executed, i.e. for each β_i there must exist a γ_j such that $\beta_i = \gamma_j$. Then by permuting independent interactions, we obtain an equivalent trace $\rho'_g = c_0 \xrightarrow{\gamma_0} c_1 \xrightarrow{\beta_1} \cdots \xrightarrow{\beta_k} \xrightarrow{\gamma_{k+1}} \cdots \xrightarrow{\gamma_{n-1}} c_n$. The sequence of interactions $\xrightarrow{\gamma_0}\xrightarrow{\beta_1} \cdots \xrightarrow{\beta_k}$ is a representation of the simultaneous set $SSet(c_0)$, while based on the induction hypothesis the rest is a representation of some trace in A_R. They all together prove our theorem.   □

4.2 Combining Simultaneous Set Reduction with Lazy Predicate Abstraction

To combine the simultaneous set reduction with lazy predicate abstraction of BIP, we modify the node expansion procedure in Algorithm 2 by replacing the function EnabledInteraction in line 2 with Algorithm 3, such that instead of creating a new successor node for each possible interaction (line 3), we create a new successor node for each simultaneous set. Notice that since a simultaneous set is a set of interactions, the successor computation (the loop in line 3) should also be slightly adjusted.

Algorithm 3 computes the set of simultaneous sets on an ART node. It uses two additional functions EnabledInteraction and DisabledInteraction. Function DisabledInteraction computes the set of disabled interactions on an ART node, which is simply the complement of the set of enabled interactions.

Algorithm 3. Simultaneous set computation

Input: an ART node $node = ((l_1, \phi_1), ..., (l_n, \phi_n), \phi)$
Output: a set of simultaneous sets $SSets$
  1: $enabled\_interactions \leftarrow$ EnabledInteraction($node$)
  2: $disabled\_interactions \leftarrow$ DisabledInteraction($node$)
  3: create a worklist of interaction sets wl
  4: push $enabled\_interactions$ into wl
  5: **while** $wl \neq \emptyset$ **do**
  6:    $current\_set \leftarrow \text{pop}(wl)$
  7:    **if** exists $\gamma_1, \gamma_2 \in current\_set$, s.t. γ_1, γ_2 are dependent **then**
  8:       $copy_1 \leftarrow current\_set - \{\gamma_1\}$
  9:       $copy_2 \leftarrow current\_set - \{\gamma_2\}$
10:      push $copy_1, copy_2$ into wl
11:    **else if** exists $\gamma_1, \gamma_2 \in current\_set$, $\gamma_3 \in disabled\_interactions$,
                s.t. γ_3, γ_1 are dependent, and γ_3, γ_2 are dependent **then**
12:      $copy_1 \leftarrow current\_set - \{\gamma_1\}$
13:      $copy_2 \leftarrow current\_set - \{\gamma_2\}$
14:      push $copy_1, copy_2$ into wl
15:    **else**
16:      **if** $SSets$ does not contain $current\_set$ **then**
17:        push $current\_set$ into $SSets$

The basic idea is that starting from the set of enabled interactions, the algorithm progressively refines this set by splitting it into two sets. If two interactions from the set are dependent (line 7), or they are independent of each other, but dependent with a disabled interaction (line 11), then this set is split into two, each of which is obtained by removing one of the interactions (lines 8, 9 and 12, 13). Otherwise, if all interactions are independent of each other and with the disabled interactions, then the set is a simultaneous set and is added into the result set *SSets*.

Assume that, given two interactions γ_1 and γ_2, it takes $\mathcal{O}(1)$ time for the dependence check with precomputed dependence relation on lines 7 and 11. The while loop (line 5) executes at most $|enabled\_interactions|$ times, where $|enabled\_interactions|$ denotes the number of enabled interactions on the input ART node, since in each loop execution at most two interactions will be split and one simultaneous set will be added into the worklist wl. In the worst case, $|enabled\_interactions|^2 * |disabled\_interactions|$ checks need to be performs to find the two interactions to be split. Thus, the worst case time complexity of Algorithm 3 is $\mathcal{O}(|enabled\_interactions|^3 * |disabled\_interactions|)$.

The correctness of Algorithm 3 is straightforward, according to the simultaneous set constraints in Definition 10.

Theorem 3 (Correctness of Lazy Predicate Abstraction with Simultaneous Set Reduction). *Given a BIP model, and for every terminating execution of the combination of Algorithms 1 and 3, the two properties of Theorem 10 still hold.*

Proof (Sketch). Algorithm 3 computes the set of simultaneous sets on an ART node. A simultaneous set on an ART node is a simultaneous set on the configurations that are covered by this ART node. Therefore, the theorem follows from Theorem 15.

5   Related Work

Although there are plenty of works on safety property verification in literature, we review the most related ones in two aspects. With respect to combining abstraction techniques with explicit state reduction techniques, the works most related to ours are [8,9,24]. In [8,9] the authors propose two ESST-based verification techniques for multi-threaded programs with a preemptive and stateful scheduler (e.g. SystemC [20] and FairThreads [7]). The work in [24] combines classical lazy abstraction and partial order reduction [11] for the verification of generic multi-threaded programs with pointers. The difference between these works and ours is that they combine the abstraction techniques with classical partial order reduction techniques, (e.g. persistent set approach [11] and ample set approach [10]) in which one reduces the interleavings of concurrent transitions by exploring only a representative subset of all enabled transitions. In our approach, we leverage the BIP operational semantics to tackle this issue by executing concurrent interactions simultaneously.

With respect to the compositional verification, the most related ones are [6,13,21]. In [6] the authors presents an assume-guarantee abstraction refinement technique for compositional verification of component-based systems. However, the target system model is finite state and without data transfer. In [13] the authors propose a compositional verification technique for multi-threaded programs based on abstract interpretation framework. This algorithm relies on solving recursion-free Horn clauses to refine the abstraction. Later the work in [21] combines this method with a reduction technique based on Lipton's theory of reduction [19]. The programming model is quite different from ours. They handle shared variable concurrent programs, whereas BIP does not provide communication through shared variables, but only multiparty synchronisation and data transfer.

6   Experimental Evaluation

We implemented the proposed techniques in our prototype tool BIPChecker, based on the symbolic model checker nuXmv and the SMT solver MathSAT. In the experimental evaluation, we took a set of benchmarks from the literature, including the untimed temperature and railway control system [18], the ATM transaction model [4], the leader election algorithm [1], and the Quorum consensus algorithm [12]. We modelled them in the BIP framework and verified different safe and unsafe invariant properties. All these benchmarks (1) are scalable in terms of the number of components; (2) are infinite-state, using potentially unbounded integer variables and (3) feature data transfer on interactions.

All the experiments have been performed on a 64-bit Linux PC with a 2.8 GHz Intel i7-2640M CPU, with a memory limit of 4 Gb and a time limit of 300 s per benchmark. We refer to our website[1] for all the benchmarks and the tool.

We run two configurations of BIP-Checker: OLA and OLA+SSR, where OLA stands for on-the-fly lazy abstraction, and SSR stands for the simultaneous set reduction. We do not compare the performance of our tool with DFinder [4] and VCS [14],

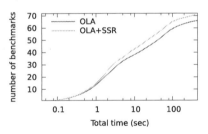

Fig. 2. Cumulative plot of time for solving all benchmarks

since they do not handle data transfer and infinite-state models respectively. The comparison of OLA and OLA+SSR on the full set of benchmarks is shown in Figs. 2 and 3.

In Fig. 2, we plot the cumulative time (x-axis) to solve an increasing number of benchmarks (y-axis), and in Fig. 3, we show the scatter plot of time for solving

---

each benchmark.[2] The plots show that simultaneous set reduction can improve the performance in general when it is combined with the on-the-fly lazy abstraction. In particular, from Fig. 3 we find that for safe models, OLA is comparable to OLA+SSR, while for unsafe models, OLA+SSR is always more efficient than OLA. In other words, OLA+SSR is more efficient to find counterexamples. This phenomenon can be explained because with simultaneous set reduction, some independent interactions are executed simultaneously, thus reducing the length of execution steps and being faster to detect counterexamples.

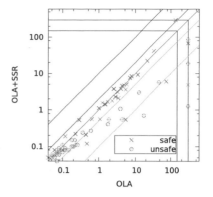

Fig. 3. Scatter plot of time for solving each benchmark

7 Conclusion

In this paper we proposed a generic approach to safety property verification of BIP models, which combines on-the-fly lazy abstraction and simultaneous set reduction technique. We also implemented our techniques in the BIPChecker tool. The experimental evaluation demonstrates the efficiency of the proposed approach. As future work we will investigate more efficient reduction techniques for component-based systems, that can boost the abstract reachability analysis, such as property guided reduction.

Acknowledgements. We want to thank Alessandro Cimatti, Marco Roveri and Sergio Mover for the instructive guidance during our collaboration that enabled this work and for their help with the nuXmv model checker and the MathSAT SMT solver, and all the anonymous reviewers for their careful reading of the paper.

References

1. Baier, C., Katoen, J.P.: Principles of Model Checking. The MIT Press, Cambridge (2008)
2. Basu, A., Bensalem, S., Bozga, M., Combaz, J., Jaber, M., Nguyen, T.H., Sifakis, J.: Rigorous component-based system design using the BIP framework. Softw. IEEE **28**, 41–48 (2011)
3. Behrmann, G., David, A., Larsen, K.G., Håkansson, J., Pettersson, P., Yi, W., Hendriks, M.: UPPAAL 4.0. In: QEST (2006)
4. Bensalem, S., Bozga, M., Nguyen, T.-H., Sifakis, J.: D-Finder: a tool for compositional deadlock detection and verification. In: Bouajjani, A., Maler, O. (eds.) CAV 2009. LNCS, vol. 5643, pp. 614–619. Springer, Heidelberg (2009)

---

[2]   Red diagonal guides provide a reference for comparison, each indicating shift of one order of magnitude.

5. Bliudze, S., Cimatti, A., Jaber, M., Mover, S., Roveri, M., Saab, W., Wang, Q.: Formal verification of infinite-state BIP models. In: Finkbeiner, B., et al. (eds.) ATVA 2015. LNCS, vol. 9364, pp. 326–343. Springer, Heidelberg (2015). doi:10. 1007/978-3-319-24953-7_25

6. Gheorghiu Bobaru, M., Păsăreanu, C.S., Giannakopoulou, D.: Automated assume-guarantee reasoning by abstraction refinement. In: Gupta, A., Malik, S. (eds.) CAV 2008. LNCS, vol. 5123, pp. 135–148. Springer, Heidelberg (2008)

7. Boussinot, F.: FairThreads: mixing cooperative and preemptive threads in C. Concur. Comput. Pract. Exp. **18**, 445–469 (2006)

8. Cimatti, A., Narasamdya, I., Roveri, M.: Software model checking with explicit scheduler and symbolic threads. Log. Methods Comput. Sci. **8**, 1–42 (2012)

9. Cimatti, A., Narasamdya, I., Roveri, M.: Verification of parametric system designs. In: FMCAD (2012)

10. Clarke Jr., E.M., Grumberg, O., Peled, D.A.: Model Checking. MIT Press, Cambridge (1999)

11. Godefroid, P.: Partial-Order Methods for the Verification of Concurrent Systems: An Approach to the State-Explosion Problem. Lecture Notes in Computer Science, vol. 1032. Springer, Heidelberg (1996)

12. Guerraoui, R., Kuncak, V., Losa, G.: Speculative linearizability. In: PLDI (2012)

13. Gupta, A., Popeea, C., Rybalchenko, A.: Predicate abstraction and refinement for verifying multi-threaded programs. In: POPL (2011)

14. He, F., Yin, L., Wang, B.-Y., Zhang, L., Mu, G., Meng, W.: VCS: a verifier for component-based systems. In: Van Hung, D., Ogawa, M. (eds.) ATVA 2013. LNCS, vol. 8172, pp. 478–481. Springer, Heidelberg (2013)

15. Henzinger, T.A., Jhala, R., Majumdar, R., McMillan, K.L.: Abstractions from proofs. In: ACM SIGPLAN Notices. ACM (2004)

16. Henzinger, T.A., Jhala, R., Majumdar, R., Sutre, G.: Lazy abstraction. In: POPL (2002)

17. Hojjat, H., Konecný, F., Garnier, F., Iosif, R., Kuncak, V., Rümmer, P.: A verification toolkit for numerical transition systems - tool paper. In: FM (2012)

18. Hojjat, H., Rümmer, P., Subotic, P., Yi, W.: Horn clauses for communicating timed systems. In: HCVS (2014)

19. Lipton, R.J.: Reduction: a method of proving properties of parallel programs. Commun. ACM **18**, 717–721 (1975)

20. IEEE 1666: SystemC language Reference Manual (2005)

21. Popeea, C., Rybalchenko, A., Wilhelm, A.: Reduction for compositional verification of multi-threaded programs. In: FMCAD (2014)

22. Sifakis, J.: Rigorous system design. In: Foundations and Trends in Electronic Design Automation (2013)

23. Su, C., Zhou, M., Yin, L., Wan, H., Gu, M.: Modeling and verification of component-based systems with data passing using BIP. In: ICECCS (2013)

24. Wachter, B., Kroening, D., Ouaknine, J.: Verifying multi-threaded software with Impact. In: FMCAD (2013)

Author Index

Bliudze, Simon   147
Bursuc, Sergiu   1

De Nicola, Rocco   16
Delzanno, Giorgio   32

Feng, Xinyu   95

Gössler, Gregor   79

Hasuo, Ichiro   112

Jensen, Thomas   63

Li, Ximeng   95

Matos, Ana Almeida   47
Melgratti, Hernán   16

Nakagawa, Shota   112
Nielson, Flemming   95
Nielson, Hanne Riis   95

Prasad, Sanjiva   131

Qiang, Wang   147

Rezk, Tamara   47, 63

Santos, José Fragoso   47, 63
Schmitt, Alan   63
Stefani, Jean-Bernard   79

Zuck, Lenore D.   131

Printed in the United States
By Bookmasters